The Post-Qualifying Handbook
for Social Workers

of related interest

Handbook for Practice Learning in Social Work and Social Care
Knowledge and Theory
Second edition
Edited by Joyce Lishman
ISBN 978 1 84310 186 4

Competence in Social Work Practice
A Practical Guide for Students and Professionals
Second edition
Edited by Kieran O'Hagan
ISBN 978 1 84310 485 8

Enhancing Social Work Management
Theory and Best Practice from the UK and USA
Edited by Jane Aldgate, Lynne Healy, Barris Malcolm, Barbara Pine, Wendy Rose and Janet Seden
ISBN 978 1 84310 515 2

The Developing World of the Child
Edited by Jane Aldgate, David Jones, Wendy Rose and Carole Jeffery
Foreword by Maria Eagle MP
ISBN 978 1 84310 244 1

See You in Court
A Social Worker's Guide to Presenting Evidence in Care Proceedings
Lynn Davis
ISBN 978 1 84310 547 3

Making an Impact
Children and Domestic Violence – A Reader
Second edition
Marianne Hester, Chris Pearson and Nicola Harwin
With Hilary Abrahams
ISBN 978 1 84310 157 4

Planning and Support for People with Intellectual Disabilities
Issues for Case Managers and Other Professionals
Edited by Christine Bigby, Chris Fyffe and Elizabeth Ozanne
ISBN 978 1 84310 354 7

Social Work Theories in Action
Edited by Mary Nash, Robyn Munford and Kieran O'Donoghue
Foreword by Jim Ife
ISBN 978 1 84310 249 6

Social Work and Disadvantage
Addressing the Roots of Stigma through Association
Edited by Peter Burke and Jonathan Parker
ISBN 978 1 84310 364 6

The Post-Qualifying Handbook for Social Workers

Edited by Wade Tovey

Jessica Kingsley Publishers
London and Philadelphia

MT

For CJ

First published in 2007
by Jessica Kingsley Publishers
116 Pentonville Road
London N1 9JB, UK
and
400 Market Street, Suite 400
Philadelphia, PA 19106, USA

www.jkp.com

Copyright © Jessica Kingsley Publishers 2007

Library of Congress Cataloging in Publication Data

British Library Cataloguing in Publication Data
A CIP catalogue record for this book is available from the British Library

ISBN 978 1 84310 428 5

Printed and bound in Great Britain by
Athenaeum Press, Gateshead, Tyne and Wear

The table on pp. 259–66 is reproduced with kind permission from the Education Standards and Information Team, GSCC.

11/15/07

Contents

Part 2 Practice

Part 3 Issues

Part 4 Doing PQ

General Introduction

You may have picked up this book because post-qualifying (PQ) social work practice and professional development are important to you and you want to find out more – knowing that there are many challenges ahead, but at the same time many rewards. You may have received confusing or even conflicting information about PQ at different times even though all the countries in the UK have used the framework of the Central Council for Education and Training in Social Work (CCETSW), and three countries continue to do so for the time being.

The General Social Care Council (GSCC) in England forged ahead with the introduction of a new framework on a full basis in 2007, and some universities achieved an early start in 2006. Scotland has taken a more measured approach with the publication of *Changing Lives,* the report of the '21st Century Social Work Review' (Scottish Executive 2006b). This proposes a five-year plan, with existing education and training arrangements (including PQ) set to continue until the review is complete. Northern Ireland introduced a new framework from April 2007, though those on the existing framework can continue with it through to 2010. In Wales there is an ongoing arrangement for mental health, while consultation continues over the future of PQ. (More details are in Appendix 4.)

This book is relevant to PQ throughout the UK, regardless of country or your area of social work practice. Continuous professional development (CPD), as you will see, can be a stimulating, even exciting, process with many benefits, which will build on your existing learning and experience, and no doubt recall aspects of your motivation for coming into social work in the first place. The CPD process of PQ will help you be more critically aware and will enhance your confidence in your abilities. Social work is a unique profession, in which personal and professional development intertwine, and the person you are now will not be the person who started on a social work programme or indeed the person you will become as you progress through your career.

The nature of the work can be so challenging that one can lose confidence in the wealth of accumulated expertise, drawing on knowledge and very real, and transferable, skills. This expertise is increasingly recognised in many settings outside traditional Social Services Departments. I recently met somebody who had worked in children's settings but, due to reorganisation (something very familiar to social workers!), had moved into managing an adults/learning disabilities unit. She was enjoying the change enormously. First she realised that she was able to transfer most of the necessary skills from her previous job and, second, she found that her fresh approach had energised and excited the workers in the unit, who had been demoralised and frustrated.

You may be a busy social worker with a challenging workload, and perhaps limited support, but a commitment to doing PQ. Your motivations may be many: you may want to learn more; move onto a higher grade; demonstrate your growing experience and abilities; maintain your professional registration; improve your CV; have some time to study and reflect critically on your practice; and, above all, you may well wish to develop your abilities to deliver more effective provision to those who use services. This book should help you with all these opportunities.

It is also, however, aimed at those who are helping you, and those who should support you in the process, to understand what PQ is all about and how you can make progress at the different levels. The first step is often the most challenging and, if subsequent steps can be made easier, the impact of your achievement can make your journey ever less effortful. If you have already completed some aspect of PQ then you can find here details of the next steps to take. This book provides the context to PQ and Part 1, 'Contexts', examines the importance of this. Almost every social worker should be able to relate to one or more chapters in Part 2, 'Practice', which provides examples of work with different groups of people who use services. In Part 3, 'Issues', we look at the issues that most social workers will encounter at some time in their practice. These three major parts provide you with examples of writing by different authors in different styles, but all demonstrate the critical and reflective thinking and knowledge that you too will need to show in order to be successful at the different levels and in the various areas of PQ awards. The chapters are sequenced to enable you to work through the process and, as the book proceeds, 'Recommended reading' at the end of each chapter suggests books and resources that tackle practice and issues in much more breadth and depth than is possible here. The final part, 'Doing PQ', provides a bank of resources for you to draw upon throughout.

Table 1 sets out the awards and requirements at different levels of PQ in England (further details of this are set out in Chapter 18). These requirements also reflect the different academic levels that could be applied elsewhere in the UK.

Table 1 PQ awards and requirements

PQ level	Focus	Academic level
The Specialist, or first, PQ level	Consolidates, extends and deepens initial professional competence in a specialist context	The minimum academic level for such programmes is honours level (the equivalent of the third year of an honours degree). Some universities may be offering this award at a higher level
The Higher Specialist, or second, PQ level	A specific focus on the knowledge and skills needed to make complex judgements and discharge high levels of responsibility	The minimum academic level for such programmes is master's level but the Higher Specialist award does not have to incorporate a master's degree
The Advanced, or third, PQ level	Knowledge and skills required for professional leadership, research and improvement of services. Incorporates managerial forms of leadership but also includes other types of professional leadership	The minimum academic level for such programmes is master's level. Only programmes leading to master's degrees will be approved as Advanced award programmes

In England, the different types of practice require the development of different types of knowledge and skills, as well as the different levels listed in Table 1. Please note that in this book there are references to the former awards, which applied across the UK. In future, other countries in the UK may follow the general direction outlined in England, but of course there is no certainty about this. With these points in mind, Table 2 shows the standards that have clear links to different chapters in this book. Chapters 1, 2, 3, 4, 5, 6, 7, 18, 19 and 20 should be useful to all.

Table 2 Specialist standards and levels for England (adapted from GSCC 2005a)

Area/chapter	Specialist	Higher Specialist	Advanced
Children and Young People, their Families and Carers	Recently qualified social worker working in this specialism Experienced social worker who has no PQ qualification or holds PQ 1 Social worker holding PQ award in a different specialism	PQSW holder in Child Care or another specialism wishing to change specialism PQ Specialist level holder in Children and Young People Experienced Children and Families social worker who can evidence they have met the Specialist level outcomes Children and Young People, their Families and Carers social worker in a specialist setting	PQSW holder in Child Care PQ Specialist level holder in Children and Young People AASW in Child Care Very experienced Children and Families social worker who can evidence they have met the Specialist level outcomes and have the ability to study at master's level Experienced Children and Young People, their Families and Carers social worker in a specialist setting
Social Work with Adults	Recently qualified social worker working in this specialism Experienced social worker who has no PQ qualification or holds PQ 1 Social worker holding PQ award in a different specialism	PQSW holder in Adults SW or another specialism wishing to change specialism PQ Specialist level holder in Social Worker with Adults Experienced Adults social worker who can evidence they have met the Specialist level outcomes Adults social worker in a specialist setting	PQSW holder in Adults SW PQ Specialist level holder in Adults SW AASW in Adults SW Very experienced Adults social worker who can evidence they have met the Specialist level outcomes and have the ability to study at master's level Experienced Adults SW in a specialist setting

Social Work in Mental Health Services	Recently qualified social worker working in this specialism Experienced social worker who has no PQ qualification or PQ1 Social worker holding PQ award in a different specialism SW who wants to become an ASW Note: 1. Course can be accessed by other MH professionals 2. Impending reform of MH legislation proposes the role of an Approved Mental Health Professional (AMHP) – specific requirements will be needed	ASW or PQSW holder in another specialism wishing to change career PQ Specialist level holder in Social Work in Mental Health Settings Experienced ASW or Mental Health social worker who can evidence they have met the Specialist level outcomes Mental Health social worker in a specialist setting	ASW or PQSW holder in Mental Health SW PQ Specialist level holder in SW in a Mental Health Setting AASW in Mental Health SW Very experienced Mental Health SW who can evidence they have met the Specialist level outcomes and have the ability to study at master's level Experienced ASW or Mental Health SW in a specialist setting
Leadership and Management	The Leadership and Management awards will be at Higher Specialist and Advanced levels. The *only* exception to this will be for social workers who are managers of registered services for whom awards at Specialist level may be offered	Newly appointed, first-line, junior or middle managers who may or may not hold PQ awards or other management awards. Senior practitioners who may wish to combine another specialism with Leadership and Management modules Inspectors and regulators of social care	Senior managers who hold strategic positions who may or may not hold PQ awards or other management awards Managers in inspection and regulation

Continued on next page

Table 2 continued

Area / chapter	Specialist	Higher Specialist	Advanced
Practice Education	Core practice education within specialisms above	Experienced mentors and practice teachers who may or may not hold the Practice Teachers award or another teaching qualifcation Experienced senior practitioners who may wish to combine another specialism with practice education modules	Very experienced practice teachers who may or may not hold other qualifications Experienced senior practitioners who may wish to combine another specialism with practice education modules Social work educators

All the contributors to this book have a wealth of PQ experience and knowledge, which we all hope will help you to overcome the challenges involved in taking the first step or the next step in the PQ process. As Robert Adams points out in Chapter 2, this 'process is stimulating, enjoyable and even exciting'. We hope that you will agree after reading the book and having taken the first step, or a further step, on the ongoing journey of your professional development.

Key terminology

The authors use some different terms for the people with whom social workers work. This variation reflects the fact that there has been much different termi-nology since social work began, and that there is no consensus or agreed terminology to date. This issue will be referred to in more detail in Chapter 17 and elsewhere. When Social Services Departments were created the term used was 'client', but this has many pejorative connotations in contemporary prac-tice and other terms came about. 'Users' was employed quite widely as shorthand for 'service users who use the services of social workers', but to many 'users' itself has a negative interpretation, so 'service user' is often used instead. Equally 'people who use services', 'customers' and 'experts by experience' are all terms that are used. It is also crucial to understand the distinction between these people and those who act, very often, as their unpaid carers. Please bear these issues in mind as you read the book.

Part 1

Contexts

Introduction

Part 1 provides a starting point for everybody in PQ. Here, we start the process of reflection through considering how we put the 'post' in post-qualifying. The process of PQ is dynamic, satisfying and individual. There are unique challenges for social workers around issues of ethics and values, and in reflecting on this one should consider the challenging question of what social work is really about. Theory and practice can be integrated effectively and this process must be ongoing in PQ practice, which should link closely to research and evidence-based practice. Some tools and reflections are provided to this end. There is a demonstration that post-qualifying education and training has significance beyond the UK and the potential for sharing learning, and finally, researching practice guidance.

CHAPTER 1

Engaging with Continuing Professional Development: With or Without Qualification?

Michael Preston-Shoot

Introduction

Once the social work degree had been configured and launched in the four nations of the United Kingdom, it was only logical that the reform spotlight should turn to the post-qualifying (PQ) framework. Arguably, the imperatives driving the reconfiguration of the initial social work qualification apply just as much to what might be termed social (care) workers' post-registration status. While strategic responsibility for the development of the social work degree in England was retained by the Department of Health, that for the design of the new PQ framework was lodged with the General Social Care Council. However, design of the new structure (GSCC 2005c) drew on the same group of stakeholders, including experts by experience.

The purpose of this introductory chapter is to set the scene; to locate for practitioners and managers, who must now engage with continuing professional development, the context underpinning the changing landscape of social (care) work qualifications. The chapter's orientation is that the profile now being given to the education and training in which social (care) workers engage post-registration represents an opportunity, although one hedged with qualification. The use of qualification in this context is deliberate. Its use highlights the two meanings of the word. First, it can be used to denote an attribute, quality or accomplishment. Second, however, it can denote reservation. In setting this scene the chapter will survey the road travelled, map the landscape that influences the route being constructed, and anticipate the horizons that beckon.

Looking back

Social work policy-makers, practitioners and managers have, arguably, enjoyed an ambivalent relationship with post-qualifying education and training, reflective more of 'qualification' meaning reservation. Other than in relation to mental health, where Approved Social Workers (ASWs) must have a post-qualifying award in order to exercise legal powers and duties under the Mental Health Act 1983, policy-makers and regulators have shied away from requiring continuing professional development in respect of specialist social work functions. Indeed, the post-qualifying Child Care award has never attained the equivalent status for child protection workers as that attained by ASWs with their mental health qualification, regularly updated, because the role of child protection practitioner has not been ring-fenced for those practitioners and managers with several years' experience and recognised continuing professional development attainment.

Staff development officers know only too well the difficulty of securing manager attendance on courses that are centrally relevant to the nature of the decisions that they must take daily, involving as they do questions of needs versus resources and risk versus autonomy. They will know, too, that organisational training needs analyses and workforce planning models have only recently become more sophisticated and begun to systematically influence agency policy. Post-qualifying consortia will have had the experience of organisations challenging requirements for being overly academic, another reflection of the clash of perspective identified by Marsh and Triseliotis (1996) and by Barnes (2002), namely that managers prioritise practitioners knowing about the law and procedures while workers stress knowledge from empirical research and of methods of intervention. In the meantime regulators have expressed concern that employers are providing insufficient support for their employees (GSCC 2006a).

While the number of candidates completing post-qualifying awards has risen slowly, overall the workforce remains known for its low skill base and lack of training, and the sector for struggling to facilitate further education and training of its existing staff (Roche and Rankin 2004). Research has identified that social workers do not feel empowered and that quality practice is hindered less by lack of knowledge than by organisational attitudes towards trained staff, restricted purposes for supervision, limited resources and agency policies (Balloch, McLean and Fisher 1999; Jones 2001; Karban and Frost 1998; Marsh and Triseliotis 1996). Moreover, it is still possible to hear social (care) workers talk with pride about not having read a book or journal since qualifying, as well as complain that they are not supported in those study programmes with which they do engage (Preston-Shoot 2002). Such anecdotes suggest that the drift towards atheoretical practice is not just one encouraged by policy-making that has sought to reduce the area within which social workers have decision-making autonomy and discretion, but one with which at least some practitioners have colluded. However, the landscape has changed and continues to evolve, such that harbouring reservations about (post) qualification study is becoming less of an option in social (care) work.

Legal imperative

The Care Standards Act 2000 created care councils, provided for protected title for social workers and established registers for social (care) workers. It enabled the publication of codes, thereby requiring continuing professional development for ongoing registration. Indeed, the codes (GSCC 2002a) are unequivocal. Workers must be accountable for the quality of their work and take responsibility for maintaining and improving their knowledge and skills. This is integral to another required practice standard, namely that of upholding public trust and confidence in services.

Employers must enable their employees to meet the standards in the code of practice. They must provide training and development opportunities to enable staff to strengthen and develop their skills and knowledge. Thus, both social (care) workers and their managers are held accountable for the currency of their applied knowledge and skills, and for whether the learning culture provides opportunities for individual and collective growth into job roles.

It is too soon to judge the impact on quality and standards of registration, title protection and regulation through the codes of practice. Roche and Rankin (2004) have suggested, however, that more needs to be done to embed the codes in everyday practice. To the degree that practitioners continue to experience difficulty in challenging agency policy and procedures that infringe the codes of practice, it is certainly arguable that current structures are inadequate for clarifying accountability and for ensuring quality practice standards.

Policy imperative

National Occupational Standards (Topss 2002) include a key role of reflecting on, and continuing to develop, professional practice. This introduces a requirement for continuing professional development, as well as ongoing learning to consolidate and extend knowledge and skills, and to ensure safe practice.

The modernisation agenda (DoH 1998) has been set out to protect people from poor practice, to raise service standards and to make welfare agencies more accountable. It seeks to improve the commissioning of personalised services and to transform people's experiences of provision by strengthening the coordination of professional activity around specific outcomes. However, at its heart there lies a contradiction. The emphasis on quality is juxtaposed with tolerance of resource-driven work. The stress on coordination sits alongside policy proliferation rather than harmonisation, whether between health care and adult services, or between youth justice and children's services. The goal of raising standards is confounded by social policies that dehumanise groups of people and that embrace too readily narrow definitions of evidence, or selectively choose their focus on research findings to justify ideological positioning. It is in this terrain that social (care) workers practise. It is a geography in which, without courage, care and commitment, staff can lose the orientation that their values and knowledge provide.

Partnership imperative

Experts by experience expect practitioners and managers to be critical fixers (Braye and Preston-Shoot 2005). This orientation integrates technical competence (knowledge surrounding what needs to be done and the skills to do it effectively) with critical analysis (knowing why it needs to be done) and partnership (how to do it together). This parallels the themes that service users and carers continually emphasise, namely the importance of user-defined outcomes and of a process characterised by relationship, human qualities of respect, empathy and listening, and skilled application of methods of working (Barnes 2002). Experts by experience expect practitioners to be confident to challenge inappropriate provision and to advocate alongside them for practice that is lawful, ethical and knowledge-informed, where that evidence is drawn from research, practice wisdom, and service users and carers.

Just as the new ways of working envisaged by government (DfES/DoH 2006) include partnership with experts by experience in both service commissioning and delivery, they also give added impetus to inter-professional practice. This is consequent upon the Health Act 1999, the Health and Social Care Act 2001 and the Children Act 2004 (DoH 2004a), the result of which has been organisational reconfiguration, growth in integrated provision, and an emphasis on new skill mixes and working models. A moment's reflection would probably highlight that, when social (care) workers engage with legal, health and education professionals, they expect advice and guidance that is informed, up to date, lawful and evidence based. A second moment's reflection would be illustrative, namely a pause for thought on the impression being conveyed to these colleagues from other professions about social (care) work's commitment to the same standards.

Personal imperative

Chances are that many social (care) workers will at some time require social care services themselves, perhaps as carers, perhaps as service users. Critical reflection at this juncture might prove instructive in connecting the professional with the personal. As potential service users ourselves, relying on the professional attitudes, knowledge and skills of others, the standards we would expect are not hard to outline. Quite probably these will relate to the process surrounding an interaction – the values that characterise it, the currency of the knowledge that informs it, and the skills with which it is facilitated. They will focus in all likelihood also on clarity and delivery of negotiated outcomes that meet the needs presented. Having configured these standards, how well does current social (care) work practice and the management of that practice measure up?

Practice evidence imperative

That quality services are offered by social (care) workers may be deduced from inspection reports published by the Commission for Social Care Inspection and from articles in academic and practice journals. Researchers have found social workers to be knowledgeable, skilled and committed to continuing professional development and to using research knowledge (Jones 2001; McNeill 2001). The Options for Excellence report (DfES/DoH 2006) contains illustrations from the statutory and voluntary sectors of leading-edge approaches to continuing professional development, support for newly qualified staff, and practice learning, as well as recruitment and retention of staff, user-defined outcomes, workforce planning and commissioning. Nonetheless, in recognition of the fact that the picture is not uniform, the report also outlines a vision of workers accessing quality teaching and research, and taking decisions based on a sound evidence base. It advocates the development of practitioner-researcher posts and the systematic use of research into good practice to inform continuing professional development. Similarly, the Scottish Executive (2006b) envisages a research strategy to develop the capacity of the workforce and to provide practice resources for front-line staff.

The necessity of this policy direction is underscored by the continuing evidence of the challenge of disseminating research findings and aligning social (care) practice more closely to evaluation findings (Humphreys *et al.* 2003; Randall 2002; Walter *et al.* 2004). At least one review of social work and social care (DfES/DoH 2006) has found that not all staff are appropriately qualified or supported by excellent leadership and management. Additionally, there is evidence that some practitioners are out of date, unclear how to update, and offered limited training opportunities – for instance, in respect of the legal rules (Braye, Preston-Shoot and Thorpe 2006) where employers are required to provide continuing professional development (GSCC 2002a). Inquiries find evidence of abusive practice across social (care) work sectors (Reder, Duncan and Gray 1993; Sheppard 1996). There are reports that practitioners collude with managers in unlawful and unethical practice (Horwath 2000; Machin 1998).

Researchers have found that the workforce is unable to re-skill at a rate commensurate with the pace of change (Balloch *et al.* 1999); this in a context of providing services increasingly to people with complex needs. The nature of practice is also changing, with increasing numbers of service users now employers themselves, as a direct result of the introduction and subsequent extension and strengthening of direct payment legal rules, and with a substantially greater involvement of experts by experience in commissioning, inspection and delivery of social (care) services.

Visioning forward

The contrast between the contemporary policy emphasis on post-qualifying education with the historical position is quite striking. Guidance from employer-led organisations is unequivocal about continuing professional development. It is seen as vital to service improvement, effective people management and recruitment and retention, meeting standards, and the development of a skilled workforce (Skills for Care/Children's Workforce Development Council 2006; Skills for Health 2006). Organisations are encouraged to have a strategy for planned learning and development for all social (care) work staff as a properly trained and skilled workforce is seen as axiomatic for effective safeguarding and quality service commissioning, development and provision (DfES/DoH 2006).

Delivering the vision will require that some barriers are more effectively addressed. There remains a large section of the workforce without appropriate qualifications (Roche and Rankin 2004; Skills for Health 2006). There are long-standing accessibility issues, particularly staffing levels and turnover, and difficulties with staff release that revolve around workloads, resources and the cost of training (Roche and Rankin 2004; Skills for Care/Children's Workforce Development Council 2006; Skills for Health 2006). One temptation to resist here will be to focus on informal learning opportunities via workplace experience, involving critical incidents, supervision and knowledge sets, at the expense of formal programmes. A second temptation to resist is a minimalist focus, perhaps on induction, the requirements for re-registration, and supervision and appraisal to meet emerging or core aspects of a role. A third is to avoid splitting and abdicating responsibility. Continuing professional development is a joint responsibility – employers to provide learning opportunities, staff to develop their knowledge and skills (Skills for Care/Children's Workforce Development Council 2006); agencies to become learning organisations, staff to value their contribution when learning and facilitating the learning of others, whether in formal roles of appraisal, supervision and seminars, or through opportunities that arise through the lived experience of work.

In this context, the analysis of the strengths and weaknesses in different models for improving the use of research in social (care) work (Walter *et al.* 2004) is instructive for the goal of maximising the effectiveness of investment in continuing professional development. The allocation of responsibility to individuals to update and apply their learning has to be accompanied by the creation of space so that they have the autonomy to use this knowledge base. Embedding professional development and the knowledge base in organisational policies and procedures requires a significant shift in the traditional structure of post-qualifying education and training to include managers alongside practitioners. Read and Clements (1999) and Crawshaw and Wates (2005) provide examples of joint involvement in workshops being used to inform action planning, while Roche and Rankin (2004) suggest that supervision and appraisal meetings can be used to monitor the use and impact of training and knowledge acquisition on practice. Such embedding also requires the application of the knowledge gained to the local context, in which experts by experience should be involved (Walter *et al.* 2004), and greater transparency about the relationship between knowledge utilisation and other imperatives to which social (care) work organisations are subject.

There is the challenge of ensuring that there is suitable and flexible provision, capable of offering higher education institutions the stability they require to invest in programme development, while guaranteeing employees and employers access to quality education tailored to workplace needs (Skills for Care/Children's Workforce Development Council 2006). This challenge revolves not just around developing the pedagogy of post-qualifying education, diversifying more substantially into blended, distance and e-learning; it centres, too, on being mindful of the difference between training and education. Meeting the needs of employers, and therefore emphasising operational knowledge for practice, competence for roles and organisational performance, must not obliterate the critical questions, the development of emotional and intellectual understanding, that are also relevant if practitioners are to manage the dilemmas with which they are confronted daily (Nellis 1999; Preston-Shoot 2000). Building the workforce requires integration rather than separation of critical thinker and fixer functions (Braye and Preston-Shoot 2005; Roche and Rankin 2004).

However, the framework will be complete only when there are complete escalators that social (care) workers can access, from their introduction into social care through different sectors or levels of responsibility, from social care into social work, or from practice into leadership, management and/or research of practice. The focus hitherto has been on social work rather than additionally social care and professional colleagues in health, housing or education – the inclusion of these perspectives more closely corresponding to the developing coordination within children's and adult services. The framework's potential will be enhanced with the creation of career pathways that enable experienced staff to develop advanced practitioner roles through which their learning can impact on service development and practice, and with a review of the fragmented regional organisational jigsaw through which the framework is currently being rolled out.

Equally, the framework's potential for improving the quality of services and the standards offered by the workforce will be realised only when it evolves through systematic evaluation of the outcomes and processes of continuing professional development. Historically there has been a lack of evidence of the overall impact of training (Roche and Rankin 2004). Single points of evaluation, usually at the conclusion of teaching inputs, should be replaced with different combinations, suitable to context, of baseline and repeat measures, and data collection that assesses impact on learning needs, attitude development and service provision (Carpenter 2005).

Conclusion

Whatever its structural and operational tensions, the result of competing perspectives and interests – for example, around control of funding – the new post-qualifying framework, and policy-makers' commitment to it, represents an opportunity. For it to be grasped requires a shift of mind from policy-makers, academics, employers and employees, to ensure that continuing professional development is fully embedded in the future of social (care) work. Using the standards envisaged by the modernisation agenda (DoH 1998), it is easy to begin to scope the questions that must be answered positively.

- Needs-led:
  - How well do universities know the needs of local services and practitioners?
  - How well do agencies know the training needs of staff?
  - To what degree are experts by experience informing training needs analyses?
- Relevance:
  - How well are experts by experience involved in planning, delivery and evaluation of continuing professional development?
  - How closely is learning and assessment aligned with practice and its management?
- Quality:
  - To what degree are outcomes systematically evaluated?
  - To what degree are experts by experience involved in research on outcomes of education and training?
  - To what degree is continuing professional development raising practice standards?
- Coordination:
  - How well do agencies and universities engage in partnership planning?
  - How far are other sectors and professional groupings involved in the post-qualifying framework?
  - To what degree is continuing professional development relating diverse forms of knowledge and evidence to policy and practice?
- Accountability:
  - To what degree is post-qualifying education addressing staff experiences of work?

- ○ To what degree are the standards expected by experts by experience upheld in the content of learning offered?

- Flexibility:

  - ○ To what degree is work-based learning integrated into the qualifications framework?

  - ○ What is the availability of e-learning and distance learning?

This shift of mind will require a critical openness and reflective self-examination on the part of all stakeholders involved with social (care) work. However, what is learned might enable practitioners and managers, together with experts by experience, to provide policy leadership (located in learning organisations), political leadership (knowledge-informed responses to questions of health, well-being, equality and social justice) and practice leadership (established credibility with experts by experience and other professions to advocate for process and outcome standards). That could make quite a difference.

Recommended reading

Adams, R., Dominelli, L. and Payne, M. (eds) (2005) *Social Work Futures: Crossing Boundaries, Transforming Practice*. Basingstoke: Palgrave Macmillan.

Brammer, A. (2006) *Social Work Law* (2nd edn). Harlow: Longman/Pearson Education.

Stanley, N. and Manthorpe, J. (eds) (2004) *The Age of the Inquiry: Learning and Blaming in Health and Social Care*. London: Routledge.

Trevithick, P. (2005) *Social Work Skills: A Practice Handbook* (2nd edn). Maidenhead: Open University Press/McGraw-Hill Education.

CHAPTER 2

Reflective, Critical and Transformational Practice
Robert Adams

Introduction

When working with people, we are expected to finish each piece of work. We are tutored in how to bring about closure. Every piece of practice has a beginning, a middle and an end. The middle is the part that concerns this chapter. The middle, as we shall see below, is about a broadening or loosening process that invites reflection and questioning, and is the opposite of tightening and closure. The question is how far we can take this broadening and opening up. The beginning and end may particularly be backed up by pieces of paper, that need completing, checklists, lists of standards, assessment schedules, forms, questionnaires, inventories, lists of aims, objectives, methods, review reports, summaries and evaluations. It is good practice to set an achievable goal that automatically lends itself to setting a limit to the assessment, the planning, the intervention and the review, so we are taught, because completion is proof of our competence. Yet we are working with people's lives which, unless the beginning of our case coincides with their birth and the end with their death, are part of larger processes. How do we tackle those tasks that are more demanding either because of their subject matter or their complexity? They are social work 'beyond the basic'; they require work at a higher level. They are 'beyond' in another sense, because they are more arguable, provisional and unfinished. The more 'beyond' they are, are they more likely to be recognised as post-qualifying?

We have to start somewhere in this book and it is not just convenient but necessary, perhaps, to begin by exploring those boundaries between levels of practice that might be used to distinguish what is 'basic', what is 'post-qualifying', 'Specialist', 'Higher Specialist' and 'Advanced'. This chapter explores these ideas, setting them against another set of ideas to do with how practitioners reflect, are critical and may act transformationally.

Post-qualifying practice: contested, provisional, unfinished

Social work, particularly at its post-qualification (PQ) levels, is a long way from those immediately definable tasks that follow guidelines, require boxes to be ticked, and have a beginning, a middle and an end. These tasks can be delegated to newly qualified staff, or even carried out by student social workers under qualified supervision. I am not saying all PQ work is necessarily open-ended, but the more *complex* nature of goals, methods and so on perhaps makes prescriptions more difficult to arrive at. In fact, PQ practice shares almost nothing with the heavily proceduralised rules that constrain some basic tasks, and in contrast has much more in common with the creative arts. This is a theme that Hugh England successfully argued a generation ago, but which has remained somewhat under-explored (England 1986). Another feature of social work research and practice shared with the creative arts has been built on by enthusiasts for the psychologist George Kelly's Personal Construct Theory (Kelly 1955). It is the notion of 'loosening' referred to above, where we allow our mind to range over possibilities, test alternative perspectives and allow for possible intuitive reframing of ideas, interpretations and practice, before asserting our rationality, 'tightening' and focusing our analysis on conclusions and implications for practice.

Another feature of post-qualifying practice that relates to some of the larger projects of creative artists is its *unfinished* nature. This is as much as anything a reflection of the reality that social work deals with the process of people's *lives*, becoming involved for short periods in experiences that are much longer. They precede social work intervention and continue after it. There are some art forms where the artist engages in a long-term, even lifelong project. In Spain, the renowned architect Antoni Gaudí conceived a design for the cathedral Sagrada Familia in Barcelona that was far from completed in his lifetime. While in Barcelona, I was very struck by the continual struggle of those engaged for the past century in completing this masterpiece. Reading about the experiences of those involved, far from the building being a failure because it was unfinished, it seems as though some vital spark of the original creativity has been sustained through its status as incomplete and, therefore, as still developing. It occurred to me that the unfinished character of some art has a dynamic quality lost in that which is complete. It enables succeeding generations of people to interact with it. In this regard, post-qualifying social work has the edge over the 'finished' status of basic qualification, by remaining unfinished and therefore a lifelong challenge for the worker.

Like Gaudí's architecture, the practice of social work at post-qualifying level is challenging by virtue of being constantly subject to *fresh questions and interpretations.* We have a view of a situation, but it is provisional. Dorothy Whitaker and Lesley Archer developed different ways of describing practice-based research through reflecting with groups of post-qualifying social workers on their various practice-based research projects (Whitaker and Archer 1989). One of the features of this is the flexibility with which the practitioner revisits the practice situation with fresh questions and hypotheses to test out in future actions, continually revising them, reflecting and revisiting in an unending cyclical process. In one sense, of course, it is not a cycle, because it is moving forward all the time. The practitioner revisits a continually changing situation, does more, reflects, more happens, the practitioner does some more, reflects, and so on. They are describing everybody, including us. In our future reflections we probably continually revise our view as fresh evidence emerges and more things happen. The so-called *academic wisdom* and the *practice wisdom* interact. This interaction can lead to fresh knowledge and research, or it can go the other way and the research can produce new knowledge and fresh approaches to practice (Whitaker and Archer 1989, p.13).

We could argue that some of social work at any level, but all of social work at post-qualifying level in particular, presents other challenges that some might say bear similarity to architecture, chiefly its complexity, and creative and contested character. The complexity arises in the situations with which practitioners engage. The creativity arises from the need for practitioners to come up with innovative ways of responding to the complexity and the contested nature of the judgements and decisions needing to be made. Social workers are challenged uniquely in their work by questions about the legitimacy of particular approaches to the work. These have knock-on effects on issues at the pre-qualifying stage of people's careers and complicate questions about what the particular 'added value' should be of post-qualifying practice. The publication of standards and curricula for the different courses at qualifying, post-qualifying and advanced levels does not end debates, but merely provides more opportunities to open them up and expose further gaps and inconsistencies.

We can push the analogy with architecture one stage further, by drawing attention to the invisible structure of complex theories and calculations that lay embedded in Gaudí's work on the cathedral, even before the first trench was dug for the foundations. The infrastructure modelled the large creation. There was more than one model. There were different forms of model applied to test how much support, for example, would be needed to ensure this or that tower did not fall down. There was an infrastructure of ideas and theories, embedded in the practice.

This is where the present handbook comes in. One way forward is to try to develop a discourse for basic qualification and post-qualification social work education and training that is both accessible and usable in practice, yet conceptually robust and rich enough to contribute both to practice development and the development of theory. Reflective practice, critical practice and transformational practice are notions with the potential to make this contribution. It is too simple to suggest that a practitioner might move through a continuum from 'simple' reflection, to critical reflection and, ultimately, to more ambitious transformational activity, for individuals, families, groups and communities. Nevertheless, there is no doubt that these different perspectives pose progressively greater challenges for practitioners. This chapter introduces these perspectives and acknowledges that they do relate to practice in some direct ways. How far they match the framework for post-qualifying practice in England and the developing equivalent elsewhere in the UK is, at present, an open question. We are not quite ready to examine them, though, because first we have to discuss some features of social work that complicate its theory and practice considerably more than happens in some other professions. I heard a student say in a seminar that it is the social in social work that creates all the controversies with others. The ripples from this insight seem to me still to be moving outwards. It makes a timeless point, examined here briefly.

The 'social' in social work is challenging and challenges social work

Ironically, while social work has a troubled image due to a small percentage of problems that lead to scandals and create the reputation of a damaged profession, the truth more often is that social work suffers from the aura around people's ills that it deals with, rather than from any intrinsic ills in itself (Parton and Franklin 1991). It is no stronger, but no weaker, than other professions. Yet it appears to be. Almost uniquely among professions, social work takes responsibility for managing the personal dimensions of multiple problems such as urban and rural squalor, deprivation and degradation in communities and societies, while attempting to empower, and sometimes intervene in the lives of, individual people experiencing personal problems (Halmos 1978). One of the difficulties social workers have faced over several decades is how to convince fellow professionals, as well as service users and themselves, that social work is an equivalent activity, as credible as others, warranting respect as a legitimate profession alongside others such as nursing and teaching. There are at least three challenges to the legitimacy of social work: in its knowledge base, the relationship between practitioners and people receiving services, and through the responses of others to shortcomings and scandals; these challenges will be examined now.

Knowledge base

The long-standing first challenge is from those who maintain that social work is a 'semi-profession' that does not have sole ownership of a particular territory of knowledge and expertise in practice (Etzioni 1969). Many areas of theory and practice in social work, including many aspects of research itself (Dominelli 2005, pp.223–36), are subject to debate. New recruits to social work on qualifying degrees sometimes find such an atmosphere of controversy hanging over the practice, as well as what we call the consumers of the practice, rather a lot to take on board. Fortunately, by the time they complete their basic qualifying degrees, most student social workers have not only grasped but joined in these debates.

That is what they are – debates. The idea that there is a stable, unchanging base for practice if only we can find it is an illusion. In the early 1970s, in the wake of the Seebohm Report, generic social work was created and practised largely from the newly created Social Services Departments. From the mid-1970s, the advent of radical and critical criminology, the National Deviancy Conference and radical social work (Pearson 1975), and the social workers' strike of 1978 were evidence of a growing mood of criticism and self-criticism by social work academics and practitioners alike. To some, 'professionals' served the bureaucracy and the status quo first and this became anathema (Bailey and Brake 1975). In the twenty-first century, Social Services Departments are disappearing, to be replaced by new directorates of adults' and children's services, many of whose providers are in the independent sector. Indeed Scotland uses the term '21st century social work' and a five-year planning cycle is in hand, whereas England has a vision in Options for Excellence for 2020 (DfES/DoH 2006).

Relationship between practitioners and 'people receiving services'

There is little doubt that the requirement to work *with* 'service users' and carers means they participate in a much more substantial way than would have been envisaged a generation ago. The word 'empowerment' is now firmly rooted in the social work literature (Adams 1996). This diversity of terms for the 'customers' of the range of partnerships and public and private providers of social care and social work services does not make for public and professional confidence in the local authorities employing social work practitioners.

In the 1970s, we still talked and wrote of social workers and 'clients'. In the revised framework for post-qualifying education and training published in February 2005, the GSCC requires that regional planning networks developing post-qualifying programmes must develop them with the involvement of service users and carers alongside employers at regional, sub-regional and local level (GSCC 2005c, para. 27, p.9).

Responses to shortcomings in services

A succession of inquiry reports into shortcomings in social work services have been published since the 1970s (Blom-Cooper 1985; Laming 2003; London Borough of Greenwich and Greenwich Health Authority 1987; London Borough of Lambeth 1987; Secretary of State for Social Services 1974), and have combined with the modernisation agenda of the Labour Government, which came into power in 1997, to force a number of major changes in the organisation and delivery of social work services.

Questions of 'level'

As one of the three editors co-writing and co-editing a trilogy of texts about social work, I have taken part in many editorial discussions, between ourselves and with the publishers, about the level at which these books should be pitched. One view, often expressed by the publishers, was that the sales of the books would be increased by use of words such as 'Basic' and 'Introductory' in their titles. Another view, particularly put forward by the editors in relation to the third book, was that this should include direct reference to 'Advanced Practice' in its title. At the same time, there was a view that all qualified practitioners should be equally competent in all the aspects, and post-qualifying, in effect, meant simply more knowledgeable and more experienced. In the event, we ducked these debates and disagreements, and proceeded by using other words on which we all agreed. I continued to consider whether it mattered or made sense to compartmentalise a more 'advanced', or 'post-qualifying', practice from 'basic' qualifying practice. The key questions in this regard include: Do post-qualifying social workers practise differently? Do they have a richer, that is distinctively different, knowledge base? Do they think, that is theorise, differently? Is there a conceptual difference, a fault line, a sharp break of level, between qualifying and post-qualifying, or is all practice simply 'post-experience', in the sense that one accumulates 'practice wisdom' by a process of gradual sedimentation up the gentle gradient of years of experience? One of the products of this chapter is the tentative conclusion that, while it is hard to answer 'yes' to these questions, many experienced and appropriately qualified social workers do work at a level beyond that of a recently qualified practitioner. A hard-and-fast distinction between basic and post-qualifying social work may be hard to maintain; nevertheless, a distinction exists. Two of the more obvious differences are in the complexity of the situations presented to practitioners and the life-changing significance for people of the decisions that may have to be made. We could argue that the framework of theories, approaches and skills that the practitioner brings to bear on these situations has to be conceptually richer, more robust, with more complex interconnections with various contexts than is required for 'simple' cases. That is easy to say but probably is impossible to categorise in any way that a majority of social work educators and practitioners would agree about.

Let us introduce a practice example, in the form of a short case study, to help us examine in more detail what it means to engage in reflective, critical or transformational practice at different levels.

Case study

Mrs Khan was expecting somebody from adult services to call to arrange for her request to admit her husband, who had a stroke last week and has just come out of hospital, to residential care, because she cannot cope. Mrs Khan has rung again to say she has made a simple request and she wants a simple, preferably immediate, response.

Regulations and reflective, critical and transformational practice

All practice does not take place on a single level. For a start, there is basic qualifying practice and there is post-qualifying practice. The post-qualifying framework for England announced by the GSCC in 2005 was the first in the UK and consists of three levels: Specialist, Higher Specialist and Advanced. In broad terms, the Specialist level equates with all or part of the final year of an honours degree or free-standing graduate diploma; the Higher Specialist corresponds with a postgraduate diploma; the Advanced corresponds with level M in the QAA framework (i.e. the academic level common both to postgraduate diplomas and degrees at master's level). However, the framework specifically states that 'only programmes leading to master's degrees will be approved as advanced award programmes' (GSCC 2005a, para. 35, p.12).

The GSCC documentation specifies that the three levels of post-qualifying education and training will be integrated with academic levels corresponding with graduate, postgraduate and master's qualifications respectively. It is more difficult to delineate the boundaries between the three levels in professional development terms. At Specialist level, the focus is on 'consolidating, extending and deepening initial professional competence' (GSCC 2005a, para. 19, p.8) and this runs on, apparently seamlessly, from basic qualifying without a gap in theoretical or practice terms. That is to say, there is no specified criterion for judging a jump up to a higher level. At the next, second, Higher Specialist, level the framework refers to three criteria: 'the knowledge and skills needed to make complex judgements', the knowledge and skills needed to 'discharge high levels of responsibility for the co-ordination of social support' and 'the management of risk' (GSCC 2005a, para. 20, p.8). At the third, Advanced, level the single criterion concerns the knowledge and skills contributing to 'professional leadership and the improvement of services'. The two aspects of professional leadership are deemed to be 'managerial forms of leadership' and 'those linked to the promotion and dissemination of advanced practice skills' (GSCC 2005c, para. 21, p.8).

It is important to recognise a tension between the fact that the revised PQ framework is designed to support modular university-based learning and, through it, the GSCC envisages professional development beyond qualification as a holistic process. Importantly, this draws on the notion of transferability, which has been present in social work education for many years. Through this, 'individuals acquire knowledge and skills in different areas, which then combine with one another to promote a deeper sense of overall professional identity' (GSCC 2005c, para. 23, p.8).

While it may seem to be relatively clear how in specific areas such as mental health or child protection a practitioner can move from pre-qualification to post-qualification in encountering the complexities of difficult cases, or in another sense can take on a post requiring professional leadership, this clearly leaves a vast territory of generic practice from which these milestones are absent. This territory will probably take years to map, as the different courses continue to develop, building on existing provision. At the same time, perhaps we need to commission one of our colleagues to examine the existing maps of social work education and training programmes in their richness and diversity to see whether there are useful concepts in common use, which can be linked more systematically to the basic qualifying and post-qualifying frameworks. The ideas of reflective practice, critical practice and transformational practice provide a useful starting point.

It is tempting but mistaken to view reflective, critical and transformational practice as 'easy' ideas to put into practice. It is entirely understandable, though, because one of the realities social workers encounter in their daily practice is that the material of their practice, the situations in which they work, can be described by anybody, as well as by professionals, the practitioners, using similar language. That is to say, while doctors and nurses use words from physiology and pharmacology to refer to their practice, social workers use words such as assess, plan, review, help and advise. You would also expect social workers who have qualified since the early 1990s to use words such as reflective, critical and transforming to describe aspects of their practice. We can use the example of work done with Mr and Mrs Khan to explore these ideas in more detail. While it would be a mistake to claim that they can be teased out entirely separately, it is reasonable to suggest that, together, they have a cross-bracing effect. Their combined effect strengthens practice.

REFLECTIVE PRACTICE: THE BASIS FOR QUALIFYING AND SPECIALIST WORK?
It is common to encounter the statement that practice should be reflective. It is more difficult to work through the meaning of reflection in particular cases. When we talk about being 'reflective', we often mean no more than 'in a thoughtful mood' or 'pensive'. However, in social work, the term 'reflective practice' can refer to several things, among which the following three are common (Schon 1983).

1. We may use it to mean thinking slowly and systematically through the options before taking a decision.

2. We may use it to describe an approach involving mirroring the practice situation in our own circumstances, so as to draw comparisons and contrasts. We are not detached from people's circumstances and the work we do with them, but are affected by it and use its effects on our own thoughts and feelings to inform our judgements about how other people are affected. We may use the term 'reflexive' to refer to this activity. Reflexivity is an important component of being reflective because, like reflection, it involves a continuous cycle of thinking, experiencing, being affected by that experience and acting before thinking further, and so on (Payne 2002a, p.127).

3.   We may use it to refer to the process of considering the piece of work we have done and alternative ways we could have done it.

It is clear that reflection means more than pondering on the case. It implies drawing on our values, knowledge and experience in a systematic way, looking back at what we have done and looking forward at what to do next. What does this mean in relation to the example of Mr and Mrs Khan? For a start, we shall consider their situation with them and enable them to clarify the different options facing them. It is hoped we can widen their choices in the process. It may not be too implausible to talk about empowering them to make decisions. If we had to select two words to sum up this reflective approach, they would be 'reflexive' and 'purposeful'.

CRITICAL PRACTICE: EVIDENCE-BASED 'HIGHER SPECIALIST' PRACTICE?

The term 'critical' has different meanings in different situations. In everyday language, to be critical often implies being negative. However, in social work the meaning of critical practice is complex and implies an enrichment of ideas going beyond reflective practice. There are three common meanings of critical: first, it means drawing on critical theories; second, it may refer to the clustering of reflections about a piece of practice that do not flatter it; third, it may mean making a considered evaluation judgement about its strengths and weaknesses. Expanding on an earlier discussion of critical practice (Payne *et al.* 2002, p.6), we can identify five main features of critical practice in social work.

1.   Comprehensive assessment: this involves us assessing people's circumstances so as to develop as comprehensive a picture as possible.

2.   Critical appraisal: this necessitates us critically appraising research evidence and bringing it to bear on possible ways of tackling the situation.

3.   Putting in context: we need to take both our assessment and this critical appraisal of research and set them in the broader context of our knowledge and understanding of relevant theories.

4.   Value-led practice: our practice needs to be informed by our values.

5.   Empowerment-based practice: the skills we draw on will include working in partnership with Mr and Mrs Khan, so as to empower them as far as possible throughout the above process.

Thus, the foundation of critical practice is the *evidence-based practice* under-pinned by research into practice and the ever-growing body of critically reflective writing on practice. This may not support the prevailing current of how things are done in a particular agency and setting, but may suggest different ways of working. We need additional knowledge – from experience and from the research evidence base – so we can access and critically review in order to develop evidence-based practice. So we can argue it is practice that goes beyond the basic qualifying level.

TRANSFORMATIONAL PRACTICE: 'ADVANCED'

The idea of transformational or transforming practice revolves around the notion of change. Usually transformation has connotations of fundamental change. Change can happen at a number of levels – individual, group, organisation, community, society, continent and globe. It can be perceived by an observer or experienced by a person receiving the service, as positive or negative, depending on the person's perspective. One of the ideas that has its roots in Marxist theory can be transplanted from its radical origins and relocated here in the mainstream of social work theory and practice, namely *praxis*. Praxis pushes beyond the notion of reflexivity we encountered earlier. It refers to our ideologies, or beliefs and values about how the world is and how we believe it should be, which feed into the cycle of our critical reflective thoughts being carried into action and back again into reflection, and so on, in a continuous process (Payne 2002a, p.127).

The key elements of transformational practice are as follows.

- It implies reframing the way we perceive the situation, in its context, thinking 'outside the box'.

- It may involve changing our response to the situation.

- It may lead the person(s) with whom we are working to a significantly different, better outcome.

Common elements of all three viewpoints include their emphasis on considered, purposeful, aware and self-aware practice. What we are implying is that some practitioners may use an enhanced level of knowledge and skill to push the boundaries of practice beyond maintenance of the status quo and act in more creative ways that may well be more rewarding for all concerned. This may benefit people using services and carers and, in challenging the boundaries of received wisdom about work with people, may move beyond existing patterns of working. The reality is that to work beyond the basis of reflective practice requires an enhanced level of knowledge, skill and confidence. This may accumulate only through time and through post-qualifying experience and learning.

Case study revisited

We shall now view the work with Mr and Mrs Khan through the three lenses of reflective, critical and transformational thinking (see Table 2.1). Let us try to put ourselves in the position of the reflective practitioner, then in the position of the critical practitioner and finally in the position of the transformational practitioner.

Table 2.1 Reflective, critical and transformational practice

Form of practice	Characteristics of practice
Reflective	Working within the status quo
	Carrying out necessary procedures, processes
	Acting thoughtfully, sensitively, self-awarely
Critical	Locating practice in policy and practice context
	Acting reflexively and self-critically
	Considering how practice could have been carried out differently and better
Transformational	Analysis of immediate and wider environment
	Empowering people who use services and carers to act collectively with others
	Challenging and changing status quo of practice

In terms of reflective practice, we might expect the practitioner to work with Mr and Mrs Khan to enable Mrs Khan to become more flexible in her assessment of her situation and in the range of options she considers feasible for Mr Khan to receive community care services.

As far as critical practice is concerned, in working with Mr and Mrs Khan, what will be the main features of our critical practice? First, we shall try to assess their situation so as to develop as rounded and full a picture as possible. Second, we shall ensure that Mr and Mrs Khan contribute to this assessment. Third, we might expect the practice to put the circumstances of Mr and Mrs Khan in the context of research evidence on the ways households are affected by one person's stroke, and work with them to reduce the negative consequences. Fourth, we would seek to empower Mr and Mrs Khan to exercise their respective choices in the options available to them. Even after a risk assessment indicating that there was a high risk that Mr Khan might have another stroke, the practitioner might be willing to take the considered risk of encouraging the couple to continue to live independent lives in the community, with support.

Finally, let us consider how transformational practice might be applied. It is possible to envisage the practitioner:

- empowering Mr and Mrs Khan by creating the conditions for them to reassess their circumstances and use direct payments to maintain their independence

- putting Mr and Mrs Khan in touch with other carers and service users, so they can share experiences

- engaging in research, analysing data from a number of similar situations to Mr and Mrs Khan's and making recommendations to the local authority concerning service development.

Now, let us have a hard look at the above. Is it really possible to make a hard-and-fast distinction, in terms of level, between being reflective, critical and transformational? To be honest, there is some difference between the first two. Our reflections do not seem to take the situation as far as possible in considering all possible outcomes, in the present – the status quo – and in the future, depending on other possible changes we might effect. However, our distinction between being critical and being transformational seems less easy to justify. It is more a matter of how far we go, rather than going somewhere intrinsically, qualitatively different. That is still justifiable, if we say that becoming more advanced as a practitioner entails accumulating and learning from the experience of dealing with more complex situations and acquiring a richer store of knowledge of research evidence on which to base our practice.

Tensions and dilemmas arising in practice

I have written a rather summary account above. One advantage of the written word is that we can construct tidy examples in which everything works out for the best. Reality is not usually as tidy as this. In practice, Mr and Mrs Khan live in the real world and the practitioner works in the agency. Let us remind ourselves of the further complexities this creates and the inevitable tensions produced.

Mr and Mrs Khan's story does not end here. Let us imagine what happens next. The intervention by the practitioner is part of a process. Mr Khan's condition improves for a while, then deteriorates again. Mrs Khan reaches a point where she cannot cope with caring for him at home. She faces the dilemma as to whether to struggle on, inadequately, or whether to break with her basic values of support through the family and ask for him to be admitted to residential or nursing care.

Meanwhile, the practitioner in the agency encounters issues concerning limitations of resources and the capacity of the agency to enable practice to continue to move in the direction the practitioner desires. The practitioner is accountable in one sense to Mr and Mrs Khan and also to professional values and practices, which are held dear. Also, the practitioner has accountability to the employer and the line manager, and has to continue to deliver services as directed by local procedures, in line, it is hoped, with national standards.

We could argue, of course, that there is no reason to prevent any practitioner reaching this point. The difference between the possible outcomes for the family will be minimised by the practitioner taking advice from team members who are more qualified and experienced. We cannot predict this with certainty. What this example enables us to clarify are the implications of different ways of responding to the situation of the family.

Reflective, critical and transformational practice at post-qualification levels

It would be too crude and simplistic to suggest that there is a correspondence between reflective, critical and transformational practice and the respective levels of Specialist, Higher Specialist and Advanced post-qualification, but there is some merit in examining links at the three levels and looking to a future where we shall be able to continue to develop discussions about the social work literature in specialist fields, at continually refined and enriched levels of conceptualisation and debate.

Conclusion

It is easier to clarify the academic boundaries between the three levels of Specialist, Higher Specialist and Advanced post-qualification in social work than to chart the distinctions in terms of practice. When it comes to practice, unsurprisingly perhaps, actual cases, rather like our own thoughts, feelings, lives and work, do not break down into categories of level or complexity. While, in many senses, the journey from pre-qualifying through the different levels of post-qualifying practice is seamless because the practitioner is engaged in a learning process, there are differences that, although their boundaries may be vague and difficult to pin down, are real. This chapter has drawn on the widely used notions of reflective practice, critical practice and transformational practice to help explore this.

In the example used above, it is noted how necessary it is for the practitioner to practise reflectively. Also, we have seen how continuous engagement in critical reflection enables the practitioner to engage with the complexities of people's lives and the difficult issues they face. However, one implication of this is the capacity of the practitioner to develop a robust practice capable of grappling with the challenges of transformation: of thinking and doing, theorising and practising. The very strength of this robustness is self-awareness of its fragility. Therein lies a paradox at the heart of post-qualifying practice. A further responsibility at this level is to engage in continuing debate about that practice and continually revisit it critically, an uncomfortable process that necessitates us continuing to gaze critically at ourselves. This critical gaze and self-awareness open up questions without answering them, raise issues but do not resolve them, and build further work on the as yet unfinished foundations of past and present practice. It is no surprise that post-qualifying practice poses so many challenges and it is equally unsurprising that this handbook contains so much material concerning unfinished aspects of theory and practice, and presents what we may call the post-qualifying agenda for practice. The most promising and exciting aspect of this agenda is that it is, and probably always will be, contested, provisional and incomplete. This maximises the potential for creative practice in the future.

Recommended reading

Payne, M. (2002) 'Social Work Theories and Reflective Practice.' In R. Adams, L. Dominelli and M. Payne *Social Work: Themes, Issues and Critical Perspectives.* Basingstoke: Palgrave.

Payne, M., Adams, R. and Dominelli, L. (2002) 'On Being Critical in Social Work.' In R. Adams, L. Dominelli and M. Payne, *Critical Practice in Social Work.* Basingstoke: Palgrave.

Schon, D.A. (1983) *The Reflective Practitioner: How Professionals Think in Action.* New York: Basic Books.

Whitaker, D.S. and Archer, J.L. (1989) *Research by Social Workers: Capitalizing on Experience,* CCETSW Study 9. London: Central Council for Education and Training in Social Work (CCETSW).

CHAPTER 3

Ethics and Values in Theory and Practice

Mary Rayner

Introduction

This chapter considers the role of ethics and values in the light of the changing world in which social work is practised in the twenty-first century. It argues that critical thinking with regard to the development of the approach to professional ethics is absolutely crucial for the post-qualified social worker.

All welfare professionals claim to have 'ethics' at the heart of their practice. There is, and certainly 'ought' to be, constant debate and discussion about 'what is right' and 'what is wrong' for each profession in carrying out their 'role and tasks'. Perhaps more familiarly, this is expressed as a concern with 'good practice' (to be shared and disseminated within that profession) and 'bad practice' (to be eliminated and stamped out). This chapter takes the view that social work, and the education and training of the profession, has always adopted a unique stance among welfare professionals with regard, not to the contested and much debated issues of 'right' and 'wrong', 'good' and 'bad' practice, but rather with regard to the system or method of deciding how such issues are to be resolved.

With a history of thought, reason and philosophical reflection spanning thousands of years it is clearly not possible to provide a detailed account or even sketch in the outline of such thought. This chapter therefore confines itself to:

- practical ethics and a selection of theories that have been and continue to be significant for social work practice; these are 'virtue ethics', 'duty-based' ethical theories and 'consequentialist' ethical theories

- consideration of these theories as *they must apply to practice;* this involves 'critical thinking'. It therefore attempts to demonstrate *how* critical thinking about ethics should be carried out, if the necessary interlocking and interdependence of theory and practice or critical thinking and critical action are to result in critical practice.

The selection of some theories over others and the aim to enhance the critical thinking skills of the qualified social worker must depend for its success on the relevance to a consideration of the world in which social workers must operate. It therefore begins with a consideration of social work and social change in the twenty-first century.

The importance of 'context': social work and social change in the twenty-first century

It is generally acknowledged that the last three decades of the twentieth century were characterised by 'change' – rapid, fundamental, and impacting on the social, political and economic structure. Additionally, factors such as increased migration and influxes of refugees and asylum seekers to the UK have enhanced changes in culture and language.

In response to these changes, as Sarah Banks (2006, p.xi) points out in her preface to the third edition of her basic text on ethics and social work, 'few professions have changed more than social work'. Two kinds of change have resulted:

1. change in the 'roles and tasks' of social workers – with increasing diversity of perspectives and heterogeneity of the social work task

2. change in the very status and identity of social workers.

The most significant questions, however, that must be addressed by the social worker operating within this are whether this also necessitates a change in core social work ethics and values and, if so, what these changes might be and who has the power to decide on them.

The answers to these questions lie beyond the scope of this chapter, but I hope in it to provide the post-qualifying social worker with the skills for considering them. There is a danger of important social work values becoming part of an old sepia-coloured 'snapshot' rather than contributing to the 'moving picture' of life in the twenty-first century. Payne, Adams and Dominelli (2002) begin with the heading and statement 'Critical practice is *still* relevant in social work' (in Adams, Dominelli and Payne 2002a). Not only is such practice still relevant, it is essential for social work in the postmodern world. The emphasis should be not on telling qualified social workers 'what to think', but rather that they *must think*. Critical practice consists of 'critical action', preceded by 'critical thinking', so we focus below on critical thinking – the 'action' being carried out by the social worker in practice. Our commentary can act as a 'critical friend', both supporting and challenging the post-qualified (PQ) social worker. It is hoped that three things will be achieved:

1.   to revitalise knowledge already gained, but that has lost clarity among the stresses and strains of practice

2.   to identify gaps in knowledge, both as an individual social worker and within the profession during qualification

3.   to develop enhanced understanding of society and the role of social work ethics within this.

Before moving on to 'unpacking' what such critical thinking might mean, with regard to 'ethics and values', in the complex world of the social worker in practice, we acknowledge the most significant changes, the notion of operating a 'mixed economy' of welfare, application of 'managerialism', multi-disciplinary partnership working, consumerism, user/carer rights and involvement, the reorganisation of social work education and training, and the fragmentation of the social work task arising from the organisational division between 'children and families' and 'adults', are not simply theoretical constructs put forward during qualification as a social worker. Rather the key constraints, conflicts and ethical dilemmas, and the associated 'guilt' felt by many social workers in practice, arise from this.

A comprehensive framework for tying ethics and values firmly to such change is clearly not possible in a short chapter. Two of these aspects of change – the application of managerialism and multi-disciplinary partnership working – have emerged from practice as particularly significant and illustrate here how ethical theory can be used to help clarify difficult latent issues.

Ethical theory

Three main approaches to ethics in practice are discussed here:

1.   duty-based or Kantian principles

2.   consequential approaches

3.   'character and relationships'-based approaches.

Duty-based or Kantian principles

The first of these – that dominated by Immanuel Kant, an eighteenth-century German philosopher – is a 'duty-based' approach. At the heart of this approach is the notion of 'respect for the individual' and Banks points to Kant's 'categorical imperative': 'So act as to treat humanity, whether in your own person or that of any other, never solely as a means but always also as an end' (Banks 2006, p.29). The relevance of this to social workers is obvious.

Consequential approaches

This alternative approach considers the consequences, or outcomes, of putting the principles into practice as a guide to action, and is typified by the nineteenth-century utilitarian philosophers. Indeed, the terms 'consequentialism' and 'utilitarianism' are used almost interchangeably in many texts. The relevance of this approach to social work is less obvious and indeed if the term 'utilitarianism' is taken as a synonym for 'consequentialism' is deeply problematic. As Banks says:

> Approaches to social work ethics that are explicitly and wholly Utilitarian have not been well developed, partly because such approaches do not lend themselves to taking account of the personal relationship element of social work that has always been regarded as so crucial. (2006, p.37)

To this could be added the key criticisms of utilitarianism as a whole, that it is extremely unfair to minorities of any kind (a particular problem for social work, with its duty to promote anti-discriminatory practice and challenge structural oppression), and that it is a theoretical and impractical economic schema that is associated with, and indeed is the foundation stone of, the notion of 'market forces' and the operation of micro-economics.

Other consequences-based approaches, such as a radical or Marxist approach, are similarly part of a treatment of individuals as a means to an end – even if the end in question would seem to be a more desirable and just society. At the same time, for social workers to suggest that they should ignore the consequences or outcomes of their actions is clearly not appropriate in practice.[1]

---

1   Both these approaches belong to a particular strand of philosophical reasoning, which philosophers call 'Theories of Moral Obligation', but that in practice in the twentieth and twenty-first centuries have become subsumed under the general heading of 'a principles-based approach to ethics', which has been highly influential. As Banks (2006) points out, most 'ethics texts', certainly outside of social work, advocate principles based on a pluralist approach to ethical theory.

'Character and relationships'-based approaches

In a theoretical sense this aspect also has a long history, stemming as it does from the Ancient Greek philosophers. A major weakness of this opposing view is that it covers, in effect, anything that is not based on establishing 'principles' for practice. Historically, the assumption behind this approach is that the complexities of real-life situations preclude any useful operation of a principles-based approach in practice. It is the contention of, for example, McBeath and Webb (2002) that the fragmentation and complexity of the postmodern world, arising from the changes outlined earlier, preclude any notion of a principles-based approach being applied to the social work task.

Social work has always maintained that values and ethics must be digested and expressed by the practitioner, because situations encountered in social work are too complex and differ far too much from one individual situation to the next for there to be any encapsulable rules that can be applied to a situation in practice. From this perspective, the defining characteristics of a profession, and indeed of any ethically sound practitioner, are to be found in the character of the practitioner and the nature of his or her relationship with service users.

Ethical practice: surveying the field

Social workers and their educators assert constantly that 'social work is, essentially, a moral enterprise' (Pinker 1990, p.14) and that 'moral issues haunt social work' (Jordan 1990, p.1). Throughout his or her social work education and training, the PQ social worker has been inculcated with the notion that values are at the heart of how they have been educated and trained to carry out the social work role, and that to be a 'good' social worker values must also be at the heart of their practice. In spite of this commitment social work has become 'detached from its ethical roots' (Bowles et al. 2006). The PQ social worker, needs to acquire greater knowledge of their own professional philosophical stance. This revolves around such issues as the importance of 'character' of the moral agent and the significance of relationships in determining 'right' and wrong' in complex situations (Banks 1995, 2001, 2006). Only then can ethics move beyond being a tool or yardstick for defining good practice to being a driving force of such good practice, which enhances both the effectiveness of multi-disciplinary partnership working and the management of welfare practice. This requires critical thinking about ethics and values.

Critical thinking about social work ethics and values

We proceed now to apply the notion of critical thinking to the application of the above theories in practice. All too often, because ethical aspects are embedded in practice, their theoretical nature is not recognised. The PQ social worker is required to 'manage complex ethical issues, dilemmas and conflicts', be 'accountable for their own work', and 'think critically about their own practice in the context of the GSCC Codes of Practice, national and international codes of professional ethics and the principles of diversity, equality and social exclusion in a wide range of situations including those associated with inter-agency and inter-professional work' (Brown and Rutter 2006, p.1).

Brookfield regards critical thinking as a lived and creative activity, not an academic pastime:

> Thinking critically involves our recognising the assumptions underlying our beliefs and behaviours. It means we can give justification for our beliefs and actions. Most important, perhaps, it means we try to judge the rationality of these justifications. We can do this by comparing them to a range of varying interpretations and perspectives...and we can test the accuracy and rationality of these justifications against some kind of objective analysis of the 'real' world as we understand it. (Brookfield 1987, pp.13–14)

Let us break this down into a checklist of how rigorous critical thinking can be applied to ethics in social work. To engage in critical thinking PQ social workers need to:

1. recognise the assumptions behind beliefs and behaviours

2. justify those beliefs and actions – in particular those most influential in social work

3. judge the rationality of this justification – in light of the changes in the world and twenty-first-century Britain.

In order to do this the PQ social worker must:

1. compare a range of varying (i.e. different) interpretations and perspectives

2. test the accuracy and rationality of the justifications – in particular cases in practice

3. test against the real world as we understand it.

From critical thinking to critical practice: case studies of the reflective process

Case study 1

An experienced social worker, engaged in discussion of a very common ethical dilemma drawn from her practice, describes a frail elderly lady who wishes to remain in her own home. Her over-burdened carer believes that this is unsafe, and that the burden of care in these circumstances is having a detrimental effect on herself and her family. She wishes the social worker to provide residential accommodation and care.

During discussion on the conflicting duties of the social worker to the user and her carer, and the use of 'ethical theory' to resolve this dilemma, there is an outburst from the social worker, which may be paraphrased thus:

> What is the point of this nonsense? I don't have the resources to provide any kind of residential care. Before I began this [ethics] course I thought I had done a 'good' job if I went on a home visit and came back with the response that 'they did not meet my agency's criteria'. All that has been achieved is that I do exactly the same thing, but end up feeling guilty. I will be expected to resolve the dilemma by organising support in her own home. The real dilemma is between me doing what is expected by my employer and what I know is my duty as a social worker. Worse still, I will end up presenting it as a compromise solution between the wishes of the user and the carer – no reference to resources at all. How ethical is that?

Case study 2

This concerns an almost qualified social worker with only placement experience, reflecting on the training she has received to carry out the social work task. Again I paraphrase:

> I left a reasonably well-paid office job to come here. I wanted a job where I felt I could make a difference. Now, I am beginning to suspect, in the light of my practice placement experience, that I am swapping one reasonably paid office job for another. I have had three years of considerable financial loss. The only difference is that I now have the skills and knowledge to be able to make a difference, but if I want to keep my job, I will not be allowed to use them. One office job for another office job, plus perpetual guilt. What have I done?

Applying critical thinking

This brief chapter does not allow a thorough analysis of how critical thinking, about ethics, could help the above practitioners resolve what was for both of them a difficult ethical dilemma, giving rise to feelings of guilt. Some points for consideration can however be made.

First, both had gone a considerable way towards recognising assumptions behind beliefs and behaviours in their reformulation of the dilemma – in the first case between resources and needs, and in the second with reference to the need to strike a balance between 'duty' to the client and duty to the employer.

Second, however, a common and endemic piece of 'practice wisdom' within the social work profession is also visible – namely that the managing of services and resources and their distribution in a just and equitable fashion is not part of the social work task. Consequently, policies, laws and organisational procedures, while part of the context in which social work practice must be carried out, are not seen as part of the ethics and value system of the competent and confident social worker. Lip service may be paid to the notion of 'distributive justice' as a key component of social work ethics but, for example, 'managerialism' is a pejorative term; 'needs-led assessment' is seen as vastly more ethical than 'resources-led assessment' and, as in the case studies provided above, responding to the demands of colleagues and employers for responsible resource allocation is seen as a factor that works against 'good' ethical practice.

Finally, far from even attempting to justify 'beliefs and action', the above case studies suggest that social work involves 'beliefs' that are in opposition to 'actions', and it is this commonly held 'practice wisdom' that must be challenged if the individual PQ social worker is to not just survive but flourish.

Critical thinking about pluralism

Duty-based approaches to ethics alone are of little help when considering the competing claims for action: between individual users; between users and carers; and between individuals and society. 'Social workers are not autonomous professionals whose guiding ethical principles are solely about respecting and promoting the self-determination of service users' (Banks 2006, p.35).

Consequential approaches, in any of the developed forms available, are inimical to social work. The key issue considered by Banks and others in terms of recognising assumptions behind beliefs and behaviours is that it is concerned with promoting welfare and justice in society – surely at the very heart of social work.

Critical thinking must reveal that both of these approaches are 'necessary' but 'insufficient' on their own as the basis for social work in practice. Perhaps we can turn to a pluralist approach for a way forward? Pluralism:

> is the presumption that there will often be genuine, independent merit in more than one of the available schemes of explanation, prediction and precept for practical (moral) action. Pluralism seeks the most plausible solution on balance, being prepared to give credence to a range of approaches and theories, while recognising that the theoretical disputes that divide them are not capable of being resolved for the time being. (Clark 2000, p.67)

Pluralism is a better method for the complex and uncertain world in which social workers operate. It 'leads to unconvincing and unworkable solutions' (Clark 2000, p.68).

Pluralism between the two competing schema of the principles-based approach is well established, but the tendency of even this pluralistic version of the principles-based approach to degenerate into 'rules' and, worse still, 'lists of rules' is one that has, quite reasonably, had great resonance with social work. Virtue ethics, on the other hand, does not lend itself either to consideration of issues of 'justice' or indeed a pluralistic approach that combines elements with views from other theoretical perspectives. The inclusion of insights arising from this perspective within pluralism is, however, essential.

Conclusion: how not to 'throw the baby out with the bath water'

I have provided in this chapter a framework for thinking and reading for the qualified social worker. This reflects a firm commitment to the notion that such activities must be inextricable from the developing professional practice of the social worker, and has attempted to emphasise the significance of both *change* and *continuity* in terms of the society in which both the social worker and the service user must live.

Social work has certain advantages in terms of maintaining core values and providing a service to society for the most oppressed and vulnerable members. These are:

- that ethics and values remain at the heart of social work and social work education

- the significance of reflection and reflexivity, and their link to critical thinking, critical action and hence critical practice, within social work education

- the importance of the concept of 'empowerment' of service user groups in the social work task.

It has also been argued, however, that ethical aspects are so embedded in practice that their true theoretical nature has not been recognised and, perhaps more importantly, that this results in a misuse of ideas and a lack of clarity about the very nature of the social work role and tasks. The effective PQ social worker needs to:

- understand the various schools of thought in the 'principles-based approach' – at least to the point where they understand where other welfare professionals are 'coming from'

- think critically about how the application of such 'principles' can be made to work with core social work values and ethics, rather than against them (see Chapter 8: Developing Inclusive Practice in Children and Families Social Work)

- enhance partnership working, by promoting notions concerned with 'virtue ethics' in those professionals, whether health care or others, into a more central position

- engage with the task of preventing principles degenerating into rules or lists of rules

- consider and engage with issues of power and professionalism in the interests of, and in partnership with, users and carers.

Critical actions require critical thinking about the social work approach to ethics. This should be regarded as an ongoing journey of thought and discovery. The issues of 'what is the right' and 'what is the wrong' thing to do in practice as a social worker are, and should remain, contested and debatable. I hope that this chapter will help to support and encourage the PQ social worker to enter into this debate from a position of enhanced understanding and knowledge. This is the critical practice to which social workers aspire and the critical thinking outlined in this chapter is the means of achieving it.

Recommended reading

Banks, S. (2006) *Ethics and Values in Social Work* (3rd edn). Basingstoke: Palgrave Macmillan.
The key text informing the structure of this chapter and providing a view of both approaches to ethics.

Bowles, W., Collingridge, M., Curry, S. and Valentine, B. (2006) *Ethical Practice in Social Work: An Applied Approach.* Maidenhead: Open University Press, McGraw-Hill Education.
Plugging a very significant gap in social work ethical discourse and an essential prerequisite for critical thinking.

Callahan, J. (ed.) (1988) *Ethical Issues in Professional Life.* Oxford: Oxford University Press.
Reader on a 'principles-based' approach to professional ethics containing extracts from many seminal works – some of which are clearly relevant to social work.

Rumbold, G. (1999) *Ethics in Nursing Practice* (3rd edn). Edinburgh: Baillière Tindall.
Professional ethics in other caring professions (for the purpose of understanding from where other partners in practice draw their ethical thinking) – nursing. Of particular note are his 'Conclusions', pp.260–1.

CHAPTER 4

The Social Context of Post-Qualifying Practice

Nigel Leech

In this chapter I am going to explore some thoughts around the loss of the social in social work. I have worked for the last 15 years or so as a non-social work trained member of a social work section in a university in the north-east of England. The main task of this working group is to provide initial education for social workers. This is done through the provision of the degree in social work as well as two joint degrees in social work and nursing (learning disabilities and mental health). As part of my role within the team I have worked as a tutor to students on social work placements. Throughout this time I have therefore been an observer of social work, albeit as an outsider and somewhat at a distance. Over the years I have developed an appreciation and growing respect for social work. At the same time I have noticed changes within the social work profession that have concerned me. My background and interests lie in human relations and psychotherapy and, as such, I see the relationship aspect of helping as crucial to bringing about meaningful change in people's lives. It is this decline, indeed loss, of relationship-focused social work in many, if not all, areas of practice that needs exploring. This can be seen as the loss of the social from social work.

For writers like O'Brien (2004) the social of social work is more about how we understand people's social lives. For me it is more at the level of personal social interactions and the emotional life that accompanies those interactions. Recently a second-year degree student, in an emotionally charged conversation, said that she had given up a very good job as an office worker to become a social worker. She now realised that she was spending years of her life studying, just to become an office worker again. This has been reinforced by comments from recently qualified social workers in practice. I have seen students close to tears as they describe how the reality of social work placements is far removed from their expectations. Many have said that once they qualify they doubt that they will actually become social workers (though of course most do).

A newly qualified joint degree graduate, regarded by staff at the university as an excellent student, has spoken of the utter frustration she feels in her job and her anger at the university for not preparing her properly, saying that what she would have benefited from is modules on 'form filling' and 'filing'. This might be regarded as a sarcastic comment rather than a genuine one, were it not for the fact that I have heard it stated, in various forms, by numerous students and newly qualified workers. What particularly concerns me is that it is just this type of person that the profession of social work is in desperate need of: students who want to engage with others at a deep and meaningful level and then reflect on their experiences of the encounter at an emotional level. Despite the rhetoric of reflection, the opportunity for this is becoming much less.

I have heard many variations on these themes and have been told how, in many cases, basic human 'relatedness' is prevented in practice because 'it is not what we do' or is more than is required in terms of managing the case. This trend away from relationships is something that has developed over the time that I have been involved in social work education and I wonder what could be behind it.

It is not that social workers have become any less caring. On the contrary, the institution of social work is struggling to maintain itself in an ever-shifting environment that is not of its making. Over the last few decades we have experienced the demise of the relatively stable post-war period, where the economy and welfare were managed for the collective good of society, to a situation where, as a result of our response to globalisation and living in a postmodernist world, 'the institutions of the welfare state are being redesigned in the image of the market' (Powell 2001, p.24). This, in many ways, is putting almost intolerable pressure on the institution of social work. One result is that it is becoming more beleaguered and bureaucratised (O'Neill 1999). Along with this increased bureaucratisation there is the trend towards more regulation, inspection and surveillance (Adams, Dominelli and Payne 2005). It could arguably be said to be experiencing an identity crisis. Among all this, social work is becoming preoccupied with numbers and competence. During the last decade or so, there has developed a reductionalist approach that sees complex behaviours and understanding reduced to competences to be 'ticked off from a functionalist checklist' (Gould 1996, p.5). Despite the introduction of the new degree, with its greater emphasis on standards, this trend does not seem to have lessened. In fact many students and newly (and not so newly) qualified workers report that there is a growing demand to meet targets and close cases. There appears to be a growing emphasis on quantity, with a risk of neglect of quality. Children's and adults' services often appear to be run more like a business so that, 'in our contemporary culture, working with people is politically and socially reduced to valuing commodities' (Hinshelwood 2001, p.182). It can seem that there is more of a concern with providing a service for some identified group than with serving the community. Also, as Jordan (2002) has pointed out, social workers are being expected to change in a way that increases outside control over their actions, with more regulation and quality assurance.

The institution of social work

There is a move from serving to servicing. The institution of social work no longer seems to be set up to serve the unique needs of 'clients' at deep emotional, and often profoundly distressing, levels of intimate relatedness, but rather to provide more surface-level care (Cooper and Lousada 2005), often in the form of a 'package of care'. It is rather like the difference between buying a personally tailored suit to buying one off the peg, and is as if social work is becoming progressively more 'McDonaldised' (Ritzer 2004), with inputs and outputs becoming more and more uniform and predictable.

It is interesting to consider this concept of providing a service and the notion that 'clients' are now service users or users of a service. This has the effect of distancing the 'client' from the 'social worker'. In many cases the actual delivery of the service is performed by care workers rather than social workers. The notion of service can be viewed from different perspectives (Waddell 2006). It is possible to serve a person by providing a service or commodity where different 'pre-packaged' items are put together to form a total package of care, offering service users a managed version of care that is at a distance from the service user themselves. It is case management rather than casework. Although, of course, casework is ancient history (Adams 2006), in that social work has moved very much in the direction of managing and supervising cases over the last decade or so, this analogy is still useful. Alternatively, it is possible to view service as serving somebody in the sense that a servant might do. In this context a social worker waits on the sidelines until needed, views and reflects on the situation, and comes forward to serve as and when required. The social worker is then able to think and wait. In doing so they are able to contain the situation and truly be of service to the service user. This does not entail physically standing aside (or not intervening when legally required to do so) so much as *mentally* standing aside and at the same time being emotionally available and 'active'. This can allow a 'containment' of the situation and a chance for issues to be worked through. Waddell (2006) gives a good example of this when she describes how on a hospital ward everybody was busy trying to help a young mother whose baby would not stop crying. Nurses and care staff were offering, and trying, practical advice, and the social worker was busy trying to resolve the mother and her husband's financial and housing difficulties. The baby's distress just increased, and no solution to the couple's difficulties could be found. The social worker then changed her approach and just spent time with the couple and their baby in a secluded room over a number of visits. She talked and listened and was able to 'emotionally hold' them. This contained and lessened their distress to some extent and the baby quickly calmed down and stopped crying. These opportunities and spaces to think and be, rather than do and act, are being lost. It is in this space that the social aspect of social work is being lost.

There is major ambivalence involved in how social workers are perceived and treated by society. It is as if they are seen both as objects to be admired and as objects to be feared and hated at the same time. Social work is the caring profession that will look after us if we are in need, but at the same time it is the profession that will punish us if we transgress social norms. Punishment might be in the form of removing our children if we are deemed to be unable to cope. In particular, this ambivalence appears to be perpetuated by the government. Although welfare is certainly about people, social work is being forced to disengage from people (Cooper and Lousada 2005). The rhetoric and the actions of New Labour do not seem to match, since on the one hand they talk of making social work more professional, by protecting the title of social worker and bringing in the new degree qualification, while proceeding to 'deprofessionalise' as fast as they can. The insistence on competency and skills (or standards), as well as the audit culture that exists, is actually very deprofessionalising, as well as being profoundly disempowering. The strong implication is that social workers do not know what they are doing and need to be told what to do by a higher authority, namely the government. For example, the GSCC has produced a code of practice for social workers to which all registered social workers are expected to adhere. Nowhere in this document (including the title) is the term 'social worker' used, even though it is now a 'protected title'. The term 'social care worker' is used throughout. So, social work is given higher status by having the protected title of 'social worker', while at the same time its status is severely diminished, since the implication is that social work is synonymous with social care work. As yet there has been no decision on the registration of social care workers themselves, and if, or when, this does happen there might be further implications for the status of social work.

Over the last couple of decades there has been a steady increase in emphasis on the individual, to the detriment of the collective good, with an attendant emphasis on the notion of personal responsibility. For example, we are held to be more personally responsible for our own health and increasingly for aspects of citizenship (as expressed in the notion that 'you cannot have rights without responsibilities'). This has spread into the workplace. There is more individual accountability, so that one consequence of the protected title of 'social worker' is that an individual social worker can now more easily be held personally accountable for their actions, rather than the organisation as a whole. Also, there is a promotion of capitalism and enterprise, and a consequential widening of the gap between rich and poor. As Young (1999) has argued, society in the UK has moved from being inclusive to being exclusive. In this climate certain groups are more readily blamed for society's problems (such as youth or those who do not show enough social responsibility). It has been observed that the New Labour agenda is very moralistic (Jordan 2002) and there is a move to separate criminality from oneself and onto the other, to see crime as being perpetrated by a particular 'underclass' that does not have the same 'values' as ourselves. Also, as many students and practising social workers have pointed out to me, economic concerns seem to take priority over social work issues. This puts mounting pressure on the institution of social work. Not only has it to deal with the usual gamut of human misery, but also growing demands from society, which often seem unrelenting. These demands can manifest themselves through changing roles and managerial pressure.

Many of the recent changes in social work practice mean that social workers are further removed from their clients. 'Clients' become 'service users' (or even just 'users' with its derogatory implications of drug abuse). 'Children in care' become 'looked after children' or 'accommodated children', which, Speight and Wynne (2000) suggest, shows a movement away from something that was child-centred and offered care and protection, towards something that is cold and implies support for abusing parents. There is an over-emphasis on managerial roles with the development of a free-standing class of management (Hugman 1998). This has eroded the professional status of social workers. More and more, it seems, social workers are required to operate in an industrial-type model with care packages being rather like products supplied to consumers. Managers maintain more centralised control. As social workers become more and more case and resource managers, and less and less case workers, and less able to use themselves as their primary resource, so the boundary between themselves and service users seems to become more and more clearly defined. I have been told by practising social workers how it seems that it is becoming more important to close cases, save money, fill in the right forms, keep files up to date and be ready for audit, than it is to have long-term, deep and meaningful emotional relationships with service users, who more often than not are in desperate need of this. Hinshelwood's comments, although made in relation to the mental health service, appear particularly poignant and relevant:

> Human values – the importance of relationships, the recognition of difficulties in human living, personal support and colleagueship, the need for help at all levels, and the place for emotional honesty – must survive against the onslaught of monetarist values. This is the predicament for all healthcare where the culture of care is opposed to the more ruthless business culture of the market, and where the survival of the fittest dominates as a principle. (Hinshelwood 2001, p.182)

Relationship and role

To me social work is ultimately about relationships. At present there is a 'culture of commodification in human services' (Cooper and Lousada 2005, p.180) that seems to encourage these relationships to be often fractured and distant. For any relationship to exist there needs to be space to think about the relationship, space in the minds of the individuals concerned and space in the organisation involved. This space is reducing. Even in a higher education institution work group tasked with social work education, the space to think and reflect is getting squeezed. In my experience it is becoming increasingly difficult to find time to think at an emotional level. This educational work group seems to mirror many of the dynamics experienced in social work settings (pressure of work, targets, bureaucracy, etc.) and yet we do not find the space to reflect on this. It is moaned about and criticised but true reflection, where one's emotional experience is heard and contained and thought about, is largely avoided. It is too painful to attempt, both at an educational and at a service level. It is truly ironic that, at a time when social workers are charged with being more reflective (Redmond 2004), the space for reflection by social workers is getting less and less.

The institution of social work has a role to play in society. Part of that role is unconscious and to do with warding off anxieties. As Young (1992) pointed out, as individuals we are constantly arranging our inner and outer lives so that we are not overwhelmed with 'psychotic anxiety'. Much of our social life is organised to defend against this psychotic anxiety, and this defence extends to social work (and other) institutions. Aspects of this psychotic anxiety are ever ready to break through into awareness (Young 1994).

> ...by 'psychotic' is meant: the fear of annihilation, the fear of being made a nothing, the fear of not being able to make sense of what realities might be, the fear of disorder and chaos, the fear of disintegration, the fear of loss, ending and death. These fears are acutely present in psychic life during earliest infancy and can be reactivated at any time in our subsequent lives when persecutory circumstances trigger them. (Lawrence 1999, p.1)

Thus, 'psychotic anxiety' stems from our undifferentiated early life experience. The time around and during birth is also traumatic (Adzema 1998) and no doubt this and other in-utero experiences contribute to our 'anxiety'. In order to function adequately it is necessary to have these primitive fears and traumas 'contained' so that they do not encroach into awareness too much. We need to keep this 'psychic anxiety' under control to prevent us from feeling or indeed going 'insane'. Also, trauma is part of life. It is part of growing up, and is a consequence of being dependent and vulnerable when we are young (Leech 2002). Of course, there are people who are fortunate enough to have been brought up in an environment that enables their 'unavoidable' hurts to be worked through and resolved. However, most of us are left to carry this unresolved pain and hurt into adulthood. It just adds to our 'psychotic anxiety'.

In times of rapid change and uncertainty, this anxiety is amplified (Cooper and Lousada 2005). Just as individuals defend themselves from awareness of unresolved hurt and pain, so too does society. It is possible that social services organisations are expected to act as a container for this pain and hurt (Leech 2002), which is due to the anxiety that is part of being human as well as the hurt and pain of unresolved trauma. Another role of social work organisations is to contain the anxiety of their workers. As individuals, we need to feel that our anxieties are containable and manageable. This is especially so in an occupation like social work, where engaging with service users can be particularly anxiety-provoking. The social environment in which social work now has to function makes this process extremely difficult and has resulted in much of the current practice of overwork, targets, bureaucracy, audits, and so on. One way to attempt to lessen the impact of this anxiety is to try to suggest that working practices exist that can help avoid this anxiety:

> The capacity to do meaningful...social care work presupposes being able to tolerate extreme states of feeling and thought... It is difficult work, often directed at helping others negotiate difficulties and choices they feel they cannot bear. Yet there is a pervasive encouragement to believe that, in all spheres, work can be made easier. (Cooper and Lousada 2005, p.198)

Parton (1996) argued that social work is changing as a response to social pressures and the contracting of the UK welfare state, and that this necessitates a shift in working practice.

He also points out that social work serves the function of mediating between those who are actually or potentially excluded from society and those who are included in society. Social work can also be seen as policing the boundaries between what is acceptable and what is unacceptable (Webb 1996). Thus social work sits on the boundary of exclusion and inclusion. Part of this boundary maintenance now appears to involve the gatekeeping of resources. Social Services Departments increasingly are having to decide who is eligible for their resources, who is to be included in social work provision and who is to be excluded. There is increased emphasis on collaborative working – for example, with social services being charged with working closely with health and education. There is the rhetoric of putting the service user first and providing appropriate care in the community. In practice provision is often driven by economics, and social workers, finding themselves on the boundary between social work and health (for example), are required to spend large amounts of time denying care (Pollock 2004), with the result that actual provision suffers.

There is an effort to limit the need for services and to shift economic burdens onto other welfare departments. In particular the emphasis, and thus economic burden, of many services have been shifting from health to social care (and therefore of course to social services) (Mandelstam 2007). Social workers are now more firmly placed in the role of boundary keeper. Also, social workers act as the guardians of the boundary between that which is unknowable (repressed into our unconscious) and that which it is possible to know about. It may be 'unknowable' in the sense that the knowledge is 'too unbearable to bear'. We can project our anxiety and knowledge of trauma onto that section of the population known as social work service users and we can project onto social workers the task of maintaining the boundary. Thus social workers have the 'real', if unconscious, task of not allowing society to become aware of all its hidden pain and hurt. They must act as an impenetrable boundary between 'unconscious' and 'conscious' aspects of society and therefore need to manage and contain that which is unknowable. This means that we can maintain the fantasy that we are not like 'them' and that, really, we do not have aspects of ourselves that are in pain and despair.

It would seem that when social workers break these unconscious 'rules' people get into a panic and extreme anxiety threatens to break through into awareness. Society swiftly attempts to cover up the exposed hurt or trauma just as an individual might do. This is seen, for example, in the media outcry that follows the public discovery of a 'failure' in child protection. We all seem unable to find the time and space to reflect and 'know' about that which is shocking and often 'unknowable'. In many ways the case of Victoria Climbié was an example of this. It might be useful to look at possible dynamics, of course recognising that faults and omissions existed. Individuals and institutions develop defences against difficult emotions that are too painful or too threatening to acknowledge (Cooper and Lousada 2005; Halton 1997; Hinshelwood 2001; Leech 1999; Menzies 1984). It is not uncommon for professional systems to mirror the distorted and abusive relationships that exist in the families that they work with (Ferguson 2005) and in many ways this was so in the Victoria Climbié case. In trying to deal with the 'unknowable', social workers found themselves in an abusive working environment. In that environment, they did not manage to carry out the most basic and straightforward of social work tasks (Laming 2003), which could well be associated with the complicated socio-dynamics of dealing with violence (Ferguson 2005), whether that violence is actual or imagined. It could be that the whole of that is part of the same dynamic. The workers found themselves in the middle of forces that demanded that they 'know' about the 'unknowable'. 'Know' means 'understand sufficiently to allow action' and 'unknowable' means that which we do not want to know about for various reasons. A different way of expressing it is that they were in a position where they were expected to speak about the unspeakable. There is a failure to see what is 'obvious' because if you did then it would involve too much 'psychic disturbance' (Rustin 2005). You could well suspect that something is happening but be too afraid to look closely for fear of what you might find: 'you know about the abuse but you don't know' (Ferguson 2005, p.792). There was no space to think and reflect, and to allow the unknown to become known.

Conclusion

This in many ways sums up the position that social work finds itself in today. We live in a complex society and social work is now a much more fragmented and networked organisation. Relatedness is now often less between an individual social worker and service user and more between various organisations (such as health, education, the different aspects of the voluntary sector, and different care and service providers). All organisations, and particularly those involved in welfare, need to defend against the anxiety that is inherent in the work that they do (Menzies 1984; Obholzer and Roberts 1997).

Social work's more fragmented nature means that the institution is now much less able to contain the anxieties inherent in its work. Society itself is also experiencing continual change and uncertainty, which increases anxiety. We can only contain and handle so much, and when the mechanisms that help us do so are less reliable we need to find ways to ensure that anxiety does not become intolerable. Relationships are fundamentally about managing boundaries, whether in the private or the public sphere. Social work plays out its many roles at many boundaries and attempts to cope with the complexities of modern life. In order to cope with the anxiety evoked by this it is as if social work has had to use borderline-type defences where the fear of knowing battles with the fear of not knowing. By borderline-type defences I mean a way of reacting to overwhelming complexity and feeling. Strong thoughts and feelings, in ourselves and others, are difficult to bear for any length of time. In order to be able to tolerate and work with strong feelings we need the capacity not only to bear but also to be able to think about those feelings. If that capacity is missing then we need to resort to borderline-type defences:

> The rich literature on borderline states of mind and pathology are all efforts to describe the complex forms of mental functioning – systems of defence against unbearable mental pain – that are seen to have taken root when conditions promoting such capacities are absent or have failed. (Cooper and Lousada 2005, p.28)

Here we want closeness but fear it. We oscillate between inclusion and exclusion. Our relationships may appear to be close but are actually conducted on a superficial level. Borderline defence is to do with the mental pain involved in the conflict between forces that oppose each other and the guilt associated with ambivalence. Ultimately these are forces of 'love and hate' (Rustin 2005). The space in our minds to hold emotions and thoughts becomes less and less because those emotions and thoughts become overwhelming. Often we are forced to fill our time with over-activity or procrastination.

The social of social work has become lost because there is little or no space to think and reflect, to allow the unknowable to become known. Due to the pressures from society social work organisations are now not able to provide the containment needed for this space. If social workers are to think and reflect then they need the mental space to do so. In order for this space to exist sufficiently, there has to be sufficient containment of anxiety. This is just not possible in present-day UK society. This is demonstrated in the seeming distancing from service users that I have discussed – the move from casework to case management. There is a fear of intimacy (compounded to no small extent by the 'risk culture' in which we live) and at the same time a fear of 'aloneness' that seems to pervade welfare work, a 'borderline' type personality state. This will change when the institution of social work finds the security it needs to become free of the fear of meaningful and deep emotional relationships in which it seems to be caught up at the moment.

Recommended reading

Cooper, A. and Lousada, J. (2005) *Borderline Welfare: Feeling and Fear of Feeling in Modern Welfare.* London: Karnac.

Hinshelwood, R. (2001) *Thinking About Institutions: Milieux and Madness.* London: Jessica Kingsley Publishers.

Jordan, B. (2002) *Social Work and the Third Way: Tough Love as Social Policy.* London: Sage.

Menzies, I. (1984) *The Functioning of Social Systems as a Defence Against Anxiety.* London: Tavistock Institute of Human Relations.

Obholzer, A. and Roberts, V. (eds) (1997) *The Unconscious at Work.* London: Routledge.

CHAPTER 5

Integrating Theory and Practice at Post-Qualifying Level

Ian Duncan

My rationale for volunteering to write this chapter arises from a very long involvement in the teaching of social work practitioners in a wide variety of fields and in several different academic settings – experience that has made me very much aware of the difficulties many social work students and candidates at post-qualifying levels have in integrating theoretical knowledge into written evidence of competence in an academic context. I have found that it is one thing for social workers to do their jobs well and yet another to have to provide evidence in the form of a theoretical reflective analysis. My experience is echoed by, for example, Paul Stepney (Stepney and Ford 2000, p.20), when he writes that theory 'is something the vast majority of practitioners find very difficult to articulate'. He goes on to argue that, because of these difficulties, many practitioners reject theory as largely irrelevant to their needs. The theme is consistent with analyses by authors such as Parker (2004), Fook (2002), Coulshed and Orme (1998), and Watson, Burrow and Player (2002), who all make similar points. There is a very wide range and variety of books about social work theory – for example, Payne (2005) and Adams, Dominelli and Payne (2002a, 2002b), Thompson (2005), Healy (2005) and Lishman (1991), to mention only a few. All, in their separate and highly effective ways, make available to social workers a comprehensive range of theoretical source materials to support social work practice. All these authors also refer to the ambiguities and complexities inherent in defining both social work and social work theory. In considering the volume of writing aimed at explaining and clarifying social work theory, and indeed social work itself, I have some sympathies with the student social worker or post-qualifying award candidate attempting to make sense of it all.

The transition from 'pre' to post-qualifying social work involves a significant change of role in relation to responsibility and accountability, if not to the actual hands-on work undertaken. In working extensively with students undertaking qualifying training I have found that awareness of the nature of the transition from 'unqualified' social work to the role of 'social worker' begins with the role of being a student social worker in a practice placement. At this point, student social workers, especially those who have been working in social care environments highly effectively but who are unqualified, develop a heightened awareness of their developing knowledge base, their professional role and their increased levels of responsibility and accountability for assessments and decisions. They are no longer simply passing on information to be used by others with greater responsibility and accountability than themselves, but are beginning to occupy and own that role. However, as students, the actual responsibility and accountability for their work remains with the qualified social worker who is the practice teacher.

Developing professional autonomy

The integration of knowledge and skills, increasing levels of complexity and accountability are illustrated by what could be a typical case facing a social worker undertaking work in community care and mental health settings not long after qualification. This will be a useful exercise for the reader to consider the amount of knowledge needed for effective practice in such a context. You may also want to undertake a similar exercise based on a familiar typical 'case' specific to your area of work.

Case study

Elizabeth is not an Approved Social Worker (ASW) in terms of mental health law so she relies on support from an ASW colleague, Peter. The initial referral for assessment is in connection with Mr and Mrs H. Mr H is terminally ill, and services are assessed and agreed to support and enhance the care being provided by Mrs H, who is finding it increasingly difficult to cope. Elizabeth remains involved after the death of Mr H because Mrs H deteriorates mentally and physically in the weeks following bereavement. Mrs H's reliance on alcohol increases and with it risks arising from possible misuse of medication, a lack of attention to her own needs and the potential for accidents in the home. As a result of Mrs H's increasing needs, Elizabeth, having built a good working relationship with Mrs H, makes referral to a psychogeriatrician. Peter, along with a Community Psychiatric Nurse (CPN), Mrs H's GP and wider family members, all become involved.

This case involves Elizabeth, in collaboration with family, social work and medical professionals, and illustrates knowledge of mental health issues, of relevant legislation, and of different professional roles and responsibilities. Also illustrated is her awareness of role and anti-oppressive practice in balancing Mrs H's independence, autonomy and rights against professional accountability for identifying and managing risk as Mrs H's capacity to care for herself decreases. Elizabeth, informed by psychosocial theories of ageing and by theories explaining reactions to loss and transition, also applies a number of methods and approaches, among them Crisis Intervention and Task Centred Working. The approaches are inherently person centred and strengths based, and as far as possible involve working in partnership with Mrs H to support her in taking steps to address her needs.

She recognises, assesses and takes action to address the risks and needs that are a result of Mrs H's mental health difficulties, her excessive use of alcohol and her capacity to manage her medication. All these elements are taken into account in formulating and agreeing a care plan in partnership with the other professionals and family members, and Elizabeth is conscious at all times of Mrs H's decreasing capacity to manage her affairs and make decisions about her own care and medication. There are times when Mrs H is reluctant to adhere to planned activities, such as day centre attendance, so Elizabeth engages friends and family as well as care staff to monitor risk and provide avenues for communication in the event of an emergency. Ultimately, as the result of a crisis one weekend, Mrs H agrees to a voluntary admission to hospital but her progress in the controlled environment of hospital is not sustained on her return home. Her needs escalate to the point where compulsory admission to hospital is probable and a nursing assessment, with a view to admission to a residential nursing home for the elderly mentally infirm, is arranged. Elizabeth advises family members about the need to make application to the Court of Protection as Mrs H no longer has the necessary capacity to deal with her financial affairs, including the sale of her home.

The transition from student social worker to professionally qualified social worker therefore involves completing a transition to a role that carries with it a very high degree of professional autonomy and accountability legitimised by 'expert' knowledge. No amount of experience or competence in an unqualified role can compensate for a legally recognised social work qualification, the 'protected title' of 'social worker' and all that goes with it. A qualified social worker must be ready to become involved in complex and demanding work involving professionals from other disciplines, and to accept a high degree of autonomy and responsibility in cases that require difficult decisions – decisions that, in working with vulnerable (and sometimes dangerous) adults or children, recognise and encompass risk in order to achieve desired outcomes or decisions that limit or override rights and freedoms. In an increasingly multi-disciplinary working environment, qualified social workers must accept a high degree of accountability for assessments and decisions, and have the confidence, skills and knowledge to justify their professional opinions in discussions with other professionals who may not always share the same views, especially in relation to the assessment and management of risk.

Demystifying theory

My own experience is that many practitioners do not consciously work within a theoretical framework but when given an opportunity to reflect on practice it becomes clear that they are relying on a sound level of theoretical knowledge. I therefore felt drawn towards a discussion not so much of theory but of reflection and experiential learning as a means of making practice theory links explicit, meaningful and relevant to practice, in the hope that such a discussion would help those involved in learning and teaching at post-qualifying levels consider 'theory' and the teaching of theory in a new light. What I did not want to do was to produce a review of the range of specific social work theories that many other authors have set out with great competence and clarity elsewhere.

Whether conscious of it or not, no one ever approaches any situation or event without a theory in mind to explain it. Coulshed (1991, p.8), in discussing theory in relation to social work, observes 'whether we recognise it or not, theoryless practice does not exist; we can not avoid looking for explanations to guide our actions'. Everyone has 'theories' or 'opinions' (dictionary definitions of the two words are very similar (e.g. Brookes *et al.* 2004, pp.836/1259)) about what 'makes the world go round' or why people behave as they do. Theories do not only address what we can see or what we have experienced. Theories do not begin life as fact – initially many theories, even those based on some evidence from observation or experience, are about 'belief' and we must look for definitive evidence or conduct research to validate such theory. Theories are hypotheses – 'statements or propositions assumed to be true for the sake of argument; statement or theory to be proved or disproved by reference to evidence or facts; provisional explanation of anything' (Brookes *et al.* 2004, p.580). Thompson (2000, p.23) echoes these definitions but reminds us that there are often competing theories addressing the same subject from different perspectives. Competing theories are the result of different minds being applied to the same problem, seeing it from different perspectives and coming up with differing explanations. Rather than being seen as confusing, competing theories are a wonderful opportunity for reflection and critical analysis as to their respective merits in relation to particular cases encountered in practice. But social work is an uneasy alliance of philanthropic endeavour and changing political ideologies, and it is based on theories that attempt to explain both subjective and objective realities in a procession of individual and social circumstances almost too broad and extensive for any one social worker to comprehend. It is therefore understandable that students and qualified social workers find social work itself, and the theoretical terrain on which it is constructed, diverse, complex, challenging and often confusing.

Where is this taking us? First, to an appreciation that social work is not simply a practical activity with functional outcomes but one that makes use of practical interventions explained and justified in the light of a social worker's knowledge of the people with whom they work and of the enormously varied contexts in which social work is carried out. Second, to an appreciation that, while the knowledge base needed for effective social work is extensive and constructed on a range of different disciplines, social work undertaken without the support of underpinning knowledge is at best difficult to justify and at worst dangerous. Finally, to confidence that the necessary theory is neither mysterious nor difficult but that social work practice does require reflection on theory, in the form of the writings and research of others, if it is to be effective and meaningful. But – and this is reinforced by my own experiences of working with post-qualifying award-level candidates – when competent social workers are asked to produce written analyses of their work, their confidence in their own abilities to theorise and make underpinning knowledge explicit seems to evaporate.

Martyn (2000) provides further reinforcement for such observations. In discussing the professional development of students undertaking Goldsmiths College's advanced programme, Martyn (2000, p.xiii) describes how 'Developing Reflective Practice' was effectively written by final-year students 'when confidence had grown to the point where it was possible to expose work to rigorous analysis and criticism from outside commentators'. Her engagement with experienced social workers in writing about their practice highlighted the anxieties that inhibit social workers (and perhaps any professional person) when it comes to making explicit the theoretical rationale for their interventions to a wider audience or readership. Martyn is analysing here her work with experienced social workers undertaking advanced studies rather than newly qualified social workers undertaking post-qualifying awards. Her observations and comments suggest a lack of both confidence and tradition among the social work profession when it comes to writing down and analysing the social work carried out.

Practising social workers know how difficult it is to find the time to theorise when faced with the pressures of day-to-day social work, which often, and by definition, involves responding to pressing needs and crises. Martyn (2000, p.xvi) uses an example from Ronald Laing who, some 35 years ago, in presenting a paper to the Association of Family Caseworkers, stated, 'We have hectic jobs; our theorising is often done in the midst of our activity, or in our own spare time when we are not too exhausted. We often discover what we do after we have done it.' Perhaps not a lot has changed in terms of pressures during the intervening years, except that social workers are now exposed to even greater pressures and a level of media scrutiny unknown 35 years ago! Yellowly and Henkel (1995) argue that post-qualifying education is an opportunity for participants to reflect on and reconsider their current roles away from the pressures of their jobs but, returning to my own personal and recent experience of delivering post-qualifying training, social workers undertaking post-qualifying awards still find it difficult to meet deadlines in presenting their portfolios. The most frequently cited reasons, in my experience, put forward by social workers in requesting extensions and deferments are 'pressures of work' and the apparently endemic 'organisational restructuring', which regularly interrupts the continuity of their work.

Making the theory explicit

Post-qualifying awards in social work have ensured that many social workers have either had to submit portfolios as part of their continuing professional development, or have chosen to do so. The demands of post-qualifying education and continuing professional development being made on social workers will continue to increase following the introduction of the requirement for them to 'register' and the establishment of a new framework for post-qualifying awards. Placing post-qualifying education within a university framework is unlikely to diminish the requirement, already being made by existing post-qualifying consortia, for social workers to evidence not just their practice competence but also the theoretical knowledge and values underpinning their practice. The reasons for this are debated below, in ways that suggest that, while there are no undisputed right or wrong answers in attempting to analyse the huge range of social contexts and human behaviours that bring people to the point at which they become users or recipients of social work services, there is a framework of knowledge built on evidence and experience that can help us analyse individual and social circumstances and come to justifiable decisions.

Stepney and Ford (2000, p.20) suggest that there is a conflict between 'theoretical knowledge and practice wisdom'. In trying to explain the conflict, they go on to argue that:

> In social work many of our ideas are borrowed from human sciences, philosophy and law and so on, which means that inevitably the theoretical knowledge base of social work is very broad. It also needs to be recognised that such ideas may be at a highly abstract level of analysis, quite speculative and fiercely contested.

This acknowledges that the limits of social work theory are difficult to identify, as are the boundaries of social work itself. Social work involves working with people in individual, family, social, medical, cultural, economic, legal and political contexts, which many different academic and professional disciplines have attempted to define. Sociologists, psychologists, psychiatrists, lawyers, criminologists, politicians, educationalists, economists, medical professionals, historians (this list is probably not exhaustive) all attempt to define and explain the human condition and/or attempt to regulate the ways in which human beings interact with their environments and with each other. Social work needs to draw upon all of these areas, and this is of course a major part of the problem: how do you put a boundary around the breadth and depth of knowledge and theory required for effective social work in all its manifestations? As Soydan (1999, p.4) states:

> The problem for social work is that what is defined as social work is also carried out within the framework of other disciplines: if sociology can be regarded as an exporting discipline, social work may be generally considered an importing discipline as far as theories and analytical methods are concerned.

If only it was a science...

There is perhaps a more fundamental reason why applying theory in social work is so difficult. Social work is far from being a rational scientific discipline, and while the scientific method of testing theories and hypotheses can be used in some situations the testing of theories and methods in a social work context is not straightforward. In a physical science the researcher can often control variables effectively in order to test or apply a theory or method. In social work, the subjects of study, service users and methods of working with service users, are almost always subject to environments and variables over which the social worker has no control. Working with people is not only a minefield of subjectivity but complicated by the fact that the majority of service users are at the mercy of structural, economic and social determinants over which neither they nor the social worker have very much control. There is an inherent dilemma for social workers in deciding whether the service user's inner resources or whether external, environmental factors are the major determinants of behaviour. It is perhaps not surprising therefore that, in a pressured, stressful and complex working environment, social work responses are reactive rather than reflective, and tend to avoid detailed consideration of how individuals address and cope with structural disadvantage or weakened inner personal resources – neither of which are comfortable areas to address in practice.

Understandably, therefore, students of social work and practitioners at post-qualifying levels have difficulty both identifying and integrating theory into reflective writing. There is, in social work, a divide between practice and the evidential or theoretical components underpinning the work, a divide that needs to be more effectively bridged by practice and academic settings. The Competence/Practice Requirement framework of the Diploma in Social Work (DipSW) ensured an emphasis on what was done rather than on how or why. The knowledge requirements set out in 'Paper 30' (CCETSW 1995) were extensive but received less priority than the practice tasks. Cox and Hardwick (2002) make the same point, that following the restructuring of the DipSW in 1995 more significance was accorded to competencies, evidence and outcomes than to process. We need therefore to ensure that the underpinning knowledge on which the 'Occupational Standards' and 'Key Roles' depend must be given a high profile so that the reflective and theoretical bases of social work are not lost.

It is, however, fundamentally difficult to apply social work theory in practice. Social workers operate in a huge range of practice situations, all with their own particular specialist knowledge areas and specific categories of service user. Social work theories attempt to explain complex human behaviours in equally complex family and social environments. Social work theories also encompass methods of intervention, but their application is often compromised because of the tangled web of subjective and objective realities of which the social worker is part and within which the social worker operates. Social workers do not frequently share their theoretical knowledge, or make explicit their methodologies or approaches to working with particular service users, even though they do attempt to work in partnership with service users. In working in partnership with service users, social workers do not want to be seen as 'experts' with (like doctors) a range of 'treatments'. Methods and theories are therefore usually applied covertly, because it is difficult and perhaps damaging to be explicit about perceived personal deficits or (an over-used description of service users) 'their lack of coping skills' when service users are often attempting to cope in very difficult social or economic circumstances. Eraut (1994, p.43), on this theme, argues that professional actions are dictated by 'theories in use which differ from the espoused theories used to explain them to external audiences or even the actor themselves'.

Social work theory – the basis on which judgements and decisions about people are made – is a highly subjective area and very much open to debate and dispute, leading to a situation in which social workers are often reluctant to commit themselves to a definitive explanation of their decisions. Could it also be that the situational and contextual diversity in which 'social work' is practised makes it very difficult to apprehend a clear understanding of not only social work itself but of the body of theory on which the practice of 'social work' is based? Like Stepney and Ford (2000, p.21), who put the term 'theory' (as it relates to social work) in inverted commas 'to denote that it is a contested concept', I feel that 'social work' itself is also a contested concept and one that is very difficult to define. The highly emotive subject matter of social work, and the tensions between understanding behaviours as 'voluntary' or 'determined' (by extrinsic factors) involved in social work judgements and decisions, make it very difficult for social workers to provide universally acceptable explanations to recipients of services. It is, I suspect, for these reasons that social workers often find it difficult to provide confident theoretical justifications for the work they do and the decisions they take in terms that are understandable to service users. Perhaps, as intended by the General Social Care Council, this is an area in which the contribution of service users to the design and delivery of the social work curriculum at qualifying and at post-qualifying levels would be of great significance.

Cox and Hardwick (2002), in analysing the use of theory in social work education, refer to the weight attached to competencies, evidence and outcomes rather than process. In moving towards reflective practice it is necessary to move towards a 'process' model to encourage reflection on practice. Working with post-qualifying award candidates, diploma and degree in social work students, I have found that facilitating critical reflection on practice in workshop scenarios encourages reflection on the processes that are taking place in social worker/service user encounters. A clear and consistent message from the large numbers of post-qualifying award candidates with whom I have worked during a period of several years is that, in most instances, qualified social workers (especially those in local authorities) are no longer exposed to 'professional reflective' supervision but to 'managerialist' forms of supervision, which are target and resource driven by 'performance management' agendas emphasising quantitative rather than the qualitative aspects of social work outcomes. In these circumstances the opportunity to reflect on process is limited but can be developed in workshop situations. I return to the comments of Yellowly and Henkel (1995), about the value of time spent away from pressured practice situations being essential to allow proper reflection on practice issues; a post-qualifying award course that provides such opportunities is an invaluable aid to professional development.

Conclusion

Approaching theory from the point of view of reflection on practice in workshop situations has been, for me, one of the most rewarding and effective ways of linking theory and practice. It is of course an interactive but simple and uncomplicated method of facilitating learning, and leads participants to the point at which they are able to arrive at their own links between practice and theory. Such an experiential and interactive approach also models partnership and participation, and reinforces the idea that the practitioners (from a very wide range of practice situations) are the experts and that they simply require the time and opportunity to engage in the reflective process that is a key stage in professional development and the enhancement of practice skills.

Recommended reading

Adams, R., Dominelli, L. and Payne, M. (2002) *Critical Practice in Health and Social Care*. Basingstoke: Palgrave.
This edited work addresses a wide range of issues in social work and is a very useful aid for anyone wishing to reflect on the meanings and contexts of contemporary social work practice.

Brown, K. and Rutter, L. (2006) *Critical Thinking for Social Work*. Exeter: Learning Matters.
A basic introduction to reflective and critical practice in social work, and a useful starting point for anyone wishing to begin the process of engaging with the concepts of critical and reflective practice.

Healy, K. (2005) *Social Work Theories in Context: Creating Frameworks for Practice*. Basingstoke: Palgrave Macmillan.
An excellent work at a reflective level, which should be very useful indeed at Consolidation, Specialist and Higher Specialist levels of the new post-qualifying award framework.

Lishman, J. (2007) *Handbook for Practice Learning in Social Work and Social Care* (2nd edn). London: Jessica Kingsley Publishers.
Formerly published as Joyce Lishman's classic and well respected *Handbook of Theory for Practice Teachers of Social Work* (1991) the current re-titled, revised and updated edition remains an excellent and accessible reference to a wide range of social work theories and policies.

Parker, J. (2004) *Effective Practice Learning in Social Work*. Exeter: Learning Matters.
This book is a very readable and useful text for students and for social workers at post-qualifying levels – especially in the context of working with students in practice learning settings. It is concise and helpful in illustrating the ways in which links between theory and practice can be used to develop reflective practice.

Payne, M. (2005) *Modern Social Work Theory*. Basingstoke: Palgrave Macmillan.
This offers a comprehensive overview of key social work theories and methodologies in one user-friendly volume. It has been a reliable and standard reference work for students and practitioners for many years and has, with several revisions, kept up to date with changes in social work practice and policy.

Stepney, P. and Ford, M. (2000) *Social Work, Models, Methods and Theories*. Lyme Regis: Russell House Publishing Ltd.
This provides a good outline of social work theory and method, which is ideally suited both to students of social work and those at post-qualifying award levels.

CHAPTER 6

Post-Qualifying Studies: European and International Contexts

Malcolm Payne

Why include a European and international perspective in PQ studies?

Why should people pursuing post-qualifying (PQ) social work education in the UK be concerned about PQ in Europe and internationally? There are three main reasons.

First, the British PQ system increasingly fits into a European structure of qualification, so it is useful to know about and consider how our own work connects with that. Globalisation means that all education is increasingly part of an international market in courses and qualifications.

Second, social workers and the people who use their services increasingly travel. We may be working alongside someone from another country, with asylum seekers and migrants from Europe and all over the world, and we might think of spending part of our career in another country.

Third, knowledge and policy development is increasingly international. In the search for answers to shared social problems, politicians increasingly look across the world. They particularly look for solutions that fit with partners in regional and international alliances, such as the European Union (EU). While social work is bound by the legal and social policy of the nations that incorporate it into their systems, it is part of an international network of organisations that interact. Examples are the International Association of Schools of Social Work (IASSW 2006), the academics' network, the International Federation of Social Workers (IFSW 2006), the social workers' associations network, and the International Council on Social Welfare (ICSW 2006), the agencies' and social development network.

Social work in the UK is increasingly specialist, after a period from 1970 to the early 2000s when it was concentrated in one local government social ser-vices agency: Social Services Departments. It is, therefore, increasingly multi-professional, because it is part of education and health care structures that connect social work more directly with other professions. These professions are also international. In both education and especially health care, specialisations increasingly see themselves as part of international movements. For example, my own field, palliative care, is now an international social movement con-cerned with better care for dying and bereaved people, a widely recognised health care speciality with a World Health Organization policy statement, a medical specialism in palliative medicine and government standards provided by the National Institute for Health and Clinical Excellence (NICE 2004). There is an International Observatory in Palliative Care at Lancaster University, tracking worldwide developments, and national and international email news-letters and conferences, involving social workers alongside doctors, nurses and other health care professionals. All this has taken place in the 40 years since the foundation, in 1967, of St Christopher's Hospice in south London, recognised as the source of this development (Hospice Information 2006).

The internationalisation of health and social care and its education has taken place mostly in the last 20 years. When welfare states were established, during the 1940s, international travel was expensive and difficult. The nation state and national borders were the basis of attempts to create global economic and political stability. The availability of cheap and quick travel, the Internet and e-mail for communication, and the developing role of transnational corpo-rations in an increasingly international economic market have made social work part of an international market in the provision of welfare, alongside practice within national legal and social welfare systems (Irving and Payne 2004).

As a result of all these trends, social workers can strengthen their post-qual-ification professional development through including within it an international perspective. In the UK, it is helpful to focus particularly on Europe, since the UK is part of the administrative structures of the EU, has links with European cultures, and travel to Europe is convenient and cheap. Many communities of migrants to the UK come from former Commonwealth countries in Africa, Asia and the Caribbean, so learning about their cultures is also a valid priority, but travel to such places is less convenient and more expensive. Extensive and advanced social work provision, such as the services in the USA or Australia, also attracts interest, because it can provide another dimension of understanding by allowing comparison with the UK system. It is not necessary to go outside the UK for comparative experience, however. Social care systems in the UK nations – England, Northern Ireland, Scotland and Wales – are diverging in policy and practice requirements, and provide interesting comparisons within a similar but subtly different cultural and service background (Payne and Shardlow 2002).

There are several uses to which we can put European and international links. They may be helpful in practice. For example, adoption, child protection and health care agencies require international investigations and transfers of care for patients moving abroad in their work. Mental health and disability movements are international in scope and connections. This chapter focuses on pursuing professional education either through courses or experience in other countries, and incorporating it into UK PQ work.

It is impossible to gain an understanding of social work PQ education in every EU country, or more widely internationally. Rather than attempt this in a brief chapter, I explore here an approach to understanding PQ systems and opportunities in other countries, using some examples of my personal involvement to illustrate some of the variations.

Europe, the European Union and PQ

The European Union is a grouping of (from 2007) 27 nations with a combined population of half a billion (see Europa, the EU website (European Commission 2006a), for more information). The EU's aims are to improve economic opportunities for its members. Social matters are subsidiary to that, being mainly the responsibility of member countries, so social care is not a major EU issue. Education developments in the EU are mainly about improving enterprise, employment and the flexibility of the workforce. The main educational development aims of the EU are expressed in the Bologna Declaration, which announced agreement to align degree qualifications and higher education structures throughout Europe. Lifelong education is a policy objective. Student and staff mobility is being encouraged to increase social solidarity and mutual understanding (Ashford 2004).

As a result, the main effect of the EU on social work education is that UK qualifications fit into a system that covers a 'European Higher Education Area' wider than the EU, of 45 countries. A European Credit Transfer and Accumulation System (ECTS) (European Commission 2006b) specifies the number of credits at different levels of qualification that a student receives for a specified amount of work on a course of learning. Increasingly, courses are advertised with ECTS credits, and national credit accumulation systems are being aligned to the same standard. This enables students to transfer credit for courses undertaken anywhere in the EU to contribute to qualifications at universities anywhere else. Where students have ECTS credits to transfer, the university they are moving to assesses their relevance to the course that they are taking up. The subject matter may allow them to substitute credits for part of the course they are moving to, or to fulfil one of the options. Usually the proportion of the course that can be credited in this way is limited. The higher education market means that universities and courses for which there is competition are less keen to accept credits for high proportions of their own courses.

The policy of encouraging mobility has also affected higher education throughout Europe. Mainly, this has come about through the Erasmus–Socrates programmes, which give grants for collaborative projects to enable staff and students to travel to other countries for part of their courses (European Commission 2006c). To discourage short visits that are little more than tourism with some educational content, the European Commission (the EU's management body) encourages universities to develop 'mobilities' (the EU jargon for travel under these arrangements) that last for several weeks or months and are part of continuing programmes. Because this mainly suits undergraduate students with few family commitments it has not affected most British social work courses. Their more mature social work students are less able to take these longer periods away from home and often do not have the language skills necessary to take advantage of foreign-language academic courses or placements in the same way as some European students placed in the UK. Generally, the UK competency-based approach to professional education is not well understood or appreciated in the academically led education of many European countries.

Consequently, many UK students have not had an experience of international education during their social work qualifying course to build on at the PQ level. Neither will this be repaired at the PQ level. In European countries where social work higher education is well developed, many students qualify as undergraduates in their early twenties and then progress to part-time study for an advanced degree or diploma, sometimes as a taught master's or doctoral degree.

However, the EU system of creating partnerships between universities in different countries has led to joint degrees developing in both particular subject areas and in general international work that can overcome some of these difficulties. Examples of several such developments are the MA in International Child Welfare at the University of East Anglia and the MA in International Social Work at the University of East London.

Understanding international PQ structures

When planning to get PQ experience and undertake training internationally, it is useful to know about the educational structures of the relevant countries. The various stakeholders are, as in the UK:

- universities, and in particular their role in qualifying education

- professional associations

- government

- agencies, often part of local government or semi-official agencies.

In each country, these combine with different responsibilities. To understand how this works in any particular country, English-language documents are available on government and professional association websites, and English-language introductions may be found on some university websites. The website of the European Association of Schools of Social Work (EASSW 2006) and the UK Social Work and Policy learning and teaching subject network website (SWAPltsn 2005) provide helpful information.

The UK is politically and administratively centralised, while all European countries have more devolved administrations. Therefore, PQ in Europe relies more than in the UK on university advanced courses rather than a national PQ system. Local universities sometimes arrange to provide courses of interest to agencies. The EU structures for transferability and the international market in qualifications mean that university credits gained elsewhere can be used to contribute to UK qualifications, or at least to the Care Councils' requirements for continuing professional development.

Some examples of how the pattern varies may help to give a picture of what happens. Regulation of the social work profession is at the regional level in Germany, and while in most European countries there is only a small non-public sector in social care, the 'corporatist' approach of German social welfare (Poole 2001) means that some social welfare services are provided through large non-profit organisations outside the public sector. Authority to use the title 'social worker', or equivalent, in many countries is in effect conferred by the award of a university qualification, rather than through a separate government regulatory process. In most countries, universities are autonomous from government, with state, private and sometimes church-based universities. For example, in Germany social pedagogy is usually taught in the universities as part of education faculties, while social work is taught in the less prestigious *Fachhochschulen*, or 'universities of applied science'. There are diocesan as well as secular *Fachhochschulen*. The arrangements develop over time as state planning and financing for universities changes. For example, in Norway, one university, Trondheim, for a long time acted as the 'staff college' for social work, and advanced courses and higher degrees were taken there. Other universities did not teach social work, and people qualified in specialist colleges. These sometimes offered PQ courses for agencies by agreement or on their own account. The colleges have recently been merging and are being upgraded to universities. As they progress, they are being approved to provide master's and doctoral education in health and social care subjects.

Looking wider than Europe, validation of social work qualifying courses in the USA is undertaken by an association of schools of social work, the Council on Social Work Education (CSWE 2006), rather than a government agency. Accreditation to work as a social worker is handled by states, each of which has its own legislation. An association of state organisations that do this – the Association of Social Work Boards (ASWB 2006) – provides multiple-choice questions for states to use in examinations for this purpose. Its website provides a summary of state legislation on social work regulation and legal definitions of social work. Reading this emphasises how, in the USA, bachelors level is distinguished from master's level social work. The bachelors level might be seen as the qualification for less qualified care management or practical social work, while the master's level is required for more therapeutic roles. In many states, clinical social work, akin to psychotherapy, is distinguished as a specialisation within master's level work; there are often also specialisations in community development, management and education. Many people who want to gain promotion or to go into social work education, research or agency management do a Doctor of Social Work (DSW) degree, which usually contains a substantial element of specialist courses and a research dissertation that is shorter than a PhD (research degree) thesis. This model is being developed in the UK, and DSWs gained in the USA, at least from the better-known universities, are valued in the UK.

Most US states require social workers to accumulate continuing education (CE) 'points' over time to sustain their qualification, similar to the requirements in the UK. Universities and agencies that provide courses can have these accredited for CE points. For example, I taught a day course on psychosocial and spiritual care in palliative care for the University of New Hampshire in spring 2007. To get CE accreditation, the professor organising the programme submitted a set of course objectives, a bibliography, evidence of my UK social work registration, doctoral degree and publications, and presented an argument that the course was relevant to US ethical and professional guidelines and standards. Certificates from such courses would be acceptable in the UK as part of continuing professional development.

Many universities offer higher degrees, including master's and doctoral degrees, in social work or related subjects, and it is often possible to take courses as part of these that can, through ECTS or similar arrangements, contribute to a British degree. Sometimes these are in English. For example, I have a connection with the department of social policy at Helsinki University in Finland (University of Helsinki 2006). This offers master's and doctoral research degrees in social work and social policy. There are also a small number of courses in English, and a wider range of English courses offered through the Faculty of Social Science. As in most of Finland, sophisticated English is widely spoken and universities encourage students to use English as the language of research theses, because this gives them a wider influence within international social science, where the English language predominates. A number of universities there, as elsewhere, offer intensive short courses, sometimes in summer schools (which can be combined with a holiday), in subjects of professional interest.

Agencies offer PQ education according to their needs, but my impression is that this is rather less common than in the UK and may be used for specific purposes. An example is a training day on multi-professional teamwork that I am teaching for Reykjavik City Council in 2007 following the merger of some health and social care functions into one department. The role of agencies in the structure of services and professional development affects the role they play in PQ education. For example, I ran a course on care management for Helsinki City Council jointly with the Swedish Institute of Social Science in Finland a few years ago, the Institute taking advantage of my availability in Helsinki and 'selling' the course to the City authorities on that occasion. Another example is the work of Professor Fabio Folgheraiter at the University of Trento in northern Italy. He developed an interest in care management and organised a series of conferences: first, a day conference run in association with the local regional council for its staff, then a more academic conference; finally, there was a three-day conference, attracting a large audience from all over Italy. UK academics and professionals took part in all these events. This shows how academic interests influence the development of social work through relationships with and development work in agencies.

The strength of professional associations varies considerably. They are an important personal support to many social workers where social work is still developing, in southern or eastern Europe, but may be weak in policy and professional influence. In countries such as Denmark, Sweden and Norway, where there is extensive government welfare provision, they are incorporated into local government trades unions and have very large conferences. I have attended annual meetings in these countries where a substantial proportion of the social work membership attends a wide range of education and training sessions. Some of these are conducted in English, often where professionals and academics from English-speaking countries take part.

Pursuing PQ outside the UK

This brief survey of the sorts of PQ education available internationally suggests various possibilities for gaining experience and education in Europe and internationally. The easiest way is to take part in an international conference. These are organised by the international social work organisations and by international groups in a wide range of health and social care specialities. Often, there is a world conference one year, followed by regional conferences the next. Many people receive funding to attend these conferences from their employers or grant aid nationally by offering to conduct a practice workshop based on their experience, or to give a paper or lecture based on their research or study. This can be a good way of gaining recognition for some academic or professional work a worker has carried out during their PQ course. At the very least, they may contribute to a portfolio of work for a British PQ course or continuing professional education for a Care Council. Listings of conferences are published in the *European Journal of Social Work* and on the websites of the main international organisations mentioned above and in Appendix 2.

The main deterrent for many social workers in taking part in such conferences is the process of submitting 'abstracts' for review by the conference committee, in order to receive an invitation to present their paper. There is a skill in writing acceptable abstracts. What is required is a clear statement of the methods, findings and importance of the paper or workshop, rather than a general account of the topics to be covered. If it is a workshop, showing how people with different languages and backgrounds will be enabled to participate is useful. Looking at the abstracts available on websites or in academic journals will give a good idea of the required approach.

However, short-term or occasional involvements in conferences overseas can provide only a partial view of how a different social care system operates. It may be more useful to pursue a more coherent strategy of long-term engagement with a particular specialisation or country, to gain greater depth of understanding and to return some UK experience to the country that we get involved with (Askeland and Payne 2001). Relevant experience and education internationally after qualification are likely to help in getting a job and in gaining promotion later in the UK. However, qualifications gained are most likely to be helpful if they are similar to the equivalent UK qualification or can be credited towards a UK qualification. Therefore, short courses should ideally have relevant transferable credits. Also, it may be more useful to follow UK higher degrees that focus on international or comparative work, European or international degrees with subject titles that clearly relate to British concerns, or research degrees or professional doctorates such as those offered in the USA and Canada where the subject matter is relevant to British interests.

Conclusion

In this chapter, I have tried to show how European structures are promoting lifelong education and increasing the alignment of qualification and education structures. I have argued that this provides opportunities for UK social workers to contribute European and international experience to their PQ education. I have given some examples of my experience of the possibilities available and discussed how to look at the structures of PQ education in European and other countries to begin the process of understanding what might be available. Finally, I have suggested various ways in which UK social workers might use some of these experiences as part of their PQ education and continuing professional development. The British social work profession and UK agencies can gain from the broader comparative perspective if we take up these opportunities. It is important to pursue a constructive programme of engagement over time, however, to avoid imposing professional tourism on our colleagues abroad – who will welcome us – and to offer something of our own experience and education in return.

Recommended reading

Askeland, G.A. and Payne, M. (2001) 'Broadening the mind: cross-national activities in social work.' *European Journal of Social Work 4,* 3, 263–274.
A useful article, which examines the pros and cons of cross-national activities.

Cochrane, A., Clarke, J. and Gewirtz, S. (eds) (2001) *Comparing Welfare States: Family Life and Social Policy* (2nd edn). London: Sage, 153–194.
A good introductory and wide-ranging book, allowing a comparison of various European welfare states.

Cox, D. and Pawar, M. (2005) *International Social Work: Issues, Strategies and Programs.* Thousand Oaks, CA: Sage.
A good general account of international issues of concern in social work.

Irving, Z. and Payne, M. (2004) 'Globalisation: Implications for Learning and Teaching.' In H. Burgess and I. Taylor (eds) *Effective Learning and Teaching in Social Policy and Social Work* (LTSN series). London: Routledge Falmer, 153–168.
A chapter that introduces issues about globalisation, and learning and teaching internationally.

CHAPTER 7

Researching Practice
Terry Murphy and David Nulty

Introduction

The role of research within social work continues to be a contested area, both theoretically and in practical terms, and is one of the most difficult areas to include within both pre-qualifying and post-qualifying (PQ) curricula. Many social workers speak of finding difficulty in relating research, and in particular research methodology, to the day-to-day social work practice that informs their professional activities. Indeed, while there is a nominal appreciation of the role of research in relation to practice, students are often unenthusiastic about undertaking research training itself, viewing research methods education at qualifying or PQ level as abstract and not engaging their interest (Berger 2002; Epstein 1987; Wainstock 1994).

Similarly, on the broader stage of professional practice itself, several studies have demonstrated a clear reluctance on the part of social workers to cite social work theory as an influence on their day-to-day practice, as has been the case in related professions (Berger 2002; Bruenlin and Schwartz 1983; Cheetham 1992; Dunlap 1993; Epstein 1987; Jones 1990; Lebow 1988; Liddle 1991; Rubin, Franklin and Selber 1992; Tyson 1992).

Responses to the issue of the practice–theory divide have fallen into a number of different camps. First, there is the response that social workers use theory implicitly rather than in an explicit manner. This, however, is an unsatisfactory response as one of the characteristics of any theory that informs professional practice must be its systematic nature and its explanatory power in allowing practice to be demonstrably related to a clear evidence base. If social workers are unable to clearly elucidate the relationship of a particular theory to day-to-day practice then we are left with the problem of theory being utilised in practice, if at all, in idiosyncratic, variable and potentially mistaken ways (Bellamy, Bledsoe and Traube 2006) (for more on theory, see Chapter 5: Integrating Theory and Practice at Post-Qualifying Level). In this chapter we offer concrete suggestions to PQ practitioners as to why the integration of research mindedness and the development of skills, including the use of modern electronic resources, can offer a more effective route through PQ development and towards the development of evidence-based practice at a PQ level. In any meaningful sense, social workers who are not regularly updating their knowledge of the literature, and engaged in a clearly understood and shared system of evaluation of their practice, are simply not engaged in evidence-based practice (Corcoran 2000; Gambrill 2003).

The pressure to complete a PQ award while at the same time working in the demanding social environment can leave practitioners wanting to move immediately into focusing on and completing individual assignments. This approach, we would suggest, is far less effective than developing, early in the course, the research skills, particularly in terms of literature review, that will enable them to have a far more effective approach both to learning and completing successful assignments. Just as case work without an element of overview and planning is rarely effective, so a PQ award benefits from the planning and preparation that the development of skills in research methods provides.

In carrying out the variety of possible types of assignment that you may engage with it is important to recognise that two principal types of research activity will predominate. The first is the literature review in which you systematically examine the literature for particular topics and, in particular, undertake the systematic examination of a particular field of social work and related literature for dissertation or detailed practice study. The second is the production of small-scale primary research, which is most commonly carried out by staff or individuals interviewing, for example, other practitioners or service users around a particular practice topic. This may more recently have been complemented by Internet- or e-mail-based research (McAuliffe 2003).

The first element of guidance for you in facing the task of demonstrating the integration of theory and practice is to develop effective research skills and approaches to the process of completing the award.

Library and information services

One of your initial planning tasks should be to familiarise yourself with the library and information services of the higher education institution with which your award is linked. You should familiarise (or refamiliarise) yourself – change can be rapid and profound – with both the physical layout of the library and, almost more importantly, with the electronic resources available to you. Within the first month of the course you should become familiar with where the physical stock of the library is located. Professional library staffs, with their high level of skill in information science, are frequently an under-utilised resource. Given the rapid changes in the form of information resources available, it will be useful for you, even if you have previously studied at an institution, to ask for an early meeting with specialist subject librarians so that they can give you an overview of the institution's information resources. The relevant library website should also be searched for information and instruction leaflets on the relevant databases, journals and access systems you will be using. It is strongly recommended that you obtain and read all the relevant information leaflets that are available as they frequently address many practical issues (e.g. how to log on to and use off-campus resources); failure to do this may delay your fully coming to grips with the resources available.

An invaluable tool will be a simple notebook, which can be used as a basic research diary. You should note any search terms you have used in searching for books or articles. Note also any databases and electronic journals that have proved to be particularly useful (save links to your PC as you work). You can also make planning notes or ideas about future research to be undertaken; as your course progresses, and given the fallibility of human memory, such a simple research tool will prevent the duplication of work already undertaken and is also a useful aid in discussions with PQ mentors and assessors, demonstrating not only the outcome of your work but also the processes undertaken in order to get there.

On-campus guidance

The assertiveness and good planning that are hallmarks of good social work practice are also appropriately applied to the PQ experience itself. It is useful at an early stage for you and colleagues on the same course to discuss your current level of awareness of research and information resources, and then present to course tutors an active list of topics on which the group feels teaching or training input would be useful. In our experience at the University of Teesside, students benefit greatly from practical hands-on training experience of using databases and electronic access systems under the supervision of a tutor at a relatively early stage of research methods training.

The next stage of taking an effective research-minded approach requires you to work, preferably in small groups, to become actively familiar with the book stock of the institution that you initially identified and equally, if not more importantly, the electronic databases and electronic journals to which the institution subscribes. You may have a tendency to remain in the 'comfort zone' of regularly examining or browsing a far narrower range of journals than an institution in fact stocks, but don't limit yourself to those journals with the words 'social work' in their titles. You will benefit by broadening your subject focus and knowledge of the library stock to include titles from, for example, the broader fields of social policy, sociology, psychology, and health and welfare. As already mentioned, early and persistent use of academic databases, in addition to browsing physical book stock, will encourage a richer approach to searching and using electronic journals as the databases you come across will cite references that span an entire relevant field of study. The ability to carry out a thorough and accurate secondary research review of the literature around a particular social work topic must be seen in the PQ context not simply as an academic exercise but as a key element in developing evidence-based professional practice.

It is extremely useful in the early stages of PQ education for you to engage in formal practice reflection in terms of your own professional history, and to begin to list the theories and theorists that you feel have concretely influenced your own practice. It is also important to identify areas of practice that you feel are in a sense non-theoretical and have been developed solely from experience or discussion with others. As you will see in other chapters, there can be a misleading faith in 'common sense' on the part of social workers, which the PQ process should challenge.

In attempting to develop more research-minded practice, and what we might call an evidence-based approach to social work, it is important to understand the purpose of systematically searching for and studying the literature on any particular social work topic.

There are two particular areas that need to be understood when examining any of the social work literature. First, there is the literature that is relevant to the social problem that social work seeks to address. This may be literature of a broader sociological/social policy nature, describing the problem (e.g. child maltreatment, drug misuse, homelessness) in which you are interested. The relevant literature may also include practice guidance or evaluation of particular social work interventions that have been designed to work with the problem (e.g. solution-focused therapy, monitoring, formal assessment). In addition to this literature, however, you need to develop familiarity with the literature on the research methodology that applies to a particular topic area.

This topic-based literature will provide the results of previous attempts to define particular social work problems or issues, and to address particular research questions. The methodological literature, on the other hand, will more typically question the underlying assumptions and arguments concerning how we can study the problem in question. An increasing number of social work journals have a particular focus on methodological debates – for example, the journals *Research on Social Work Practice* and *Qualitative Social Work* (both published by Sage).

Being able to research literature around your own area of practice offers a number of advantages. As already mentioned, it enables you to identify work already done or in progress that is relevant to your practice, and can help you avoid the unnecessary duplication of research that has already been undertaken. It can illustrate some of the difficulties and problems that have arisen in previous attempts to address or understand particular social work problems. It will also help you to understand that, in terms of evidence-based practice, the research evidence is much stronger for some social work practice approaches than others. Given the sheer complexity of human need and the complex causation of social problems, there are inevitably significant gaps in the existing research across a whole range of the problems with which social workers engage. In real-world practice, then, a research-minded approach leading to a knowledge of relevant literature in a social worker's field of practice can help avoid approaches to practice that are known to be ineffective, and can challenge the social worker's own assumptions about individuals, families, communities and indeed social work itself.

Internet-based research

The Internet itself has brought a number of advantages. However, as is usually the case with such advances, these are balanced by a number of potential pitfalls. A particularly useful and generally available Internet tool is the Internet search engine, of which Google is probably the best-known example. Any words entered into the search box on Google will return anything between a few and a few million results. This illustrates one of the major potential pitfalls of the contemporary information age: information overload. For example, the search term 'social work' entered into Google in 2006 resulted in 511,000,000 results being returned; this overwhelming number limits their effectiveness, but taking the time to look at the help section on the Google help page could considerably improve future searches. (Google, unlike some other search engines, includes Google Scholar (http://scholar.google.com), which refines searches considerably, especially when 'Advanced search' is used.) A further complication arises with the use of conventional search engines in that there is, in effect, no quality filter, and the idiosyncratic, the ideologically motivated or the incorrect website can appear next to the results of the most carefully researched study. For this reason, using conventional Internet search engines should never be the principal tool used in carrying out research.

Electronic journals and databases

As with all new technologies, users typically demonstrate greater familiarity and comfort with particular elements that resonate with existing skills or beliefs. In general you begin learning while being more comfortable with the elements of electronic resources that resemble the printed word. Electronic journals have now made available off-campus all the resources of specialist publications that would once have required a journey to a physical library. You can instead access journal articles directly via an Internet service that enables them to be downloaded direct to your PC. Within the United Kingdom the recognised system that makes available a university's purchased print resources is the Athens authentication system.[1] You can gain access via the Athens system to all the journals to which a particular institution subscribes.

In the case of most courses based within higher education, current technologies mean that a student has access to some hundreds of relevant journals within social work, psychology, health and related disciplines. The fact that the electronic journals mimic the format of print journals makes them relatively user-friendly and, once logged on via the Athens system, you may use one of the journal access systems, such as SwetsWise, Ingenta Direct or Science Direct, or the direct links to major publishers, to access all the relevant issues of the journals a higher education institution subscribes to.

In routinely examining students' work, I have found that the principal use of electronic resources consists of browsing the electronic journals available. However, results are improved considerably by students doing a preliminary database search of the several excellent online social science and social work databases available, in order to target articles more accurately. In carrying out any of your PQ assignments you will significantly increase the effectiveness of your study time by including in your planning the use of databases such as Social Care Online[2] and CSA Illumina.[3] These let you rapidly examine the entire social work and related literature for particular topics. Social Care Online was itself developed in the UK by the National Institute of Social Work and the

---

1   Athens © Copyright Eduserv is an Access Management system for controlling secure access to web-based services. It is available at http://www.athens.ac.uk/.

2   Social Care Online is available at http://www.scie-socialcareonline.org.uk/.

3   CSA Illumina, Bethesda, Maryland 20814, USA.

Social Care Institute for Excellence, and is a freely available social care and social work specialist database, whereas commercial databases such as the social science database platform CSA Illumina cover a broader range of social science material and allow multiple database searches simultaneously.

Most commonly, these databases are accessed via the aforementioned Athens authentication system within the United Kingdom. One of the most useful developments in library science in recent years has been the development within database systems such as CSA Illumina of Internet links that allow the user, with a single click, to link directly to any article the database has found within any journal for which the host library has a subscription. Databases enable candidates to carry out detailed and comprehensive literature reviews far more rapidly than in the past. However, as the way they are used is perceived to be more technical than the process of browsing through electronic journals, course staff must put teaching time aside at the beginning of the programme to allow their students time to practise and acquire database skills.

It is important to become familiar with the tools available within individual databases, such as advance search tools, which can provide far more filtered and specific results than basic search engines; it is also important to become familiar with the use of the database's in-built thesaurus. You should develop the ability to perform and understand citation searches so that you become familiar with the idea that some research articles are far more influential than others. In the UK context it is also important that you can use the database thesaurus to perform searches based on the (sometimes significantly) different terms and key words used in US articles; these may differ markedly from the terms you may be familiar with in your practice.

Primary research

Primary research, which involves gathering original data from real-world subjects such as service users or other professionals, raises its own set of issues and in particular the issue of research ethics. It is important to recognise, when undertaking primary research, the need to have the ethical aspects and viability of your proposed study scrutinised by a research ethics committee at the earliest possible stage. This should ensure that proper research governance of the topic is guaranteed, and is particularly important where research involving service users or vulnerable children or adults is concerned (Melville 2006). You must be able to demonstrate that you have ensured that any primary research you carry out clearly demonstrates informed consent on the part of the research subjects and also that you understand the potential range of consequences likely to arise during the research process.

Try to complete documentation for research ethics committees with an awareness that many of the members of such committees may not have a social work background. They are perhaps more likely to be from a psychological or health service background, such as the medical and health professions; these have a significantly longer history of research ethics and governance committees than is the case in social work and social care. In this sense preparing for an ethics committee hearing while carrying out a piece of research for a PQ award is in itself an inter-disciplinary task. In particular social workers in statutory settings may, on a day-to-day basis, have to address the issues of mandated practice with involuntary clients. While these issues form part of your everyday practice, for many other professionals from health, medical or psychological backgrounds the issue of carrying out a piece of research in a service user setting that involves a degree of legal coercion presents new challenges and a degree of understandable discomfort, which may translate into a reluctance to give ethical approval to areas of social work research within the statutory arena.

It is necessary, then, in order to engage in a successful manner with research ethics committees in completing research ethics documentation, that you write your proposal for a multi-disciplinary audience. Above all, it should seek to explain the nature of the social work practice setting within which you will be carrying out the research and not assume prior knowledge on the part of committee members, however distinguished they are within their own field. In the United Kingdom the distinctive aspects of social work and social care research have been recognised by the production of the government's 'Implementation Plan for Research Governance in Social Care' (DoH 2004b).

Good research skills are useful both in terms of the more academic parts of the PQ award and also in terms of work-based elements such as practice projects, which normally attempt to examine particular theories or concepts in social work and the utility of these to practice. Work-based elements of programmes are normally more practically orientated, aiming to analyse the causes of a real-life situation or social work problem, and develop or improve the social work service designed to meet that problem; however, the research-based review of the literature can be equally important. It should aim to highlight examples of good practice and how changes to an organisational procedure or structure have resulted in the provision of a better service. In this sense researching practice literature gives us an opportunity to gain vicariously from the experience of others, as well as examine theoretical structures.

Conclusion

Research mindedness in PQ should not be seen as a theoretical abstraction removed from the 'messy realities' of practice, for engagement with the related research literature enables us to learn from a far wider range of social workers and others than we will ever meet face to face. Research may challenge us to question the utility of practice or our approach to social work; it may also offer us independent validation for a practice approach we have found individually to be of use. The increasing demand for independent evaluation of practices and procedures encourages us to empower ourselves to deal with the information that is so readily available. It is necessary to develop our research skills to be able to filter and focus on the huge volume of material available via electronic sources and the Internet. We can then use those that help us most to offer more effective services to our service users. Finally, we need to remember that research mindedness can place not only a practical but also an ethical demand on PQ candidates to develop their research and information skills.

Recommended reading

Hart, C. (1998) *Doing a Literature Review*. London: Sage Publications Ltd.

Silverman, D. (2007) *A Very Short, Fairly Interesting and Reasonably Cheap Book about Qualitative Research*. London: Sage Publications Ltd.

Part 2

Practice

Introduction

Part 2 provides a range of critical reflective studies on a range of social work practice based on the main groups of people who use, or are engaged with, social work services. This book cannot cover every type of service user group, but almost all social workers should be able to relate to at least one chapter. This process of exploring contemporary issues will provide an example of analysis and critical reflection related directly to the reader's work, which in turn should assist in their thinking and preparation of their PQ assignments or portfolio. These chapters are not intended to go into the breadth and depth of practice with 'particular' service users as there is insufficient space to do so, but the reader is encouraged to use the recommended reading and references provided to deepen their own particular specialism and expertise. Chapters commence with, or contain where appropriate, a brief example of a case with which a practitioner might be engaged, providing a context for the chapter as a whole and confirming its relationship with contemporary practice. Many aspects of being assessed on a PQ award require succinct summaries of cases but, crucially, the chief requirement centres on the much fuller analysis of and critical reflection on the case.

CHAPTER 8

Developing Inclusive Practice in Children and Families Social Work

James Reid

This chapter considers the development of contemporary policy and standards as an aid to inclusive practice and how these same policies and standards, including the General Social Care Council (GSCC) Code of Practice, can work against this aim if used uncritically.

An example of a non-resident father and contested contact is used to illustrate the general points that apply in achieving inclusive practice.

This chapter should also be read with reference to Chapter 3: Ethics and Values in Theory and Practice.

Case study

Peter and Sarah had been married for five years before their relationship failed, and they separated and subsequently divorced.

There are two children, Sally (11) and Amy (5.) Sally is Sarah's child and Peter's stepchild. At the time of the separation there was agreement that the children would live with their mother on the understanding that Peter would have frequent and unhindered contact, and this worked well for over a year.

However, on the first contact, following an argument between them, Sarah informed Peter that the children were ill and would not be coming to stay. Over the next year the relationship between Peter and Sarah continued to deteriorate with contact with the children being used as a weapon. Contact between the children and Peter was minimal or non-existent for months on end. Illness was a frequent reason cited and the children also missed periods of school.

Peter applied for a contact order and proceedings began. Sarah refused contact during the proceedings, alleging that the children were being adversely affected by the stressful situation. The court eventually agreed a contact order and Peter saw the children again, but only briefly as Sarah made a serious allegation against him and an investigation began.

The need to work inclusively with service users is acknowledged and accepted by the social work community. Inclusive practice is a main tenet of policy and procedure, and is engrained within the laws, regulations and requirements of the profession – for example, as one aim in the introduction of the *Framework for the Assessment of Children in Need and their Families* (DoH 2000). This aim is further seen in the values prescribed by the 'Codes of Practice' (GSCC 2002a) and in requirement 5 of the *Specialist Standards and Requirements for Post-Qualifying Social Work Education and Training: Children and Young People, Their Families and Carers'* (GSCC 2005b). Additionally, the accompanying documentation for each of these provides direction as to the nature of practice that enables inclusive practice – for example, 'honesty and openness' (GSCC 2005b, p.14). Positively, there are now indications that the development of working practices in this context is providing benefit to service users; Cleaver and Walker (2004) discuss service users' reports of greater partnership with social workers following the introduction of the framework for assessment, and Millar and Corby (2006) highlight the potential 'therapeutic' benefits.

Millar and Corby also discuss the circumstances in which service users feel genuine partnership and empowerment by social workers, including:

- when honesty and trust has been developed

- through open and clear communication

- through genuine involvement in the process

- when empathy and genuine concern is evident

- when practice is accountable – enabling the service user to challenge what is said and written.

These findings are consistent with the existing literature on the subject and serve to reinforce the validity of the documentation governing the profession, but questions remain about the developing practice context. Parents and carers have reported greater partnership with social workers following the introduction of the framework for assessment. It is not clear whether perceived benefits are as a result of routinised, behaviourist practice, or through a genuine development in the understanding, values, ethics and professionalism of practitioners in developing inclusive practice. Peter, in the case example above, did not feel he was empowered or a partner in any of his interactions with social workers.

The remainder of this chapter will consider the issues that may impact upon inclusive practice, beginning with a discussion about those instruments that govern practice.

The Codes of Practice represent both the values expected of the worker, (what is good and desirable), as well as the standards that should inform their practice (ethical conduct). There is a question of balance between the autonomous professional and the mores and practices required as an employee or agent of the state. This is unproblematic until one begins to consider further the focus and function of the Codes of Practice – in particular, the ideological shift in focus away from practice based on explicit principled beliefs to that concerned with standardisation and adherence to procedure. While standardisation through the Framework for Assessment was necessary and achieved benefit for service users, professionals should be allowed to exercise judgement and discretion in their assessments (Coulshed and Orme 2006). As such the codes reinforce the existence of 'managerialism' and routinised practice within social work – that is, the control of practice by procedure and accountability through measurable outcomes. In the case study above, the social workers followed procedure and were pressurised to deal with the situation quickly.

The GSCC is forthright in declaring that the Codes of Practice are part of an overall strategy for workforce 'regulation' through which the social worker is aware of the conduct expected by employer and service users (GSCC 2002b). This demotes the social worker from a 'professional', autonomous worker to an 'employee', and assumes that both employee and employer share the same aims, objectives, reasoning and modus operandi. Of particular concern is the potential for tension between the practitioner's own sense of autonomy and the employer's wont to control and regulate (Mullender and Perrott 2002), reminiscent of the rational hierarchical management structures that are designed to achieve the objectives of the organisation with little or no room for innovation or improvisation. This is demonstrated in the more quantifiable measures, such as performance against timescales rather than the quality of the assessment or interaction between the service user and practitioner, that achieve reward for the agency. Accountability, of course, has a role, but standardised and routinised practice can lead the practitioner into being uncritical and may negate the very qualities that service users value in practitioners (Bilson and Ross 1999). This all raises a question about the sufficiency of the Codes of Practice as a holistic and effective foundation for the traditions, values and principles of social work practice.

The Codes of Practice influence organisational behaviour and (organisational) 'culture, the collective identity of members of the organisation and formal and informal groups within' the organisation (Payne 2002b, p.229), but it is the relationships between people carrying out tasks within the organisation that are crucial to the success with which objectives are met. Beckett and Maynard (2005), for example, warn of the dangers of the psychological defence mechanism whereby managers and front-line workers distance themselves from the responsibilities of each other's role. Thus, managers can distance themselves from the daily realities of difficult practice and even seek to blame front-line workers when things go wrong (the case of Victoria Climbié is an example). Equally, front-line workers can blame their managers for the lack of resources that hinders their practice. There is a need, therefore, for shared recognition and responsibility in social work organisations, and in the management of the work to do with the work to be done. In fact, the responsibility is a moral one – you have an ethical responsibility to think critically about the organisation you work in and how far the work undertaken supports the aims and purpose of that organisation. In the case study above, the workers were driven by the demands of their manager and organisation, and not the full needs of those involved. This can be achieved only by a shared language and trust between worker and manager, driven by a shared purpose. This may be difficult to achieve, but it is an important foundation for inclusive practice as it will help to establish the openness, trust and honesty expected by service users.

Of course we know that organisations have a formal structure, particularly in terms of stated aims and purposes, as well as in the use of differentiated roles. However, 'all agencies have informal structures which are more fluid and more closely linked with members' personal attributes' (Hanson 1995, p.210). Informal structures can be revealed by observing who you talk to and where you go for advice, and how you actually do your job in practice. The workplace culture refers to 'the learned and shared assumptions that regulate people's behaviour, such as communication styles and levels of co-operativeness' (Hanson 1995, p.210). Although workplace cultures reflect the values of the organisation at a formal level, they become reinterpreted at an informal level, and thus there may be a disjuncture between the stated (formal) goals of an organisation and how it is actually experienced in practice. Since we bring 'ourselves' to the workplace, with our personal histories and identities, our insecurities and belief systems, workplaces are just as likely to reinforce dominant modes of behaviour and dominant social norms (Mullender and Perrott 2002). Explicit awareness of such behaviour is crucial to integrity and practice that is honest, accountable and open to genuine inclusion.

In discussing values it is important to consider that the GSCC has not limited its focus to the Codes of Practice alone, as similar concerns are applicable to requirement 5, the 'embedded values', of the *Specialist Standards and Requirements* for the post-qualifying (PQ) programme for children and young people, their families and carers (GSCC 2005b):

In addition to the general underpinning values associated with the GSCC Codes of Practice there are a number of specific user-focused values which need to be firmly embedded in social work practice with children and young people, their families and carers. These are:

engaging with others to develop trust;

exploring ways to share control over decision-making with young people and their families;

respect for others, including respect for difference;

honesty and openness; and

an ability and a willingness to look at the needs of children and young people in a holistic way, setting problems alongside overall interests, talents and abilities and drawing on an awareness and appreciation of the diversity of lifestyles and experiences of children and young people in our society. (GSCC 2005b, p.14)

These too are action orientated, concerned with outcome, and therefore ignore the important issue of the practitioner's motives and personal values or ethics. It is noticeable that in the development of the current codes and standards the one value from the previous era that required social workers to consider their personal history, values and vigorously held beliefs, 'identify and question their own values and practices, and their implications for practice' (GSCC 2001, p.5), is absent. This is a worrying omission as it is almost impossible to be free from our personal values in our practice – they will always influence how we see a situation or the people involved. Rather than denying their influence or pretending to be value-free, you need to be able to critically evaluate the values you bring to your practice and consider their practice implications (McGowan 1995; Shardlow 2002). In doing so, you can begin to decide whether these are the values and behaviours that you think are appropriate to inclusive practice (see below).

In Chapter 13: Assessment, it is acknowledged that a feature of standardised tools is seemingly bureaucratic and rigid timescales. In addition, procedures do not allow assessment in ways that fully integrate all the potential features within a situation, or indeed allow the service user to define their needs and solutions within that assessment. Consequently the danger exists that assessment is not undertaken organically or inclusively but information is collected uncritically and simply because the pro forma and agency require it to be collected. Rigidity, lack of integration, narrow definitions and an uncritical approach all present barriers to effective inclusive practice. These features are examined here in the context of non-resident fathers, particularly where conflict over contact arrangements is present, the case study at the beginning of the chapter not being untypical. The issues, however, can be applied more widely.

There is a wide consensus that fathers have an important role to play in parenting and that they represent a resource to their children (Burgess and Ruxton 1997; Lamb 1987, 1997; Turnell and Edwards 1999); however, studies have also shown a reluctance on the part of social workers to effectively engage with fathers (O'Donnell *et al.* 2005) – indeed child care and protection practice is characterised by its consistent marginalisation of the father, both as a potential asset and as a potential risk (O'Hagan and Dillenburger 1995). As a result many fathers are excluded from the assessment process, which is obviously problematic for the fathers themselves. However, it is also an issue for mothers as gender differences and biases are to the fore, with a tendency for social workers to view the mother as responsible for parenting, with the father's role secondary or deemed unimportant (Risley-Curtis and Heffernan 2003). There is a great deal of discussion concerning the reasons for this within the literature; however, these may also include a tendency towards a behaviourist approach to work with families, in particular when the restrictions of time and a standardised approach determine that the social worker follow the path of least resistance – to concentrate on work with the child and resident parent, including the non-resident parent only when circumstances allow.

An integrated, accurate and systemic assessment will be difficult to achieve where equity and the qualities for inclusive practice, described above, are not perceived by one or more of the parties involved. Inclusive practice with non-resident fathers will be difficult to achieve where social workers view the needs of the child sufficiently or wholly met in the care of the other parent; particularly when the feeling is not that the non-resident father cannot also meet the needs of the child, but that dealing with the conflict in the adult relationship is too problematic. In such cases the social worker may also be relying on an uncritical, too narrow definition of the 'welfare principle'. That the welfare of the child is paramount is not open to debate, but when welfare only includes parenting by the mother it is. This is because a lack of contact between a child and a non-resident parent (father) usually also means no contact with the child's wider paternal family, including potential loss of identity and cultural mores.

For some social workers the fact that arguments are taking place becomes more important than understanding the debates and themes within those arguments. Rigid, standardised approaches to such situations may mean that the stereotype of the difficult father is further reinforced and unchallenged. Social workers need to develop a forensic, critical approach to their practice in order that they understand the meaning and function of, in this example, parental discord. Social workers should, for example, be aware of the difference in emotional expression between groups and consider whether, in parenting, 'women's modes of expression have been taken as the benchmark against which men are to be evaluated' (Fletcher and Willoughby 2002, p.41). The complexities of father identity and involvement have been underestimated and severely limited within the legal framework, aided by the attitudes and beliefs of the professionals, including social workers, who practise within that framework (Daniel and Taylor 2001). Some fathers are seen as too difficult to engage and resistant to change, leading to perceptions that any deficits to parenting arising from non-engagement are inconsequential to a child's development. As a result fathers are often problematised or ignored, and fatherhood is considered only in terms of quantifiable involvement – for example, the amount of time a father spends with a child. The outcome for fathers is that they feel disenfranchised, invisible or irrelevant to the development of their child. The outcome for the child is that their perception of their father is affected and access to a range of socio-cultural opportunities is restricted. The outcome for the mother is that she is perceived as wholly responsible for parenting and all that that entails.

As a critically reflective practitioner one needs to evaluate the nature and context of practice, including those codes and standards that influence practice as well as those professional and personal factors that ultimately determine positive outcomes. The use of standardised practice formats may ensure greater equity in service provision, but they tend to emphasise quantifiable outcomes and they should not negate a consideration of the role of values and ethics in practice and the decision-making process. Indeed, a danger lies in thinking that personal and professional values need to be scrutinised less, as the element of 'personal' bias is increasingly being taken out of the social work relationship in preference for agency pro forma instruments. The social worker's own experiences can affect judgement; so that if someone has learnt certain dynamics and 'normalities' within their own family of origin, or substitute care situations, these can bias their practice and decisions about what is normal or acceptable (Connolly, Crichton-Hill and Ward 2006). Social work is not only a cerebral process; emotions and prejudices can affect outcomes and how inclusive practice is understood and practised. Inclusive practice, therefore, requires explicit knowledge and awareness of the social worker's personal biases, prejudices, values and ethics, which we will now consider more fully.

The ethical element of social work is not just that you tread an awkward line between society and the individual, but more that you are frequently in positions of power compared with your service users. The decisions and choices that you are faced with may seem obvious or inconsequential to you, but can often represent a difficult process for the service user to engage in. The danger lies in making decisions on the other's behalf without due consideration of their effects on the individual concerned. Rothman's (1998) four components of ethical decision-making are a good starting point in identifying the areas for reflection on practice:

1. defining the ethical problem

2. gathering information relevant to the problem

3. an appropriate theoretical base must be determined, then professional values explored, client values understood and the impact of personal values recognised

4. options must be weighed and a sound decision reached.

Helpfully, Meyer and Palleja (1995) identify four key stages of an assessment that have parallels to the ethical decision-making process identified above.

1. *Exploration:* 'listening to the service user and understanding their narrative, helping to organize it, and hence making sense of past events that are affecting the presenting problem' (p.117).

2. The *assessment phase*, or a search for meaning – where 'the practitioner uses knowledge and judgment to interpret or make sense of the story' (p.119).

3. *Focus and plan* the intervention strategy – this draws on our knowledge base and consideration of what works and best practice ideals, and 'must take into account the resources that are available in the community and in the client's life' (p.121).

4.   *Termination and review:* given their inevitability, endings in all cases should always be kept in mind, even from the beginning, so that both practitioner and the service user can focus on the outcome of the work together.

These require a means of making explicit our choice of intervention and thus make our work available to scrutiny, which has the effect of increasing account-ability and effectiveness. However, ethical decision-making is also a critical process that involves being reflexive and reflective (see also Chapter 3: Ethics and Values in Theory and Practice). This suggests a flexibility of thought and analysis that is context specific and time related rather than fixed by a standard-ised approach. In ethical decision-making there is 'no ultimate principle or set of rules that can tell us how to do this in every possible type of case' (Banks 2001, p.36). Banks further suggests it is possible to determine four 'basic or first order principles' (2001, p.37) to promote ethical practice in social work. Clark (2000) also includes 'discipline' as a principle concerned with the development of professional knowledge and expertise, which is an equally important principle and is added to the list below:

1.   respect for and promotion of individuals' rights to self-determination

2.   promotion of welfare or well-being

3.   equality

4.   distributive justice

5.   discipline.

However, we should be mindful that principles are also open to interpretation – for instance, the principle of self-determination can be interpreted negatively (allowing someone to do as they choose) or positively, such as through the process of empowerment. Equally, the principle of equality is open to interpre-tation: equality of treatment, which is commensurate with the principle of respect of persons; equality of opportunity, which refers to equal access to resources and is typified by equal opportunity policies; and equality of outcome, which is a principle that underpins anti-discriminatory or anti-oppressive practice principles. Importantly, it is also necessary to be aware of the limitations of the principles listed above as there is a tendency in ethical decision-making to focus on rules or duties as the defining factor for determin-ing actions that allow a person to decide how to behave in any particular situation. As such there is a need to consider the social worker's behaviour in terms of motive rather than outcome.

When we talk about personal values in social work, we are referring to the personal belief systems of the social worker, which may be formalised, for example, through the medium of a religion or cultural mores, or less formalised, such as when the social worker feels they exercise their choice in terms of a particular client group that they prefer to either work with (or not). In such instances it is perhaps more difficult to discern an identifiable belief system if the practitioner does not articulate a clear objection to a particular client group – instead personal preferences are more likely to be positively expressed by identifying who one prefers to work with (the resident mother) rather than not (the non-resident father). Obviously, such choices do reveal value biases. However they manifest understanding, how these beliefs and values impact upon the intentions of the social worker and how they actively impact upon the social worker's decision-making are key to enabling inclusive practice. Only by explicitly understanding your values and beliefs and acting upon them will you be able to work with openness, honesty, respect, empathy and genuineness.

Conclusion

The introduction of the Codes of Practice, new standards and assessment tools is designed to enable inclusive practice with service users. However, we have explored how these, if accepted uncritically, can also mitigate against inclusive practice. These instruments have an important role to play in formalising our beliefs and highlighting ways in which we are expected to behave, both in relation to the service user and the agency. There is also some evidence of positive outcomes for service users because of standardised approaches to practice. However, we must be careful that the customs and practices required as an employee or agent of the state do not overwhelm the professional integrity and autonomy of the social worker. An inability to strike a balance between these will endanger inclusive practice. If we accept uncritically the introduction of such seemingly ethical instruments we may simply and without debate accede to prescribed and routinised practice. The assumption that the motivation of the agency and the practitioner are the same is a dangerous one. One approach will not fit all service users, nor do all social workers hold the same values, beliefs or prejudices. Only in beginning to understand what influences us both professionally and personally, in seeking ways to bring together our personal morals with our professional ethics and values, will we truly create a context for inclusive practice.

Acknowledgement

I would like to thank Juliette Oko, without whom this chapter would have been very different.

Recommended reading

Banks, S. (2001) *Ethics and Values in Social Work* (2nd edn). Basingstoke: Palgrave.

Connolly, M., Crichton-Hill, Y. and Ward, T. (2006) *Culture and Child Protection: Reflexive Responses.* London: Jessica Kingsley Publishers.

Payne, M. (2002) 'Management.' In R. Adams, L. Dominelli and M. Payne (eds) *Critical Practice in Social Work.* London: Palgrave.

Turnell, A. and Edwards, S. (1999) *Signs of Safety: A Solution and Safety Oriented Approach to Child Protection Casework.* New York: W.W. Norton & Co.

CHAPTER 9

Community Care
and Care Management
Martin Leveridge

Introduction

Community care for adults has been beset by problems in its implementation, despite a rhetoric that accords with current professional and political values. Social workers acting as care managers work at the interface between health and social services, and face a number of dilemmas and tensions, including the rapidly changing legislative and policy framework. These issues will be discussed in this chapter through a focus on inter-agency work, 'needs-led' assessments, and the single assessment process (SAP). As the population is ageing, with older people being a major resource issue, this group of service users will be referred to, along with issues around carers, direct payments and safeguarding adults.

What is community care?

Since it was first evolved as a concept in the 1970s, community care has come to have some very particular outcomes, each with different implications for service users and service providers, with cost saving being an element of the policy.

A key outcome was the move to care *in* the community, in the sense that the home is located geographically in the community, but the extent to which it can be said to *belong* to the community is more problematic. A major example of this is the move away from the large institution of hospital accommodation for people with severe learning difficulties to 'domestic scale' accommodation among ordinary housing.

Community care was to be local authority funded through the Social Services Department (now Adult Services or equivalent) rather than by the NHS. This has two implications: first, it enabled central government to show savings, while at the same time accusing local authorities of spending more. Second, it meant that service users could be asked for a contribution to the cost of service provision. This of course raises the key question of how the boundaries between health care (free) and social care (chargeable) are to be defined. Guidance has sought to clarify this boundary (DoH 2001a) with limited success.

Community care policy also sought to maximise informal care provision. This is perhaps where most savings could be made, since care by family, friends and neighbours, if recognised as part of the plan of care, represents a considerable saving to formal services. The importance of this can be seen in the time and effort that has been spent in recognising the contribution of informal carers, in legislation, guidance and other ways (see, for example, the carers' pages on the Department of Health website, http://www.carers.gov.uk).

Community care policy also entailed the diversion of those more vulnerable adults from expensive hospitals, and relatively expensive homes, by the provision of more intensive domiciliary services, although many authorities placed a ceiling on such provision at the cost of care in a home. The effect of this 'targeting' was that fewer resources were available for those with lower levels of need. More recently, the importance of low-level service provision as a preventive measure has been recognised (see, for example, SEU/ODPM 2006, pp.24ff). In general, however, this 'maintenance at home' aspect of community care has been welcomed by service users and professionals: older people in particular remain independent for longer in familiar surroundings, and most wish to do so (see, for example, Sixsmith 1986).

The social market and privatisation

Under the 1990 Act and accompanying guidance, local authorities were charged not to be providers of services, but commissioners, with a duty to enhance the role of the independent sector, thus producing a 'mixed economy' in care services. Unless the service user can afford to purchase care services directly, the local authority will provide the assessment 'of need' (under s47 of the 1990 Act) and then draw up a care plan involving services purchased from the private sector. The service user's contribution to the cost is provided by a financial assessment.

This promotion of private-sector provision can be seen as one of many ways in which community care introduces privatisation. Other ways include the expectation of an element of informal care in the care plan, the transfer of costs from central government (NHS) to the service user (via the local authority), and the provision of direct payments as an alternative to direct purchasing of services (see the section on direct payments, below), all of which are intended to reduce costs, improve efficiency and give more choice to service users. There has been huge growth of private and independent provision, but increasing regulation from the Commission for Social Care Inspection (CSCI) and the rises in costs through the national minimum wage make for challenges for home owners as well as for the workforce.

The White Paper *Our Health, Our Care, Our Say* emphasises the importance of local commissioning that will 'help local people keep well and stay independent, and will provide real choices for their populations' (DoH 2006b, p.161). The White Paper also notes the significance of the role of local authorities in stimulating the market in social care provision in order to enhance choice for service users. This will include 'strengthening local capacity through using the voluntary, community and independent sectors' (DoH 2006b, p.162), and this process is to be informed by local community needs assessments carried out jointly between the local authority adults care services and the Primary Care Trust (PCT). The White Paper (DoH 2006b, p.157) notes that 'Individual Budgets will put far more control in the hands of people who use social care services...markets will have to be developed to ensure that they have an appropriate range of services to choose from' (there is more on this in the section on direct payments, below).

Care management

This system originated in health maintenance organisations in the USA, and is intended to provide the assessment of need, and the coordination, planning and review of care to meet that need (DoH 1991). In practice, the role of care manager has generally been undertaken by social workers but, more recently, following the National Service Framework for Older People (NSF/OP) (see below) and the Single Assessment Process (SAP), community nurses have taken on these responsibilities in certain cases. The 1991 guidance includes the schematic diagram reproduced here as Figure 9.1.

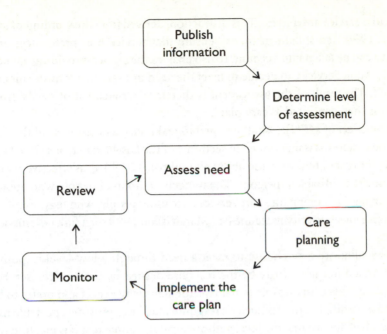

Figure 9.1 The process of care management (adapted from SSI/DoH, 1991)

Although not often considered as part of the process, it is important to be aware of the first stage, 'Publish information'. Service users and their carers are now offered a great deal of information through leaflets (and often websites), and it is this information that may often determine the expectations of service users and carers.

The second stage, 'Determine level of assessment', can seem a little illogical: how can the scope or level of assessment be decided before commencing the assessment? The intention is that service users with a relatively low level of need should not be subjected to a full and comprehensive (and unnecessarily intrusive) assessment, although this must be viewed flexibly. Some service users may not be aware of more serious underlying issues; some may approach the agency with minor requests for assistance (e.g. a 'blue badge' or disabled parking permit) first, before being able to acknowledge an underlying problem.

Assessment of need

Assessment (see also Chapter 13: Assessment) for community care services, under s47 of the 1990 Act, is a service that must be provided if the person 'appears to be in need of community care services' and cannot be charged for (Mandelstam 1999). The assessment itself (stage 3) is 'of need', not 'for a particular service or services'. This distinction, derived from the wording of s47 of the 1990 Act, should in theory ensure that service user preferences and choices can be taken into account. It also enables the service-providing agency, usually Adult Services, to decide to meet the need in a way that is more suitable to itself. The result of the assessment is therefore a 'statement of needs' from which is then generated a 'care plan'.

The effect of s47(2)a, 'shall proceed to make such a decision as to the services he requires as is mentioned in section 4 of the Disabled Persons (SCR) Act 1986', is to cut out the decision about eligibility (s47(1)b), thus effectively giving priority to 'disabled' persons. The remaining group of people who appear to be 'in need of community care services' are older people, who may therefore be given a lower priority in statute (see Mandelstam 1999 for a fuller discussion of this).

The authority may choose to meet a need through a low-level response, which would not necessarily be the response desired by the service user. For example, a service user unable to manage the stairs may expect and prefer to be offered a stairlift, but the authority's response may be to provide a portable toilet and a bed downstairs; the local authority can still argue that it is meeting the identified need. Under s47 of the 1990 Act, local authorities can also choose which needs they will agree to meet, and guidance suggests that it is the local authority that ultimately decides what needs service users have, not the service users themselves (DoH 1991). This last gives rise to 'eligibility criteria', which are interposed between identified need and the service response. Hence, in the above example, the provision of a stairlift will be subject to eligibility criteria that go well beyond just being unable to manage the stairs. Guidance indicates that local authorities should set eligibility criteria for service provision that will enable them to balance their budgets. This was tested in the Gloucestershire case (R vs Gloucestershire CC, ex parte Barry). A local authority decided, because of budgetary constraints, to reduce the domiciliary support given to a young disabled man. RADAR, the organisation that represents disabled people, took up the case with him, and it went as far as the House of Lords. The eventual decision was that the local authority could take budgetary constraints into account in deciding on eligibility criteria, but having set fresh criteria in response to a new financial situation, it should then have reassessed the service user against those new criteria.

In 2002 eligibility criteria were rationalised by the Fair Access to Care Services guidance (FACS) (DoH 2002b). FACS seeks to harmonise criteria by a banding system according to the extent to which the service user's independence and health might be at risk if services are not provided. An unfortunate effect of this has been to encourage a procedural model (Smaile and Tuson 1993) of assessment that can be reduced to little more than a counting of tick boxes (see Lymbery 2005, p.181, for example), which is frustrating for the practitioner, especially one at PQ level, as well as the service user. So, in practice, individual local authorities have considerable discretion in deciding what level of need will be met, and 'moderate' and 'low' needs are unlikely to be met (Lymbery 2005, p.159). The CSCI report on local councils' performance in 2005/6 (CSCI 2006a, p.4) notes that 'the threshold for care-managed services was set at 'substantial' and a number of councils are expecting to raise their eligibility thresholds in 2006'. The CSCI 'found examples of people "slipping through the net", and some instances where "people's safety and well-being were compromised by inadequate support...the appreciation expressed towards individual workers is often tempered by concerns, usually associated with a perception that care workers are rushed" (CSCI 2006b, p.5). Social workers carrying out assessments may find themselves in a dilemma: as employees they may feel an obligation to underplay the seriousness of need as a rationing device; but in the interests of the service user, they may be tempted to overstate needs in order to maximise provision.

The Single Assessment Process (SAP) was introduced as part of Standard 4 of the NSF/OP (DoH 2001c). It was supposed to be a single and collaborative approach to assessment, involving multiple agencies but coordinated by the social services care manager. However, such a key opportunity does not seem to have been realised in many areas, with separate assessments – sometimes in different IT systems – continuing, often with little sharing of information. The Personal Social Services Research Unit (2005) reported that there was a repetition:

> of the assessment process performed in hospital, once an older person returned home. The lack of successful structures to enable information exchange was closely linked to and frustrated by inter-professional mistrust. The introduction of information technology was considered...to have huge potential to overcome some of the structural obstacles to information sharing...this potential will not be fulfilled unless professional values and cultures also merge. (p.2)

The PQ social worker will have a key role in developing the effectiveness of the SAP, reducing repetition, and liaising with other professionals to make the process more effective for the service user.

Direct payments

Direct payments were introduced by the Community Care (Direct Payments) Act 1996 (and extended to older people in 2000) as a means of making a payment to a service user in lieu of the provision of services, so that service users can arrange services to better suit themselves. This possibility must now be offered, following an assessment, to all service users who are able and willing to take on the responsibility (directions under the Health and Social Care Act 2001); but as Glasby and Littlechild (2002) point out, the responsibilities and requirements can be onerous. Direct payments may also lay service users open to abuse. The CSCI (2006b) reports that only 7000 older people were using direct payments in 2004/5, compared with more than 300,000 receiving state-funded home care.

A number of voluntary organisations provide assistance (often commissioned to do so by local authorities) to service users in organising direct payments due to the complexities involved, especially of the service user becoming an employer. Despite this support, the take-up of direct payments has been less than expected for this reason. In addition, even a moment's reflection can reveal the challenges in the training and retention of personal assistants employed in this way. The government is now piloting a scheme of 'Individual Budgets' as proposed in the Green Paper *Independence, Wellbeing and Choice* (DoH 2005b). These are to be administered by local authorities, incorporating income streams from various sources, allowing the service user to use budgets with some autonomy and flexibility. Pilot schemes (13 at present) are expected to report in April 2008, when a final scheme is expected to be implemented.

Services for carers

It has been estimated (Carers UK 2005) that 1.25 million people provide more than 50 hours of unpaid care per week, and that six million (one in eight) adults are carers, saving the economy £57 billion each year. The Strategy for Carers (DoH 1999a) promised a 'Carers' Charter', setting out what people can expect from long-term care services, and earmarked £140 million to be spent specifically in providing breaks for carers. The carers website (http://www.carers.gov.uk), hosted by the Department of Health, is another aspect of support introduced by the 1999 paper and is a useful resource.

The Carers (Recognition and Services) Act 1995 defined informal carers as those providing substantial care on a regular basis and not employed or organised as a volunteer to do so. Carers falling within this definition are entitled to an assessment of their ability to provide the amount of care they intend to provide, so long as they request this at the time of the s47 assessment of the service user. Local authorities were instructed under later guidance to ensure that carers were told of their right to request such an assessment. Despite its title, the 1995 Act did not allow local authorities to provide any services directly to carers. The assessment of their ability to care was to be 'taken into account' in drawing up the care package.

The Carers and Disabled Children Act 2000 dissolved the link with section 47 assessments and gave local authorities the power to provide services directly for carers. The Act describes such services as 'physical help and other forms of support', but current guidance does not specify forms of support, except to suggest that 'The local authority may provide any services…which in their view will help the person care…for example, a gardening service or assistance around the house for a carer who devotes most of his or her time to providing intimate care to the person cared for.' (DoH 2005a)

Two categories of carer are mentioned in the 1995 Act: those caring for adults and those for a disabled child. A serious omission is that of young carers, who are children supporting a parent or sibling in the community; there are significant numbers of such young carers. The 2001 census suggested that there were some 175,000 young carers and, moreover, many may not be known even to their teachers. The Princess Royal Trust estimated that, in one area, 75 per cent were not known to their teachers (http://www.youngcarers.net/professionals/119/). The practice guidance to the Carers (Equal Opportunities) Act 2004 states that local authorities should have 'a protocol, shared between adults and children's services, for identifying and assessing young carers'. Guidance suggests they may be 'children in need' under s17 of the Children Act 1989 (Mandelstam 1999). The social worker in an adult service, faced with a young carer, may well need to work closely with her counterparts in children's services.

Carers can be offered direct payments in lieu of services, and this also applies to carers of disabled children who might have been offered services under s17 of the 1989 Children Act. To the dismay of the Carers National Association, the Act also allows the local authority to charge for services under this 2000 Act (by reference to the Health and Social Services and Social Security Adjudications Act (HASSASSA) 1983).

The 2000 Act allows services provided for carers to be delivered to the person cared for: a good example here might be respite care, which is generally for the benefit of the carer but actually provided to the person cared for. Because of the charging implications, the Act specifies that the local authority must show which services are provided to the service user and which to the carer. Services 'of an intimate nature' must be provided to the service user (see the guidance in DoH 2005a for a definition).

The Carers (Equal Opportunities) Act 2004 inserts three duties into the 2000 Act: a duty to inform carers of their right to an assessment; the duty to take into account whether the carer is able or wishes to work or study or follow leisure pursuits; and a duty to cooperate, in planning and providing services, with education, housing, health and other local authorities.

Given budgetary constraints, local authorities are unlikely to pay for services that a carer is currently providing, despite an assessment under the 2000 and 2004 Acts. The dilemma facing many carers therefore may well be to continue to care with little support or relief, or to withdraw care in the hope that formal care services will fill the gap. The CSCI report (CSCI 2006a, p.106) suggests there is 'often a fragmented and limited response to carers' needs…the danger, as ever, is that carers are only seen as a "resource"'.

Health or social care?

The distinction between health and social care has always been a difficult one, although, as we have seen, it can have major consequences for the service user who may be required to make a contribution towards the cost of social care. Many discharge arrangements can be planned in advance (e.g. for hip replacements), provided there is an adequate joint planning process. The unfortunate term 'bedblocker' describes a patient who no longer needs a hospital bed on health grounds, but for whom alternative support services have not been arranged. This had become a particular problem for an NHS concentrating more on acute services[1] and more aware of unit costs. The Community Care (Delayed Discharge etc.) Act 2003 was intended to overcome this problem: once notification has been given by the hospital that a patient is fit for discharge, social services must arrange appropriate care services within two days or be liable to a fine. The evidence base for this legislation has been called in question by, for example, Vetter (2003) and Glasby, Littlechild and Pryce (2004) but these situations will continue to provide many challenges for the social worker.

Hospital discharge arrangements will inevitably be linked to decisions about the boundary between health and social care responsibilities and, as we have seen, the SAP should assist in this process. The challenges also arise from

---

1   According to the Royal Commission on Long Term Care, numbers of NHS long-stay beds declined by 38 per cent from 1983 to 1998 (Sutherland 1999).

changes in the way nursing is defined (see, for example, Kelly, Mabbett and Tome 1998). They may also be due to the application of more stringent eligibility criteria to care services – especially residential care – as it is necessary to be more dependent to get into a care home (local authority funded), so this level of provision becomes more appropriate for patients who have a high level of dependency. This boundary has been subject to a number of attempted definitions, the latest of which is still undergoing consultation (September 2006) but there had been no outcome at the time of writing. Following the report of the Royal Commission on Long Term Care (Sutherland 1999) the nursing component of residential social care in England and Wales was made free, by means of an assessment against three bands of contribution towards care costs. An assessment against the Strategic Health Authority's (SHA) continuing care criteria must be made before (in the case of someone who does not qualify) an assessment of the appropriate contribution towards their nursing needs in social care, following the Grogan judgement[2] (DoH 2006b). This guidance also notes:

> SHAs, PCTs and local authorities should work together in partnership to ensure that the needs of their local population are met, and to ensure that service users do not fall into a 'gap' between services as identified in the judgement. No treatment or care should be delayed by uncertainty or ambiguity about funding responsibilities. (DoH 2006b, p.1)

The Health Act 1999 (s27) enabled joint funding of services to help eliminate gaps, and this has enabled the development of Intermediate Care projects, introduced in the NSF/OP. Intermediate Care provides inter-professional assessment and rehabilitation services for adults coming out of hospital or needing a period of intensive support in the community; the objective is to reduce the need for hospital or residential care. It remains to be seen if the Delayed Discharge provisions result in intermediate care facilities being used as a 'holding area' post-discharge. The Royal College of Physicians of London described Intermediate Care as:

> one of the new buzzwords, which came into prominence with the National Beds Inquiry... To some it is used as a pretext for stripping more beds from acute hospitals to create 'innovative community services', to others it serves as an excuse for not providing acute services for the elderly. On the more positive side it may encompass 'hospital at home', early discharge procedures, low dependency care, convalescence and rehabilitation to name but a few. (2000, p.1)

2   See http://www.bailii.org/ew/cases/EWHC/Admin/2006/44.html.

Safeguarding adults

Social workers practising in community care have long recognised that there were vulnerable adults in the community, as well as in homes and hospitals. The introduction of 'No Secrets'[3] guidance by the Department of Health aimed to ensure that key local agencies, particularly but not solely health, social services and the police, are able to work together to protect vulnerable adults from abuse, by developing local multi-agency policies and procedures. The Association of Directors of Social Services produced 'Safeguarding Adults' (2005) as a national framework of standards for good practice and outcomes in adult protection work. Such an approach has not yet been incorporated into legislation as has been the case in child protection, but there is evidence of a substantial incidence of abuse and Action on Elder Abuse (a campaigning charity, www.elderabuse.org.uk) is spearheading a campaign to address this. Workers in the sector will be aware of the Protection of Vulnerable Adults (POVA) scheme, which was introduced in July 2004 to protect vulnerable adults aged 18 years and over in care settings in both England and Wales. It provides a process for the drawing up of a list, which needs to be checked to ensure that people working with adults have not been found guilty of any misconduct that has harmed a vulnerable person or placed them at risk of harm. This area of practice is increasingly challenging, not least as it requires additional skills in working with different professionals and agencies, usually at the level of a PQ practitioner, but there is insufficient space to go into further detail here.

Conclusion

Community care is a challenging area of practice for social workers. It is increasingly demanding due to the complexities and limitations of the resources available and the need to work with many different agencies, usually including health services, and the many different professionals who may be involved with a range of service users and their carers. The introduction of direct payments may be helpful to many service users, but of itself demands different approaches to the use of resources and support. Many adults, and especially the growing older population, will experience periods of vulnerability and sadly there are those who will exploit this and abuse them, often financially but also in a variety of other ways. Those social workers working with adults need to be highly skilled and vigilant to help maintain people's

3   HSC 2000/007: No Secrets – guidance on developing multi-agency policies and procedures to protect vulnerable adults from abuse.

lives in the community for as long as possible, as well as supporting them and their carers through the process of managing the many dilemmas and tensions this creates.

Recommended reading

Glasby, J. and Littlechild, R. (2002) *Social Work and Direct Payments*. Bristol: Policy Press.

Mandelstam, M. (1999) *Community Care Practice and the Law*. London: Jessica Kingsley Publishers.

McDonald, A. (2006) *Understanding Community Care: A Guide for Social Workers* (2nd edn). Basingstoke: Palgrave.

Pritchard, J. (2001) *Good Practice with Vulnerable Adults*. London: Jessica Kingsley Publishers.

Symonds, A. and Kelly, A. (eds) (1998) *The Social Construction of Community Care*. Basingstoke: Macmillan.

CHAPTER 10

Mental Health Social Work

Linda de Chenu

Many of the people that mental health social workers are privileged to work with have experienced extreme mental distress, oppression and social inequality. The aim of this chapter is to paint a picture of how social workers can take action in partnership with service users to challenge such forces and to support user-inspired initiatives to achieve a recovery of hope, discovery, sense of self and an 'ordinary life'. It will initially explore contemporary policies and practice, against the backdrop of the new post-qualifying (PQ) framework, and then consider their relevance to working in partnership with a service user on the road to recovery.

Developing a social and anti-discriminatory model of mental health has been central to the practice of social workers in the mental health services (Gilbert 2003). This has involved a shift from a model emphasising social problems that have 'caused an illness' to a model in which discriminatory societal responses to mental distress, which oppress and institutionalise people, are challenged. In recognition of this the GSCC guidelines for PQ mental health training recommend that social workers take a lead in promoting the social model and in countering social exclusion and discrimination.

However, rather than being seen as leaders, social workers' presence is barely mentioned in many contemporary government policy documents (Duggan, Cooper and Foster 2002). Always part of the background landscape, but barely recognised in policy as part of the action, social workers have reported feeling marginalised as their expertise has not been recognised. Also, following the restructuring of services following a market model, social workers and other professionals have been caught up in adapting their language and practice to fit these new structures.

The position of English health authorities as 'agents' of a 'strong state' means that health organisations and other stakeholders have less say in whatever policy is required by a government, in comparison to many European countries, where 'experts' and authorities participate more in policy development (Heclo 1974). Similarly, within central government there are relatively few points where most professions can influence or initiate new policies, and the historically favoured relationship between medicine and government marginalises other interests (Pierson 1994; Smith 1993). Consequently England has a policy system in which new policies can be rapidly introduced without 'testing' or consensual negotiation, and it can be argued that the 'strong state' has been intensified with the increased deployment of managerial methods and powers.

In the current situation of rapid policy change the development of the new post-qualifying training is paradoxically (Allen 2006) an opportunity for mental health social workers to develop their practice and professional identity in order to respond effectively. In addition, the Care Services Improvement Partnership (CSIP 2006), involved in the National Workforce Programme (NWP) for mental health, has recently emphasised the need to support the contributions of different professionals. Alongside the GSCC PQ framework, New Ways of Working (NWW) advocates the promotion of teamwork in mental health services and the promotion of a project aimed specifically at support for social workers to articulate and develop their contribution. Although the PQ framework presents even more change, at the same time it offers timely opportunities to consolidate post-qualifying specialist identity and skills, to offer leadership, to gain qualifications and to benefit from continuous professional development (CPD).

The guidelines for the content of the PQ award have been developed by the GSCC in consultation with the DoH and stakeholders, and particularly service users. It draws on the National Occupational Standards for Mental Health (NOSMH), which are shared with other health professions. Linked to the requirements of restructuring, a theme of the guidelines is a move to the 'uniprofessional' worker who has a grounding in different professional backgrounds but then shares training and tasks with other professions. There is concern that this erosion of difference, which previously offered a wide choice of expertise to meet a wide range of different needs, will produce a less holistic service for people (Loxley 1997). A manifest concern for social work is that it will be swallowed up and incorporated into a 'medical model' within mental health services.

In recent years major organisational changes and tasks mean that as a quali-fied mental health social worker in the statutory sector you are most likely to be based in an inter-professional team. It is important that the employing organi-sation endorses the value and nature of social work, and ensures professional social work supervision for social workers even if the line manager is not a social worker (BASW 2003). You are likely to be based in a relatively new men-tal health trust that has been established following the NHS Plan (2000) and the Health and Social Care Act (2001), which allows local authorities and health authorities to pool their resources and form partnerships. At a senior management level social work is likely to be represented by a lead in social care at trust level who maintains links with the local authority, and initiatives are being suggested and tested in the form of consultant social work and advanced practitioner roles (Hope 2006).

Perhaps in response to the fragmentation of Social Service Departments (SSDs) the GSCC emphasises that the themes of inter-disciplinarity should be developed across all the PQ pathways. Moreover, students from the different social work disciplines are encouraged to study together so that there is under-standing and sharing of knowledge and practice between the disciplines of mental health, children and families, and adults. Such inter-disciplinary study should, for example, enable sharing of knowledge and practice issues around risk assessments of parents with mental health problems and children at risk.

You will be working in accordance with the National Service Framework for Mental Health (NSFMH) (DoH 1999c), which gives the outcomes that are to be achieved by mental health services. The NSFMH has been supplemented by policy papers that give related outcomes – for example, *Inside Outside* (DoH 2003a) advises on anti-racist and culturally competent mental health work, *Into the Mainstream* (DoH 2003b) gender sensitive services, the *Mental Health and Social Exclusion* report (Social Exclusion Unit 2004) inclusionary services, and finally the *Journey to Recovery* (DoH 2001f) brings together different policies within a recovery framework. It is important to reflect critically on such policy 'discourses' to evaluate their substance rather than absorbing their rhetoric. Hence, it is important to develop critical social work practice that is based on social work values and to have an interest in international practice, which helps to generate ideas and a comparative critique.

To achieve the outcomes of the NSFMH new teams were proposed by the Mental Health Policy Implementation Guides. These are Assertive Outreach, which reach out to people in their own community (DoH 1999b), Crisis Inter-vention Teams, which work with people in the community to resolve a mental health crisis (DoH 2001d), Early Intervention Teams, which intervene when younger adults are becoming mentally distressed (DoH 2001e), and the

Generic Community Mental Health Teams (DoH 2002c), which are increasingly shifting into primary care. Hence, the aim is that, increasingly, mental health services are not based in buildings. In pursuing critical and reflective practice it is important to evaluate the 'fidelity' of new models, and whether they adhere to key principles and values or develop institutionalising and coercive practice in the community (Onyett 2003).

The 'recovery' approach is an increasingly important framework for all mental health services, and it embraces many social work values and skills. It is an international movement inspired by service users and different mental health professionals, which is briefly reviewed here and then explored as a practice example below ('The "Whole Life Project": example from practice'). The recovery approach articulates a paradigm shift from people as passive recipients of care who are 'institutionalised' within buildings, and perhaps also within the care 'management' structure of assessment and planning procedures. This paradigm questions the 'institutional' approach that encourages people to be passive 'patients' and, within the medical model, 'objectifies' people. It highlights the opposite of a subjective 'lived experience' of ordinary life and argues that the professionals should work in partnership to support people moving to a middle ground or 'recovery' position (Glover and Kalyanasundaram 2006). It is suggested that a social worker works with a person to co-create strategies to overcome these problems. Blocking the initiation of institutionalisation is paramount so that social roles, skills and networks are not damaged or lost due to a hospital admission or the use of institutionalising services.

The implications are that the social worker becomes what Glover and Kalyanasundaram (2006) describe as a 'micro-enabler' rather than a 'micro-disabler' as they relate to the person's needs, seek to actively empower the person in relation to institutions, and support the articulation of personal hopes for the future. The partnership approach supports people in coping and living with their mental distress, and avoiding or challenging institutionalising services that can lead to social exclusion. A 'spiral of precariousness' (Paugam 1995) often leads to social exclusion when the person experiences stress such as a loss, then develops mental distress, loses their job, becomes homeless, more mentally distressed, loses friends and cannot regain employment.

PQ mental health pathways

The aim here is to identify knowledge and skills that can be deepened at PQ level and contribute to developing innovative practice, which is illustrated in the practice example below.

Consolidation module

At the beginning of the mental health pathway there is an emphasis on identifying the signs and symptoms of mental distress and the user's experience of
mental distress. Social workers need to understand service users' and carers'
perspective of services, their experience of stigma and discrimination, and the
legal and ethical context of mental health practice (GSCC 2007). The Ten
Essential Shared Capabilities (ESCs) (NIMHE 2004) for mental health services,
which are common to other mental health professionals, are included in the
consolidation module. A focus for the consolidation module is *holistic assessment
and care planning.*

The Care Programme (Effective Care Coordination in Mental Health Services 1999) approach provides the framework and procedures for mental
health practice. It is important to understand the perspective of long-term users
and to use the recovery and anti-discriminatory practice approach (Warren
2003). Underpinning all the activities of the social worker are their skills in
making an effective partnership and therapeutic alliance (Onyett 2003). The
aim is to work with users' strengths and expertise to ensure the care programme
system is orientated to a needs-led and empowering approach, and to create or
commission personalised services that respond to the person's view of their
needs (Perkins and Repper 1996; Barnes and Bowl 2001).

Statutory mental health social work

Despite much long debate about changes in the legislation, the 1983 Mental
Health Act Approved Social Work (ASW) Mental Health Social Work Award
still applies to PQ in the standards published in January 2007 (note these
recognise that, in due course, the role of Approved Mental Health Professional
(AMHP) may be established). The ASW role involves a synthesis of social work
skills and knowledge, particularly of mental health legislation. Essentially the
ASW is concerned with the least restrictive provision of assessment and any
subsequent treatment for people experiencing mental distress or 'disorder'.
Hence, the ASW has a pivotal role in promoting an alternative to a potentially
exclusionary process of compulsory admission. By drawing on social work
skills and inter-professional collaboration, admission can, it is hoped, be
avoided with negotiation of alternative forms of assessment, treatment support,
care and supervision in the community. The ASW has a range of responsibilities
under the 1983 Act and has a pivotal role in deploying their legal knowledge
to ensure that the Act and Codes of Practice are followed correctly and in the
interests of the person being assessed. Under the Mental Health Act 1983 each
local authority is required to provide ASWs and their training, and approval

will take place within the PQ framework; the focus of this chapter is on contemporary practice and policy issues that are 'synthesised' in statutory work.

Inquiry-based learning

This offers opportunities to develop evidence-based practice following a systematic analysis relevant to an area of practice from which plans for an assessment and intervention are developed. It has been increasingly recognised that social work needs research to both inform and develop practice (Duggan *et al.* 2002). For example, the practice example cited in this chapter involved a search for internationally based evidence of projects and a search of literature developing the principles of the recovery model, which also facilitated the building of a supportive network.

Positive risk taking, assessment and management

Risk assessment and risk management are built into the care programme processes of assessment, planning and review, and involve working collaboratively with the user, carer(s) and other professionals. It is important to acknowledge that a discourse of risk, uncertainty and dangerousness has surrounded people experiencing mental distress (Pilgrim and Rogers 1996) and, at a social level, this perpetuates the 'otherness' and stigma of people with mental health problems (Rose 1989). This has been described as a moral panic and also seen as having the ulterior purpose of rationing resources so that only those perceived as being at high risk receive services (Kemshall 2002). It is important to remember that risk assessment is not an 'exact science' and draws on probabilities of people with different symptoms becoming suicidal or homicidal, and it has been demonstrated that these assessments cannot predict future behaviour (Alberg, Hatfield and Huxley 1996).

A focus on risk work can be over-controlling and can increase social exclusion if used as a rationale for discouraging people from activities they wish to pursue. An ethical understanding of the dilemmas of such control is important as 'risk' is fundamental to mental health policy and legislation, and the GSCC Code of Practice 1.3 advocates 'Supporting service users' rights to control their lives and make informed choices'. Hence, it is important to develop a positive risk-taking rather than a risk-avoidance (Davis 1996; O'Sullivan 2002) approach, and to build on the strengths of people to reduce the hazards of potential dangers concurrent to the care planning process (Doyle 1999). A positive risk-taking approach can support the social rights of a user to parenthood;

it can support a user's life goals in living independently and so add to their social inclusion, and this is central to the recovery principles.

Crisis intervention

Crisis intervention teams have been developed in mental health services with the aim of providing home treatment and avoiding hospital admission (Mental Health Foundation and the Sainsbury Centre for Mental Health 2003). Mental health services are also now more aware of the importance of working in partnership with users to make plans for potential crises. A critical approach recognises that crises are socially constructed by all the different people involved, including professionals. From this perspective the primary aim is to meet the service user's needs rather than assuming that individual or family therapeutic interventions are required. Crisis intervention can involve recognising and developing deeper skills in working with crisis as an opportunity for positive change (Leiba 1999). It is often associated with 'risk' such as suicidal behaviour and, within the US model of crisis intervention, enables the practitioner to work with the essential psychological ambivalence of the suicidal person (Schneidman 1989).

Work with individuals, families and carers

Social workers have worked with families and carers both in their role of assessing the needs of carers and developing supportive services such as carers groups and advocacy (DoH 2002a). Social interventions are often very important in a family crisis situation and also in working with families to support work with individuals. Developing skills in more specific family interventions, which draw on psychosocial models of intervention as well as educational and supportive work with families, can be very helpful in supporting people to live in the community (Barrowclough et al. 1999).

Social exclusion and inclusion

Social inclusion has become a mantra underlying mental health policy (Social Exclusion Unit 2004), but how do we understand this contested concept as critical practitioners?

Levitas (1998) argues that the discourse of social exclusion presents poverty as a peripheral problem with a minimalist solution of supporting a transition across a social boundary to become an insider. This avoids challenging the 'massive inequalities' and 'chronic social deprivation' within wider British society. Levitas suggests that there are three perspectives of social exclusion and inclusion, and it is important to critically evaluate which is manifested in particular mental health policies and practices.

The first model is a redistributionist discourse (RED), which is concerned with reducing social inequities by extending and advocating social rights to counteract poverty. This model is clearly linked to redistributive policies and the anti-discriminatory social model in mental health. A key feature of social work is that it engages with social rights that are integral to membership of a community, such as rights to employment, housing, health services, education and training. Such social work skills in community development and group work, networking, negotiating, brokering and advocacy, gain access and extend social rights.

The European social integrationist discourse (SID) model regards poor social integration as the cause of social exclusion, which can be challenged through employment and employment-related activities. Social work in mental health has traditionally encompassed support to people in the process of re-entering employment. The US moral underclass discourse (MUD) regards the cause of social exclusion as individual pathology, which can be compounded by a welfare dependency culture. Here there is an emphasis on individual pathology and the use of workfare policies to create incentives for the underclass to gain employment, and disincentives to those remaining dependent on welfare. Social welfare and social work in England has had a focus on individual pathology and can be interpreted as supporting this model.

Mental health policies and practice are often ambiguous so that the *Mental Health and Social Exclusion* report (Social Exclusion Unit 2004) and *Journey to Recovery* (DoH 2001f) may contain a mix of these models of social exclusion. To develop critical practice it is important to go beyond general goals that we can all agree with, such as 'promoting social inclusion', and question the underpinning models and values. As social work practice engages with social 'models' and models of social exclusion, it is important to evaluate their implications, particularly for social work values and ethics. This critical activity has been demonstrated in social work opposition to removal of the autonomous advocate role of the ASW and the other disempowering changes proposed in forthcoming mental health legislation and aspects of the Mental Capacity Act 2006.

Interventions with groups and networks

An important area of social work is the development of social capital, which involves the support of social networks and 'bonds' between people, and also access to wider resources across 'bridges' between user groups and community resources, particularly employers. Social capital is important in preventing stress, which is detrimental to mental well-being, and also in challenging the social exclusion of users by enabling access to resources (Phillipson, Allan and Morgan 2004).

Skills of facilitating groups and networks are central, as the experience of groups where users and carers can articulate their experiences and share support is fundamental to the development of social capital. Social work also has a pedagogical strand as social workers support individuals and groups of users in gaining future-orientated knowledge and skills to control their situation. Such social interventions complement each other and the 'social action' approach developed by Sue Holland (1996) is an example of how social work can work in partnership with individuals, and facilitate support groups and social action groups to develop social capital, and the empowerment and social inclusion of women with mental health problems.

Inter-professional and inter-agency collaboration

Inter-professional work, a key PQ element, and inter-agency collaboration are fundamental to negotiating needs-led person-centred services with other organisations. Within the new mental health teams the challenge for the newly qualified social worker in mental health is to both establish an identity as a specialist mental health social worker and also as a 'uniprofessional' worker who shares many skills and areas of practice with other professionals. The mental health social worker needs to develop their collaborative skills with other professionals, as well as users and carers (Weinstein, Whittington and Leiba 2004), in order to develop the work of the new integrated teams (Onyett 2003). An understanding of the knowledge base, skills and ethics of other occupations and professions supports successful cooperation. Collaboration can achieve synergy (Leathard 2003) when the combined efforts of the different stakeholders create new and innovative ways of working that simply adding up the different contributions cannot achieve.

Developing inter-professional and inter-agency networking skills can support social workers taking a leadership role in developing projects, and indeed the GSCC suggests that social workers offer leadership and act as 'culture carriers' (Hope 2006) in developing the social model. The NWW project sees inter-professional teamwork as fundamental to new ways of working, and that different professionals contribute by offering leadership in their areas of expertise.

The 'Whole Life Project': example from practice

The 'whole system approach' linked to the recovery movement is one that facilitates holistic recovery of the 'whole person'. Here an 'aggregate' example of practice is based on a local 'Whole Life Project' (Rix, Jenkins and Mahoney 2006) of the National Institute for Mental Health in England Eastern Region (NIMHE), in collaboration with the Hertfordshire Partnership NHS Trust. The project has involved different professionals so that creative inter-professional practice has been fundamental to the project. From the social work perspective, Woodward and Burnage (2006) argue that the GSCC Codes of Practice provide a foundation for the Whole Life Project by treating each person as an individual, supporting service users' rights to control their lives and make informed choices, recognising that service users have a right to take risks, and helping them to identify and manage potential and actual risks to themselves and others.

The aggregate example concerns a young woman, 'Sue', who experienced agoraphobia, was unemployed, had no formal educational qualifications, had a high alcohol consumption and no close relationships. The mental health services had focused on her agoraphobic 'symptoms', but when using the 'Whole Life' model the aim is not to 'objectify' a person and impose a 'passive' patient role, hence rejecting the individual pathology MUD model of social exclusion. Instead, a constructionist and therapeutic counselling approach enabled Sue to share her story and to put issues that are important to her 'on the table' to discuss with the social worker (Woodward and Burnage 2006). By building a 'therapeutic alliance' she entered into a dialogue and was able to discuss traumatic incidents of bullying at school, which had led to a spiral of serious trauma and school non-attendance, which in turn led to difficulties with literacy and numeracy, which then contributed to her unemployment and social isolation, loss of confidence, dependence on alcohol and aggression, all of which seemed to be underlying the agoraphobia.

This 'self-assessment' led to a co-creative dialogue and then a coaching process with the worker, using 'modules' produced by the Whole Life Project. Using a 'Hopes and Dreams' module Sue talked about her hopes for the future and revealed for the first time her ambition to become a hairdresser. By using other 'modules' using cognitive behavioural therapy (CBT) principles she was able to build better self-coping strategies and lowered her alcohol consumption. Working in partnership, Sue developed the skills to manage systemic 'transitions' such as enrolling in college so accessing her social rights within an RED model of social inclusion and the SID model of social integration. She has now enrolled on hairdressing and literacy/numeracy courses at college, made new friends, and has formed her first close relationship.

Conclusion

The PQ framework offers an opportunity that mental health social workers should take in order to further engage with policy developments, and to develop innovative practice that not only deepens social work skills but co-creates with service users critical forms of practice, such as the Whole Life Project. This chapter has explored new approaches and ways in which mental health social workers can work in greater partnership with service users and make increasingly effective progress in the delivery of better services to them and to their carers.

Acknowledgement

The author would like to thank Jan Woodward for her inspiration and support, and for sharing her reflections on practice and her experience of leading a Whole Life Project.

Recommended reading

Gilbert, P. (2003) *The Value of Everything: Social Work and its Importance in the Field of Mental Health.* Lyme Regis: Russell House.

Repper, J. and Perkins, R. (2003) *Social Inclusion and Recovery. A Model for Mental Health Practice.* London: Baillière Tindall.

Tew, J. (ed.) (2005) *Social Perspectives in Mental Health: Developing Models to Understand and Work with Mental Distress.* London: Jessica Kingsley Publishers.

CHAPTER 11

Learning Disabilities Today: Integrated Working

Mike Wren

For Charlotte; with love, warmth and 'positive' reflection.

This chapter explores collaborative working in learning disabilities through a case study in relation to the transitions planning process between children, education, adult health and social care services. It will also examine what can be learned from the delivery of a joint social work and nursing learning disability programme in which the aim is to create workers for integrated services. This experience reinforces the view of Davies (1995, p.20) that:

> the boundaries between both social work and nursing in the area of learning disabilities are especially fluid, with real possibilities that by the end of the 1990s the differences in the work of the two occupations could have blurred to the point where professional separation (and therefore training distinctions) are no longer defensible.

Professional practice should, according to the Department of Health (2001g, p.49), strive to ensure that transitions planning should start with the individual, and take account of their wishes and aspirations. Person-centred planning is a mechanism for reflecting the needs and preferences of a person with a learning disability; it covers such issues as housing, education, employment and leisure, and is reliant on the 'collaborative working' arrangements that should exist across the inter-professional boundaries of learning disability social work and nursing practice. These arrangements are shaped by changes in legislation, organisational and professional body requirements.

Case study

Kevin (the case is a compilation) is 18 years old, and had a road traffic accident when he was eight, as a result of which he has lost his sight, and suffered a brain injury resulting in learning disabilities, severe epilepsy and the need to use a wheelchair. He has not had any social work input since his 14+ Review recommended admission to an out-of-area school specialising in the residential education and care of children and young people with multiple needs like his. He currently lives in self-contained and adapted accommodation attached to the school. He returns home for intermittent weekend leave and holidays only, and is due to leave school next year. Kevin needs a specific regime of medication and associated monitoring, an environment adapted to respond to his specific needs, his physical disability and sensory loss, and considerable general support.

Kevin's mother is anxious about his potential return home as she feels that major adaptations are required in the family home to fully meet his needs. In addition, she is struggling to hold down a part-time job, even with limited support from her own mother (who is not in good health) and a cousin of Kevin's who visits every weekend. She is overwhelmed when Kevin is home for holidays, even with support from volunteers from her church. The case is referred to the Community Team for People with Learning Disabilities.

This case provides the focus for the remainder of this chapter in considering how learning disability social work and nursing practitioners can work together to meet the needs of people like Kevin and his mother.

The challenges are to provide Kevin with a 'seamless' transitions process, gradually moving from a universality of service delivery, free at the point of delivery at least until the age of 19, to the point at which he will enter the adult world of means testing and charging for services given that: 'Person-centred frameworks will need to be fully compatible with the locally agreed joint eligibility planning criteria which councils and local health bodies will be asked to develop' (DoH 2001g, p.51).

These guidelines encourage the exercising of choice, promoting independence, cost-effectiveness and consultation. There is an increased risk to Kevin, as he will be required to change the routine he has had for several years at school, with many of the same care and teaching staff, as he is propelled into the adult world. This transitions process is set within a challenging time frame as there is just a year before Kevin is due to return to his family. During this time the social worker must work closely with Kevin, his family and a range of professionals, including learning disabilities community nurses and social workers with particular skills in sensory loss. They will need to build rapidly on what Kevin has learned at school, and complete a thorough assessment of his personal, social and medical care needs in the community.

The modernisation agenda: challenge or opportunity?

The policy background in which these professionals are engaged is the modernisation agenda, which is continuing to be implemented and developed at an unprecedented pace. There is a relentless plethora of legislative reforms impacting upon a whole range of health, education and social care services, which may improve service delivery in the long term but cause intitial confusion as many aspects of this agenda collide with role re-design and organisational change that will raise higher expectations from people who use services in the short term. Davies (1995) asserted that collaborative working arrangements are inevitable and essential components, and are set to become even more of a requirement for the future delivery of inter-professional practice (particularly between social work and nursing practitioners), relating in turn to their professional and post-qualifying training and educational development.

Each aspect of the various legislative reforms consistently articulates that 'collaboration' must be at the heart of this work and the key legislation will now be examined.

The Carers and Disabled Children Act 2000 requires the involvement of carers and children with disabilities in the assessment process, and provides some elements of choice in the provision of services they require. The Health and Social Care Act 2001 requires local authorities, health authorities and trusts to develop joint plans for services; enabling the establishment of Care Trusts while the National Service Framework for Children, Young People and Maternity Services (DoH 2004c) provides standards for the interface between health and social services and education.

Such legislation has contributed to the strengthening of integrated collaborative working arrangements in the Children Act 2004 (a response to Every Child Matters (DfES 2005) and the Laming Report (2003)), which led to the need for a framework of children's services, bringing together education and children and families social work. The policy driver to enhance collaboration in order to reduce risk from abuse and to safeguard children and young people, *Working Together to Safeguard Children* (HM Government 2006), was designed to replace previous Area Child Protection Committees with Children's

Safeguarding Boards. These will set out integrating collaborative working arrangements, procedures and protocols between agencies. This more joined-up approach should in theory help Kevin and those like him in the future, but much remains to be done.

Furthermore the integration of collaborative working arrangements is likely to intensify from April 2008, with the arrival of Children's Trusts; although these are not statutory bodies, they will pool budgets and resources. They will also jointly commission services, with the aim of establishing an integrated model of service delivery across education, children's social services, Connexions and some health services. This core of agencies will be responsible for all aspects of the transitions planning process, with five specific outcomes for children and young people (Children Act 2004 (DoH 2004a)) (see Table 11.1). Each provides personal milestones for the individual, as well as professional benchmarks, by setting objectives, priorities, targets and funding streams. These outcomes can be compared to the seven equivalents for adults.

Table 11.1 Outcomes compared for Safeguarding Children and Adults

Children	Adults
Being healthy	Improved health
Staying safe	Freedom from discrimination or harassment
Enjoying and achieving	Improved quality of life
Making a positive contribution	Making a positive contribution
Economic well-being	Economic well-being
	Exercising choice and control
	Personal dignity

These link to the equally wide-ranging reforms for all adult health and social care services within the White Paper *Our Health, Our Care, Our Say: A New Direction for Community Services* (DoH 2006b). These government strategies are all very well, but the process of change, while it may lead to long-term benefits, might actually reduce the capacity of services, and the workers within them, to maintain high-quality services in the meantime. In addition, the professionals involved, and arguably their professional bodies too, will have some concerns as to the potential impact upon their roles, and associated conditions of service, while different value bases, codes of practice and the like may lead to some increased tensions and conflict.

From both a learning disabilities social work and nursing perspective, each profession will also have to consider the principles of the White Paper *Valuing People* (DoH 2001g) in relation to Kevin's individual rights to an assessment that encourages independence, and promotes choice and the inclusion of people with learning disabilities into local community life. This links into the transitions planning process through the Special Educational Needs and Disability Act 2001 (SENDA), which requires a multi-agency review meeting, integrates disability discrimination law into education settings, and informs the framework for all transitions planning processes.

The Community Care Services for Carers and Children's Services (Direct Payments) Regulations 2003 would certainly encourage the use of direct payments for employing close relatives (so Kevin's cousin or one of the church volunteers could be considered), meeting the obligation of the council to offer direct payments as an alternative to existing services. However, there are many people who might not have relatives or others who can help in this way. There is also the question of Kevin's capacity to make such decisions, even with the help of workers employed specifically to provide such advice. Suitable personal assistants can be hard to find and, in addition, there is a range of issues to do with their training, support and potential career development. The needs of Kevin's mother to maintain her own independence and economic well-being through maintaining her part-time job should also be considered but she could, potentially as Kevin's carer within these regulations, continue to access employment. Learning disabilities social workers and nurses should work closely with Kevin, his family and perhaps with a number of the following people: an independent advocate, a Connexions adviser, housing with care providers, and social workers specialising in sensory loss. This process would allow all parties to tentatively explore any longer-term housing with care options available locally and align these to the Supporting People Programme (Supporting People, Supporting Independence (Officer of the Deputy Prime Minister 2003)) which aims to provide housing-related programmes to support vulnerable people to maintain aspects of independent living with appropriate support in their own community. This approach fits with the White Paper (2006) in which people during consultation said that they were looking for 'seamless health and social care to support them to stay healthy and to lead independent lives; more services provided locally; and services that are fair to all with more help for the people who need them most', continuing with a resounding clarion cry to all colleagues by further stating that 'the White Paper vision is achievable. It empowers the thousands of staff dedicated to improving the support and well being for people in their communities to use their creativity to improve care' (DoH 2006b, pp3–4).

What is evident and consistent about this blueprint for modernising adult health and social care services, in particular, is that the service development initiatives and consultation processes in the publication of the White Paper *Valuing People* (DoH 2001g) clearly suggest that a significant revision of the care management process as the 'cornerstone' of the NHS and Community Care Act 1990 reforms is required to strengthen and reinforce the core principles of this White Paper, including a detailed analysis of those core areas that represent 'major problems that need addressing to achieve inclusion in society' (Thomas and Woods 2003, p.245). What is not so clear is what increases in resources will make these ideas achievable in the near and distant future.

Major problems outlined by the Department of Health (2001g), with particular reference to aspects of service provision linked to integrated collaborative working arrangements, provide an increased impetus to the modernisation of the transitions planning process, particularly in relation to:

- poorly coordinated services for families with children with disabilities, especially those with severe disabilities

- poor planning for young disabled people at the point of transition to adulthood

- insufficient support to carers

- substantial health care needs of people with learning disabilities, often unmet, and

- few examples of 'partnership' working between health and social care services, or involving people with learning disabilities and their carers.

Williams (2006) summarises this strategy for learning disabilities into the twenty-first century as it relates to inclusion, person-centred planning and the future role of care management in a community team for people with learning disabilities. He says that 'whether person-centred planning is compatible with care management has been a topic of debate and uncertainty since *Valuing People* was first published' (Williams 2006, p.93), and goes on to illustrate this debate and uncertainty further by providing suggestions for achieving some elements of compatibility between person-centred planning and care management within the context of contemporary learning disabilities social work and nursing practice. He cites further references to a series of evidence- and practice-based suggestions discussed within the Valuing People Support Team's *Workbook on Person-Centred Care Management* (2004), which should be read as an addition to this chapter, along with *All Change – Transition into Adult Life* (Mallett *et al.* 2003) and *Person-Centred Planning and Care Management with People with Learning Disabilities* (Cambridge and Carnaby 2005).

To ensure this vision of collaborative working and person-centred planning arrangements coming together as a reality will undoubtedly require a consistent, vibrant and sustained focus, including pooling of vital individual, collective, organisational and community-based resources being brought together. In order to endure the relentless pace of change and the challenges it creates, there are opportunities and rewards for learning disabilities social work and nursing practitioners. However, 'Working in the helping professions is neither simple nor straightforward. The demands and challenges of such work are often of major proportions and can test us to the limits' (Thompson 1996, p.112).

One way forward is to use the strengths-based perspective to assess individuals, their families and circumstances. Here we can devise strategies to actively empower individuals to take more control over their lives and the decisions made about them. Informed practice is described by Thompson (1996) as 'being achieved through a process of "thinking" and "doing"'. He suggests that, when people undertake practice, they should think about how they have been working and reflect fully on that practice: 'A reflective approach enables practice to be explored and adapted to meet the needs of the person being supported and to provide insight into areas of oppression and discrimination that need challenging' (Thompson 1996, p.112).

This reflective process is essential for any learning disabilities practitioner as they embark on their own personal development. Those who undertake joint degrees see at first hand the two professional perspectives, values and codes of practice, and reflect from the outset on the differences and similarities as they develop into the integrated worker that service users and carers are asking for. It is to be hoped that an environment of collaborative working and shared learning can progress into PQ and CPD.

Shared learning and post-qualifying training: rhetoric or reality?

The work of Thompson (1996) can be further enhanced when read in conjunction with *Critical Thinking for Social Work* by Brown and Rutter (2006), which explores descriptive styles and levels for PQ social work through reflections from practice into learning. It is equally useful from a learning disability nursing perspective when contrasted with the reflective cycle advocated by Gibbs in *Learning by Doing* (1988).

The PQ framework expects inter-professional education and shared learning. It can also be evidenced within the requirements placed upon students to achieve graduate status. Both the GSCC (2002) and the NMC (2004) approved a small number of joint programmes. Furthermore these are delivered from both an academic and a practice-based perspective, through a competency framework that is comprehensively mapped across both domains of practice-based evidence and that is assessed by both a practice assessor for social work and a practice mentor for nursing. This approach is possible as there are so many common strands between the disciplines, but there is an additional and complementary benefit as students learn even more by comparing the two disciplines as well as integrating them.

Both post-registration and PQ training for learning disabilities social work and nursing practitioners go beyond inter-professional working and towards integrated working. On joint programmes students register with both professional bodies and commit to their codes of practice. These joint programmes were developed as the concept of working in integrated teams developed, and the perspective of the service user, like Kevin, is considered more and more. The ongoing challenge is that the two professions still see their differences rather than the areas of similarity that allowed the professional bodies to approve such programmes. In some areas the model works very effectively, with professionals from both sides seeing themselves as joint care managers, but in other areas the 'integrated service' is in reality far from that.

This shared learning environment also requires an 'openness' to the reality of the inter-professional conflicts, tensions and dilemmas that will invariably arise, when the overlap between social work and nursing cannot and should not be transcended, when resources are subject to extreme pressure and scrutiny, and where either the social work or nursing paradigm seeks to be dominant over the other.

These aspects of shared learning also require specific 'people investments' of appropriate skills, knowledge and attitudes to strengthen this collective commitment to 'collaboration' (Quinney 2006), which is encouraged to develop and grow for the benefit of personal, organisational and professional development purposes. It primarily aims to strengthen the integration of collaborative working arrangements with colleagues in allied helping professions, and with people like Kevin and his immediate family, who use services.

Conclusion

It is fitting that, having started from Kevin's perspective as a person who uses services, in concluding this journey through the transitions planning process, collaborative working arrangements and shared learning experiences, I come to my own perspective as a carer for someone who uses services. I see the clear need as a result of this experience as a carer, as well as a practitioner of some experience, for seamless services and shared learning whenever possible:

> ultimately, professional barriers are our own constructs, they can be broken down; but it requires vision at senior management level to create the service people really need and I know from my own experience of working across the country that a lot of people haven't yet got that vision. (Ward 2004, p.9)

The effective and efficient reality of delivering the transitions planning process is challenging (Ward 2004). The shared learning programme delivered across the professional boundaries of learning disabilities social work and nursing professions respectively is, Davies says (1995, p.x), very much reliant upon good social work and nursing practice, which 'must combine intelligence and warmth. Both qualities are crucial; without intelligence or critical sensitivity social work loses its way; without warmth, commitment or feeling it loses its identity.'

The challenge that remains for educators, managers and practitioners when implementing collaborative working arrangements must be to ensure that the feelings and aspirations of people who use services and their carers, become a reality out of the rhetoric of a monumental modernisation process that is deemed 'necessary, not only because the needs of today's and tomorrow's users of health and social care services are very different from those of yesterday' (DoH 2006b, p.3).

Recommended reading

Brown, K. and Rutter, L. (2006) *Critical Thinking for Social Work*. Exeter: Learning Matters.

Cambridge, P. and Carnaby, S. (2005) *Person-Centred Planning and Care Management with People with Learning Disabilities* London: Jessica Kingsley Publishers.

Mallett, R., Power, M., Heslop, P. and Lewis, J. (2003) *All Change: Transition into Adult Life*. Brighton: Pavilion Publishing.

Quinney, A. (2006) *Collaborative Social Work*. Exeter: Learning Matters.

Valuing People Support Team (2004) *Workbook on Person-Centred Care Management* London: Valuing People Support Team.

CHAPTER 12

Working with Young Offenders

Denis Hart

This chapter aims to give a brief background to youth offending services and a critical overview of contemporary practice with youth offenders, for practitioners, particularly social workers, working towards PQ. A case study will be used later to highlight some of the key issues and examine some of the future challenges.

Less than ten years ago youth justice was delivered by qualified social workers operating as part of a generic brief given to local authorities by the Local Authority Social Services Act 1970. These youth justice workers saw themselves as 'specialist', trying to juggle the eternal conflict between 'justice' and 'welfare' but always seeking to resolve the conflict by erring on the side of welfare. Custody was to be avoided at all costs; the relationship with the police was often one of mutual mistrust at best, and the service operated, more often than not, in isolation from other key agencies.

Enter the Crime and Disorder Act 1998: a completely new system was created, overseen by the Youth Justice Board (YJB), which required each local authority to set up a multi-disciplinary Youth Offending Team (YOT). Each YOT was to have at least one social worker, a police officer, representatives from the then Probation Service and the Education Department, and a health worker. A representative from the Children and Adolescent Mental Health Service (CAMHS) and a designated housing specialist were added more recently.

The YJB envisaged the practical problems likely to be encountered in bringing together people from such diverse backgrounds and aware that, traditionally, professional training has adopted a narrow focus characterised by a particular subject matter and a unique orientation to that subject matter. The result is that each academic professional discipline tries to maintain its own identity, leading to what has been termed 'academic territorialism'. Payne (1982), Hunt (1983) and many authors since have explained how this process undermines multi-disciplinary working in practice. Weinstein (1992) summed up the problem neatly: 'Members of multi-disciplinary teams walk a tightrope between maintaining their professional identify on the one hand and sharing skills or blurring professional boundaries on the other hand' (p.6).

Hallett and Birchall (1992) argue that people working in multi-disciplinary settings need additional skills to those required for their own profession, and identified the policy goals that collaborative working should aim to achieve. These centred on more efficiency in the use of resources, reductions in the gaps in delivery to give a more holistic service and, crucially, the roles and responsibilities necessary to avoid 'frontier problems' and demarcation disputes between professions and services (Hallett and Birchall 1992, p.17). The PQ social worker needs to be able to deal with the sorts of challenges that inter-professional working brings.

To achieve these ends the YJB required everyone who was to work in a YOT to attend multi-disciplinary training, along with members of staff from secure estates, to create a better understanding of issues, including risk and custody. The latter provision was considered especially important as the Crime and Disorder Act 1998 introduced a new custodial sentence, the Detention and Training Order, which could be used for children aged 12 and above. The aim of the training – Assessment Planning, Intervention and Supervision (known as APIS) – was to help the new multi-disciplinary workers work together to focus on the key aims of the new act to be tough on crime (justice) and tough on the causes of crime (welfare), and to prevent offending and reoffending by children and young people. It is also worth noting that this act led to the YOTs being renamed Youth Offending Services (YOS) due to the variety and number of workers needed to deal with the work.

The contemporary YOS worker will have their daily tasks very carefully regulated and prescribed, which will for some be helpful but others may find this inhibiting and limiting as they engage with individual offenders (for example, National Standards set the ground rules for the time in which tasks should be performed: National Occupational Standards prescribe the knowledge and skills to be acquired by individual workers). Their workplace will be one of vibrancy, with police, nurses, mental health and workers in housing, education welfare and drugs sharing information, and should be focused on the common purpose of reducing offending. Sound leadership and a common purpose should help and, over time, many of the different workers have learned to work together more effectively than was the case when YOTs were launched. YOS managers tend now not to be qualified social workers but rather have a police or prison service background, which perhaps fits with the key role of protecting the community. Social workers are very often a minority within the YOS, and have often developed around a specialist role in child protection and safeguarding.

The YJB had devised an important assessment tool, known as ASSET, to use with all young offenders coming into contact with youth offender workers (there is more on ASSET in Chapter 13, p.xx). The ASSET (sometimes referred to as the Core ASSET, as additional requirements can be made) model was developed from McGuire (1995), Utting and Vennard (2000) and Raynor (2002), who have explored 'what works' in reducing reoffending, the DoH (2000) *Framework for the Assessment of Children in Need and Their Families*, the work of Chapman and Hough (1998) on evidence-based practice, and pioneering work by Hoghughi (1980), who first established an objective framework to be used to assess individual young offenders.

ASSET has been called:

> a tool that facilitates the systematic assessment of the circumstances and characteristics of offending young people with each factor scored according to its degree of association with the offending behaviour, providing an overall score of the risk of each young person re-offending. (Burnett and Appleton 2004, p.33)

The APIS training uses case studies to learn how to complete ASSET. In turn participants should see how, when and why they need to liaise with others, notably 'specialists', as well as looking at the young person's own perception of their problems and needs. The latter is addressed by getting young offenders to complete a 'What Do You Think?' assessment. This not only encourages participation by the young people at an early stage but also enables issues of diversity to be addressed as some young people write things like, 'Being black I've often been stopped by the police for nothing – so I thought I'd get my own back.'

However, ASSET requires time to complete and was greeted with some scepticism as Burnett and Appleton (2004) discovered in their evaluation of it: 'ASSET is linked to perceptions of it as needlessly detailed, not to benefit practice but to serve as a research tool for performance monitoring and to supply statistics to the YJB.' Some practitioners 'Objected that their judgements were being forced into tick boxes to feed the government information machine', while managers found 'the tool generated invaluable aggregate information [and] added to the YOT's database for monitoring work and for estimating resource requirements' (Burnett and Appleton 2004, p.33).

My own research indicates that this perception of ASSET by YOS staff is somewhat outdated and that the development of risk awareness, and its management, has contributed to a sea-change, with ASSET being used more effectively. The Audit Commission (Burnett and Appleton 2004, p.33) also concluded that 'ASSET is completed in most cases usually to an acceptable standard'. (p.74)

A further feature of ASSET requires workers to look at 'indicators of serious harm' as the young person might cause serious physical or psychological harm to somebody else as well as to themselves. Practitioners identifying indicators of harm should complete the separate Risk of Serious Harm ASSET or, if the risk is to self or from others, a risk of vulnerability assessment.

Bean (2001) has explained how we now seek to intervene preventatively in the area of risk in a way that would have been regarded as inconceivable just ten years ago. Public safety has become a major concern and the YJB has not been slow to recognise the need to respond, so the intention of the 'risk of serious harm' component is to assess the risk posed in order to manage it effectively and thereby reduce the risk of actual harm occurring. Intervening on a preventative basis offers many challenges for the YOS worker, especially one undertaking PQ. There are a number of ethical issues and dilemmas that the YJB recognised to a degree but that you may not have fully resolved. NACRO, in its *Youth Crime Briefing* (June 2006), mentions some of the key issues:

> At a practitioner level it raises the question of whether there is too much focus on risk, are we becoming risk averse resulting in instances of risk inflation? It will require a degree of rigour in individual practitioner's daily work for defensible decisions not to become defensive decisions. How is significant disadvantage due to labelling to be avoided? (p.6)

The YJB (2005) identified a number of principles and values to be applied to inform the concept of risk, which it regards as relevant to all young people in the youth justice system, and stated that its assessment should be an ongoing process involving the young people themselves. The central importance of risk of serious harm has been carried forward into the legislation in the form of the Criminal Justice Act 2003, as it requires courts to consider 'dangerousness' whenever a young person commits a specified or serious specified offence. The court must consider if there is a 'significant risk to members of the public of serious harm occasioned by him of further *specified* offences, with the key being risk of *any* specified offences'. This act defines no less than 153 offences, mainly of a sexual or violent nature, as 'specified'. Specified offences are those that carry for an adult a sentence of two years' imprisonment or more, and serious specified offences are those that carry for an adult a sentence of ten years' imprisonment or more.

To add to this growing complexity, there are two new sentences available, though only in the Crown Court, that involve detention for public protection. The first is an Indeterminate Sentence with a minimum term that must be served to the full, and subject to review; and an Extended Sentence with an 'appropriate custodial term', with an extension period added (up to five years for a specified violent offence or up to eight years for a specified sexual offence). The act has had a profound impact on the prison population as Paul Cavadino, Chief Executive of NACRO, commented in a press release (29 January 2007; on the guidelines issued by the Sentencing Guidelines Council with 15 per cent reduction in sentences intended to compensate for the longer periods of post-release supervision introduced by the Criminal Justice Act 2003):

> It is no surprise that these guidelines have been ineffective. Courts are unlikely to comply with guidelines requiring shorter sentences while they are subject to a constant barrage of statements from Government and Opposition politicians urging greater toughness towards offenders. This has been the climate of the last few years and courts have responded with more punitive sentencing, giving the guidelines little chance to work effectively.

Practitioners will always be aware of these tensions, but will have to continue with the process whenever a young person becomes known to them who has committed a specified or serious specified offence. First, they will, as usual, interview the young person, get their point of view, collate information from a variety of sources, and so be able to complete the ASSET. However, they must also complete additional Risk of Serious Harm and/or vulnerability ASSETs, and submit a Pre-Sentence Report in the normal way to help the court in sentencing. This report provides background information about the young person, their welfare, problem areas, needs and risks, and professional views on the realistic options available. However, it is the court's responsibility to determine 'dangerousness' and practitioners need to be careful, as ever, as to how they phrase reports and present evidence. NACRO (2006) explains:

> The YJB clearly sees a pivotal role for YOTs in the Crown Court in sentencing where 'dangerousness' may be determined. However, this has to be arranged in a considered way with informed analysis of the relevant protective and risk factors presented to the court. There are significant issues here relating to…the portfolio of skills, experience, training and knowledge of risk assessment required before a practitioner can present a fully informed opinion. (p.6)

NACRO is reminding us here that, under the terms of the Human Rights Act 1998, we must ensure that everyone receives a fair trial. Potentially, the report writer could later be sued if a young person receives a lengthy custodial sentence because the writer deemed them to be dangerous, if later, on appeal, it is determined that the court was wrong to make such a determination and had been misled by the report. Hence:

> It is clear that a determination of 'dangerousness' has substantial implications for any young person who commits a *specified* offence, leading in effect to a mandatory custodial sentence which in many cases will inevitably be lengthy. In such circumstances YOTs will need to ensure that any assessment likely to lead the court in such a determination is well founded and reasons for the view are clearly presented and justified. (NACRO 2006, p.6)

To help practitioners from other backgrounds gain a greater insight into the issues that are relevant here I will now use a brief case study.

Case study

Joshi is a 14-year-old male of mixed race. He lives with both his parents, but there is a history of domestic violence in the home. Joshi has two younger sisters and has never been in trouble with the police before.

Joshi has been arrested following an incident at school. He appeared to be highly animated as a result of taking drugs and attempted to steal money from a classmate in the playground using a knife to 'scare him into paying up'.

The YOT has a number of obligations here, as described by Watson (2001), herself a former YOT manager:

- provision of an appropriate adult service undertaking police interviews with children and young people
- the assessment of children and young people and the production of rehabilitation programmes associated with final warnings
- bail support service for children and young people on court bail
- the placement of children and young people on remand in local authority accommodation
- the provision of court reports or other information

- the supervision of community sentences and court orders

- the supervision of detention and training orders, both in custody and following release from custody.

Since then, the following tasks have been added, making the YOS worker's role even more complex and demanding. There are the needs to complete an assessment of risk (as stated earlier) and to participate with the Local Safeguarding Children's Board to try to prevent offending by early intervention and to ensure the well-being of the child.

The YOT worker, in Joshi's case, is likely to have to attend the police station and sit in as the appropriate adult, required by the Police and Criminal Evidence Act (PACE) 1984, as Joshi's father had refused to attend and his mother was instructed by him not to attend. The worker will endeavour to help Joshi be granted bail but, as the home may not be a suitable place, the worker may need to liaise with children's services to see if alternative suitable accommodation can be found.

A Core ASSET will be produced, which will examine Joshi's offending career, living arrangements, neighbourhood, education, lifestyle, physical and emotional health, substance use, perception of self and others, thinking behaviour, and attitude and motivation to offending. He will be asked to complete a self-assessment, a 'What Do You Think?' pro forma, and each aspect will be scored from 0 to 4. This area of practice can be variable even though APIS training is designed to reduce the differences in subjective interpretation of scoring by different members of the YOT.

Joshi does, however, by virtue of the offence, warrant only a further specialised assessment of serious harm and completion of the appropriate ASSET. The key issues here are:

- a knife was used to make threats

- he was on drugs at the time of the offence

- it was a first offence

- he later expressed considerable remorse.

The YJB has produced detailed guidance as to how YOT workers should assess risk of serious harm, including the likelihood of future harmful behaviour. Some relevant issues to be considered include:

- Was the offence planned, calculated or reckless?

- Were there any ritualistic or bizarre elements?

- Was any victim 'vulnerable'?

- Was the behaviour deliberate or intentional?

- Who is at risk from the young person?

Joshi would be assessed accordingly in terms of level of risk, from low (level 0) to very high (level 3), with imminent risk of harm and reoffending identified with serious impact and need for immediate multi-agency action. The YOT worker, in producing the Core ASSET and the Risk of Serious Harm assessment, will need to consult widely within the team, drawing on specialist knowledge:

- the drugs worker to look at the level of Joshi's drug-abusing behaviour

- CAMHS to appraise Joshi's mental health

- children's services to advise on the suitability of home as a placement, and to look at appropriate alternatives should placement with parents be deemed unwise.

The information obtained will go into the pre-sentence report to assist the court when sentencing, but here we encounter a significant difficulty as a result of the Criminal Justice Act 2003: Joshi's offence is a specified offence, which means, should he be deemed to be 'dangerous' by the Youth Court, he could be referred to the Crown Court and given an extended sentence of up to five years' detention over and above the sentence he is given for the offence itself.

The situation is made worse as Joshi is a first-time offender and the Youth Court can sentence him only to a Detention and Training Order for up to 24 months or a Referral Order for up to 12 months. Some YOT workers may hold the view that Joshi does not warrant a custodial penalty at this stage but will have 'second-guessed' that the magistrates will consider a 12-month Referral Order to be insufficiently robust. As a result they will have asked for the case to be referred to the Crown Court, where a greater range of sentencing options are available, without realising that they thereby increase the possibility that the court will determine Joshi to be 'dangerous' with all that entails – a very challenging situation for Joshi to be in, so the YOS worker must take great care.

In addressing risk, YOT workers need to be aware of two comparatively new bodies with whom they may need to liaise. First, there are Multi-Agency Public Protection Arrangements (MAPPA), which have their origins in the *Health Service Guidelines for the Induction of Supervision Registers* (DoH 1994), whereby the pending Mental Health (Patient in the Community) Act 1995 required certain mental patients to be compulsorily monitored in the community after discharge. Later, further groups were made eligible – namely registered sex offenders and those who have previously received a prison sentence of 12 months of more for a violent or sexual offence.

In 2006, the YJB made it compulsory for YOS workers to refer young people to MAPPA if their Risk of Serious Harm assessment indicated the risk from the individual was high or very high. This additional complexity and inter-disciplinary working is entirely consistent with the requirements of the PQ practitioner in the case of social work.

In the case of Joshi, it is unlikely that he will be referred to MAPPA as the assessment will regard him to be of medium risk, but this classification may be moved upwards or downwards depending on the specific situation faced by Joshi as the assessment process proceeds. Referrals to MAPPA may be made upon the making of any order or as part of an after-care release package from any custodial sentence. MAPPA itself decides at which level (from 1, ordinary risk, through to 3, supervision by the panel itself as risk to the community so high) to pitch intervention once an individual case has been referred.

Second, there are Safeguarding Children Boards. The Children Act 1989 created Area Child Protection Committees (ACPCs) to address the 'welfare of the child'. The Children Act 2004 (DoH 2004a) created new requirements, whereby each local authority must establish a Safeguarding Board that must include the YOS as members. The objectives of the Safeguarding Board are to coordinate what is done by each person or body represented on the Board for the purpose of safeguarding and promoting the welfare of children in the area and to ensure the effectiveness of the resultant actions.

Essentially these boards oversee the way each children's services authority works to promote cooperative working and the effectiveness of the arrangements made to *improve* the well-being of children.

Here YOS workers are very much likely to get drawn into the prevention of 'crime' (i.e. anti-social behaviour of children under ten) and the potential use of Anti-Social Behaviour Orders (ASBOs), which are being taken up more and more by the current government.

YOS workers already have considerable routine contact with children's services agencies and indeed, remembering Joshi, areas of concern about vulnerability through domestic violence in the home should have been passed on. National Standards (2004) require YOS workers to liaise specifically to determine whether individual young people are on the Child Register, regarded as a 'child in need' (under Section 17 of the Children Act 1989), and subject to any education, social intervention or family work plans.

By involvement on Safeguarding Boards YOS workers will need to be able to appropriately broker what is available to what is needed, a particularly challenging task. This will often require working in partnership with children's services to address anti-social behaviour by children under ten. In addition, there is a need to provide services in appropriate cases, while being conscious that their service is funded only to work with children and young people over ten years of age, a particular challenge. Finally, there is a requirement to liaise more effectively on issues around child protection, young carers and children in need.

YOS workers therefore need a depth of knowledge and a high level of skill to perform all these tasks effectively. The YJB recognises that all qualified social workers need to undertake continuing professional development (CPD) to stay on the GSCC Register. It acknowledges, too, that the post-qualifying (PQ) framework takes account of changing social work qualifications and the need to support the continuing professional development of social workers working across and within other professions. This includes workers in YOTs or the juvenile secure estate (YJB, May 2006, *Professional Certificate in Effective Practice in Youth Justice*).

Currently, the GSCC is working with the YJB to establish how the Professional Certificate will be incorporated and recognised in the revised PQ framework, and is ensuring that the Occupational Standards identified by Skills for Justice (the Sector Skills Council for those in the justice field) will be incorporated.

Conclusion

The past ten years have seen youth justice totally redefined in practice, the creation of a central Youth Justice Board, which both monitors and directs practice, and the creation of dynamic and highly effective multi-disciplinary teams. The YOS has itself had to develop new relationships with MAPPA and Safeguarding Boards, which should provide more coordination and consistency. Social workers have gone from being in the overwhelming majority in the YOS, often acting as team managers, to a depleted presence and one at the margins concerned mainly about child protection issues. To regain their impact, social workers need to embrace the new culture, play a wide-ranging role in crime prevention and avoid falling into the trap of searching for long-gone, more halcyon days. It is essential, however, that they retain their own value base and continue to comply with the GSCC Code of Practice as they develop an ever-widening knowledge base in their work in the YOS.

Recommended reading

Dugmore, P. and Pickford, J. (with Angus, S.) (2006) *Youth Justice and Social Work*. Exeter: Learning Matters.

Kemshall, H. (2002) *Risk, Social Policy and Welfare*. Buckingham: Open University Press.

Payne, M. (2000) *Team Working in Multi-Professional Care*. Basingstoke: Macmillan Press.

Pickford, J. (2000) *Youth Justice: Theory and Practice*. London: Cavendish Publishing.

Part 3

Issues

Introduction

Part 3 provides another perspective on critical reflective practice to complement those provided in Part 2. The process here will be to examine some areas of practice that every social work practitioner is likely to encounter in their work at some time or perhaps even frequently, depending on the nature of their setting. These issues are chosen with no particular emphasis but are those that can and do provoke concerns and debate.

The first of these is assessment, which all social workers practise and many regard as a key social work function. Anti-discriminatory practice (ADP) and anti-oppressive practice (AOP) are also vital to social work, but because there is insufficient space to cover them in detail here, we will consider sexuality as an example, which confirms that, despite ADP/AOP being so important, there are still many who feel discriminated against or oppressed.

Loss is something that will affect us all as individuals but also as social workers at some point.

Practice learning has been experienced by every social worker as they go through their professional training and education, and many go on to 'give something back' by 'taking a student'. This process has become even more crucial for social work students.

Finally, participation by people who use services and carers is in every aspect of the development of services in social work and social care, as well as health, education and many other services.

These chapters can thus be drawn upon to further develop the reader's critical reflection on another dimension of their own practice, and also to assist in contributing to PQ requirements.

CHAPTER 13

Assessment

Brian Littlechild and James Reid

This chapter considers some of the issues that are important in the context of the social worker described in the case study below, and for any practitioner undertaking an assessment.

> **Case study**
>
> Social workers in all settings are familiar with the centrality of prescribed assessment frameworks and process – for example, the *Framework for the Assessment of Children in Need and their Families* (DoH 2000), the Common Assessment Framework and the Single Assessment Process. Helen is a social worker with 12 years' experience and is the longest-serving member of her team. She has cultivated a good relationship with her manager and other social workers in her team, who rely on her for advice and guidance. She practises in a multi-agency setting and remains sceptical about the effectiveness of the inter-disciplinary process. Her line manager is not a social worker and there are constant debates between services about funding and wider responsibilities. While she has good relationships with her colleagues from other agencies there are professional differences and, although assessments get done, they are not unproblematic.

The *Framework for the Assessment of Children in Need and their Families* (DoH 2000), comprising three interacting domains, standardised forms, and time-limited initial and core assessments, is by now very familiar to social workers in that field of work. Developed to address concern about assessment practice in the 1990s, the framework has achieved a number of its aims, including greater partnership with parents and carers (Cleaver and Walker 2004). Furthermore, when used skilfully, the framework can have (in the broadest sense of the term) a therapeutic impact (Millar and Corby 2006). Nonetheless, important questions remain about the framework's focus and assessment practice.

Although seen as positive by parents and carers, practitioners have been concerned about prescription and timescales (Corby, Millar and Pope 2002). Disquiet has also been expressed about refocusing assessment practice from protection to need (Laming 2003), and the existence of performance assessment targets sets the framework within the context of managerialism. As an ecological model the framework also lacks substance as it does not include a 'social worker' domain, to include questions on topics such as mores, values, preferred practice methods and impact. It also assumes truthfulness on everyone's behalf and a level playing field in terms of competence.

The issues highlighted above will resonate with all social workers. This chapter addresses the general issues that social workers, at post-qualifying level, need to address in undertaking assessments. It will look at generic issues for assessment, and refer to examples of assessments in adults and children services by way of illustration of the main points.

Background

Assessment is a key social work activity and has been so since the rise of casework as a method of social reform at the turn of the twentieth century. Concern with personal morality and interpersonal relations was the context for the development of models of assessment in the 1920s (Jones 1998), with the notion of 'social diagnosis' at the fore (Richmond 1922). Subsequently, assessment practices and processes have been adapted and developed in light of the prevailing paradigms. Social work in the period following the Second World War was associated with the emerging 'welfare state' and the wish to promote individual and national growth through social solidarity. Medicine, psychiatry and psychology were influential, and psychodynamic approaches were important within assessment practices. The 1970s saw the introduction of the first Social Services Departments, accompanied by increased legislative and policy frameworks (Parton 1994). More recently, government policy has led to increasing specialisation in social work and, in turn, the assessment task has become increasingly prescriptive (e.g. DfES 2006; DoH 2000).

Within the new post-qualification framework, practitioners are expected to provide evidence of their assessment practice, which takes into account such contemporary developments. Point 6 of the General Social Care Council (GSCC) Codes of Practice states that 'you [the social worker] must be accountable for the quality of your work and take responsibility for maintaining and improving your knowledge and skills' (GSCC 2002a, s6).

The concept of 'evidence-based practice' implies a professionally competent social worker should be able to identify the knowledge and research bases that inform practice, including those relevant to assessment. Given the literature that accompanied the introduction of the current assessment frameworks we assume that your existing knowledge base includes the structure and research underpinnings relevant to these frameworks. The remainder of this chapter, therefore, is designed to assist you in making explicit the links between this existing general knowledge base and a number of differing themes relevant to an understanding of assessment practice.

The process of assessment

Despite the influence of both moral and political ideals the core elements of the assessment task remain constant, typically:

- collection of relevant information

- analysis of the information collected

- forming a judgement or decision that is explicitly and openly based on the analysis.

O'Connor *et al.* (2006, p.83) propose a model for assessment that has the following stages.

- Identify the key players, their views of the problems and key aspects of the situation.

- Integrate information, particularly the nature of the transactions with social arrangements that affect the tensions or difficulties involved.

- Negotiate and establish outcomes, with service users or groups, and develop a plan of intervention.

What this emphasises is the need for professionals to use their judgement and knowledge in formulating areas for assessment, what to take into account, and how. One of the criticisms of many assessment tools is that they are too prescriptive, and do not allow the social worker to make an assessment in ways that fully integrate all the potential features within a situation, or indeed allow the client to define their needs and solutions within that assessment (see e.g. Hawley *et al.* 2006; Langan and Lindlow 2004). This situation is not helped by the existence of seemingly bureaucratic and rigid timescales and procedures. These can create tensions within the assessment process and can lead to information being collected uncritically and simply because the pro forma has been designed to require it to be collected. In addition, such bureaucratic guidelines may mean that assessments are not seen as an organic, developing process within agency responsibilities, and work with clients; assessment is not a one-off process at the beginning of contact, but should be built upon over time, by taking into account new information gained in work with the client, and with other professionals and agencies.

What O'Connor *et al.*'s model may not stress enough, however, is the dual role of social work in assessments. Social workers have to balance the rights of the identified client with those of carers and the wider community – something other professionals do not have to do in the same way (GSCC 2002a). So while social workers' assessment strategies are formed within ideas of client involvement and control, their statutory and agency duties under, for example, the Children Act 1989 and the Mental Health Act 1983, and professional duties under the Code of Conduct (GSCC 2002a), require them to sometimes undertake powerful and intrusive actions against clients' wishes. This will obviously affect the assessment tasks and strategies of social workers acting in this mode. Even when clients experience the controlling assessments mentioned earlier, what is appreciated in social workers carrying out such roles is openness, honesty and concern (Coulshed and Orme 2006; Langan and Lindlow 2004; Littlechild 2005; O'Connor *et al.* 2006).

Collecting information for assessments

There is currently a wide range of tools available to social workers as an aid in the collection and collation of information. In child care social work, deriving from the assessment framework there are Initial and Core Assessment forms, Assessment and Action Records, and the Assessment of Family Strengths and Competences materials, among others. In seeking to ensure that all relevant information is recorded and that nothing of importance is missed, the collection of information has become systematised and structured. The inherent danger is that social workers come to see the completion of the assessment pro forma as the end of the assessment process. This is particularly likely where the tools attempt to combine the process of collecting and analysing information, and do not allow for the unique circumstances of a situation to be fully examined. It is always the case that the completion of an assessment pro forma subsequently requires analysis of the information to understand its meaning and the plans and actions necessary for a successful outcome. Social workers can become constrained in a tick box, checklist mentality (Coulshed and Orme 2006). For example, in the *Framework for the Assessment of Children in Need and their Families* (DoH 2000), while being very comprehensive, and helpful for the development and achievement of children within most situations (including the great majority of children in need), it does not adequately address issues of power and abuse within families where child protection is an issue (Littlechild and Bourke 2006).

However, there are arguments for some standardisation of areas to be considered, while allowing professionals judgement and discretion in their assessments, as set out by Coulshed and Orme (2006). While risk assessment has become a key feature within social work and social care agencies' assessments and decision-making procedures in recent years, and is an increasing feature of government concern, methods of assessment of risk vary from service to service. One recent research study of risk assessment tools utilised in NHS Mental Health Trusts in England discovered that there was great variation in the content of such tools across the different agencies. They also rarely gave any evidence of how clients/carers were included in such assessments, which relates to the issues of client empowerment discussed elsewhere in this chapter. In addition, there was little standardisation, so that someone who is a mental health service user in one geographical area may have a very different assessment than if they lived in another area. Also, the great majority of forms gave no indication as to on what basis the assessment was being made, despite an obvious need to do so – for example, on the basis of previous history of the individual's behaviour (Hawley *et al.* 2006).

Perhaps the most important part of developments in the risk assessment field is that such tools highlight relevant areas of potential risk, and ensure that professionals think through and justify their decisions within their agency's aims and procedures, and should challenge them to be able to say how they have made individual decisions concerning service users. This is true for all forms of assessment – practitioners are expected to be able to justify on what basis and on what evidence they made their assessment judgements.

There are a number of structured assessments used nationally. One of these is ASSET.

ASSET

ASSET is an example of a structured assessment tool used by Youth Offending Teams (YOTs), which in a recent evaluation was found to be relatively effective in its use in a number of the areas that it sets out to address (Baker *et al.* 2005). This risk assessment is used by all staff in the multi-professional team, with the purpose of standardising the types of risk assessed. The tool takes into account a young person's offence or offences, and factors that may have contributed to the offending behaviour. The information gathered is used to inform pre-sentence reports and in drawing up intervention programmes, including addressing any particular needs a person might have – for example, lifestyle, mental health or drug use issues.

This tool sets out specific areas for practitioners in terms of the factors/risks they should be considering in terms of assessment, and particularly in terms of risk of reoffending, which may have to be addressed in any intervention programmes recommended. These include areas such as:

- living arrangements
- family/personal relationships
- statutory education
- lifestyle
- substance abuse
- physical health
- emotional/mental health
- perception of self and others
- thinking and behaviour
- attitudes to offending
- motivation to change.

For details of the ASSET assessment and pre-sentence report preparation, see the Youth Justice Board website (www.youth-justice-board.gov.uk/) and the Board's National Standards for Youth Justice.

However, even in relatively well-formulated and developed risk assessment tools, there are a number of areas of bias that can occur that those carrying out assessments need to be aware of. These are addressed in the following section.

Biases in assessment

A number of biases have been recognised that might affect social workers' assessments. While it is not possible to eliminate such biases, it is incumbent on professional workers to be aware of the biases they have in relation to assessing need and carrying out plans based on that assessment. This awareness can be developed through reflective practice, information gathering and challenging their own assumptions by way of using supervision and/or consultation processes as well as training (again, as required by the GSCC Codes of Practice 2002a; see also Fook 2002). These processes are important in order for social workers to be aware of, and make changes to, perception and action, so that assessments are as objective as possible and not influenced by biases they are not aware of or have not confronted. Individuals' own experiences can affect their judgements; so that if someone has learnt certain dynamics and 'normalities' within their own family of origin, or substitute care situations, these can bias their assessments about what is normal or acceptable (Connolly *et al.* 2006).

Assessment is not only a cerebral process. Emotions and prejudices can affect assessments – for example, fear of clients (Smith and Nursten 1998), or where social workers may have beliefs that certain types of families generally provide better care than others, or where they view elders in a paternalistic and ageist way (Middleton, Clyne and Harris 1999; O'Connor *et al.* 2006).

Assessment practice that is reactive to purely external demands, rather than practice that is proactive and responsive to the needs of the client, and takes into account biases in individual workers, can lead to information being collected that suits our hypothesis or unconsciously held ideas. This can lead to a distorted analysis and poor judgement. The work of Milner and O'Byrne (1998) in identifying two groups of assessment distortions – personal and inter-agency – is helpful in developing our understanding of these issues. Each type of distortion, with an example or explanation, is highlighted below; this is followed by a paragraph that focuses on an issue relevant to good assessment making.

Personal distortions
SELECTIVE ATTENTION

Historically, greater expectation has been placed on the protective behaviour of mothers than of fathers, to the detriment of both groups. Assessment should be aimed at the strengths and potential as well as the needs and deficits of a person or situation. It is very easy to focus on areas of concern, and while these might be the areas to be tackled, the service user can perceive an overemphasis on their shortcomings and limitations. Conversely, an approach that is based on uncovering and enhancing strengths can increase the likelihood that people will reach the goals and sustain the level of change required of them.

STEREOTYPING

Stereotyping refers to the unique features of an individual that may be missed, over- or underestimated and may induce fear or anxiety. The father who is articulate about his rights, and who demands an appropriate service, may be labelled as 'angry', 'manipulative' or 'difficult'.

ATTRIBUTIONAL BIAS

Social workers have sometimes been shown to have a tendency to hold the service user personally responsible for their situation because it is much easier to manipulate the person than the situational factors, and when the focus is away from these factors we are not required to consider the possibility of our own vulnerability in similar circumstances.

The model developed by Pincus and Minahan (1973) suggests that people involved in any change effort (including the assessment process) can be located in one or more of four systems; it is particularly helpful in aiding understanding in situations where power, conflict and differing perceptions prevail. Whatever the vehicle used as the basis of understanding, the need for an explicit knowledge base is reinforced.

SENSORY DISTORTIONS

Such distortions relate to people's willingness to categorise others by the way they look, smell or speak. In a society obsessed with personal cleanliness just think about your reaction to someone with poor personal hygiene who has unpleasant body odour.

EXPLAINING THE PURPOSE AND NATURE OF ASSESSMENT

Wholesale collection of all presenting information – visual, auditory or otherwise – or without a clearly defined purpose, will lead to a poor assessment. The service user should know the purpose of the information required and recorded, and should feel that the social worker is working in a spirit of partnership. This, of course, is not always easy to achieve and requires a process of communicating, exploring, listening, understanding and adaptation. The balance of power between the social worker and service user depends on a range of factors, including each other's willingness to share information. Those who present as 'angry' or 'loud' may be doing so through a sense of powerlessness, which in turn can leave the worker feeling anxious or frustrated. However, the assessment process develops the foundations on which partnership is created and it is therefore necessary to understand the range of distortions that may impact upon the social worker's ability to make impartial judgements. Additionally, analysis of the tenets of the social worker–service user relationship can provide each with a different perspective from which they are able to positively grow.

Inter-agency factors in assessment

Inter-agency working is now seen as key to all assessments (Barrett *et al.* 2005). This is emphasised in the safeguarding of children (HM Government 2006), in mental health work (Jones 2004), in work with older people, and in the youth justice field (see the section on the ASSET assessment tool earlier in this chapter and www.yjb.gov.uk) – in fact all areas of social work. Indeed in the area of safeguarding children and promoting their welfare, *Working Together to Safeguard Children* (HM Government 2006) is part of legislative provision under the Local Authority Social Services Act 1970, and emphasises the organisational and legal duties for agencies to share information for full assessments, as does the Children Act 2004 (DoH 2004a).

One example of government guidance in this area is the Single Assessment Process (SAP) for older people, which was introduced in the National Service Framework for Older People (DoH 2001c).[1]

The purpose of the SAP is to try to ensure that older people receive appropriate, effective and timely responses to their health and social care needs, and that professionals and agencies carry out assessments across their organisational boundaries effectively. In order to achieve this, several key themes are set out as part of the process.

- Individuals should be placed at the heart of assessment and care planning, and assessment and planning processes are timely and in proportion to individuals' needs.

- Professionals should be willing, able and confident to use their judgement.

---

1   For detailed discussion of this guidance, see www.dh.gov.uk/en/Policyandguid ance/Healthandsocialcaretopics/ Socialcare/Singleassessmentprocess/Index.htm.

- Care plans or statements of service delivery should be routinely produced and service users should receive a copy.

- Professionals should contribute to assessments in the most effective way and care coordinators agreed in individual cases when necessary.

- Information should be collected, stored and shared as effectively as possible and subject to consent.

- Professionals and agencies should not duplicate each other's assessments.

What is important to note here is the emphasis on the second point in this list – for professionals to be confident in using the judgement – which has been a criticism of some assessment tools. While emphasising this element, the guidance is also highlighting the need for structured assessments to make sure that there is a standardisation of the areas of assessment government has determined as important in the assessment of older people's needs, no matter who they are or where they live.

However, interagency distortions can affect assessments in such circumstances, and can arise in the following circumstances.

GROUPTHINK

Tensions created by timescales and rigid procedures lead to shared rationalisations and acquiescence to those with influence or greater experience. There is little room for debate, or for exploration and learning.

It is important therefore that social workers identify power relationships, and recognise and make explicit the roles and influence of other professionals. Vickery (1976), for example, emphasised an approach that stressed the need for an analysis that determined workers' responsibilities rather than, as with groupthink, responsibility and position determining the analysis. Vickery suggests the following components as essential to her approach:

- a social systems understanding of the world

- the service user may not be the focus of the work; someone else may be identified as the change agent

- a problem-solving approach characterised by partnership, clarity and agreement, and continuous evaluation.

PROSPECT THEORY

This concerns our willingness to take risks based on how a concern is framed – for example, where maintaining a young person in an abusive home is seen more positively than the young person coming into care, than the profession-als' decision-making is likely to be cautious, whereas if the option is seen negatively than the professionals are likely to be more open to risk.

Child protection assessments are focused on the likelihood of harm and are therefore negatively framed, suggestive of risk-taking behaviour on the part of the social worker. To avoid this dilemma social workers should seek to reframe the options in terms of certain and uncertain gains.

GROUP POLARISATION

This relates to the potential for members of the group to be more risk-taking than will be the case if decisions were made on an individual basis. It is crucial, therefore, that social workers consider and evaluate the basis for decision-making not only with their own potential biases in their thinking and feelings, but also in relation to work with other professionals and with other agencies; and that assessment is seen as a process rather than an event, which not only takes account of new information that emerges in the work with client(s), but also the potential effects of such personal biases and inter-agency working issues.

The ability to develop and test hypotheses, whether they are constructed individually or within a group, based on objective facts and using a sound knowledge base, is a key skill. Sheppard *et al.* (2000) identified a process of 'critical appraisal' in which social workers:

- focus their attention on particular aspects of the information available to them

- question the accuracy and completeness of the information available to them

- evaluate the quality of that information

- begin to identify causal influences that might be operating in a particular situation.

The objective is for the social worker to think reflexively about the task of assessment, 'theory knowledge' and 'practice wisdom'. Assessment is affected by both individual and group behaviour, by the mores, experience and expecta-tions not only of the service user, but also of the social worker, and it is because of this that any critical examination of practice should include reflection upon assessment as a subject, as well as the values, knowledge and skills used in assessing. This will greatly enhance objectivity in the subsequent collection and recording of information, and serve as a basis for the understanding of the meaning attached to events by relevant parties.

Client empowerment within assessments

It is also important to consider the policy and legislative context in which assessments are carried out. There is now, more than ever before, a professional and governmental realisation that social workers need to work with clients in an empowering and inclusive way, and way from the 'expert' role social work was for many years associated with. There are, for example, moves towards making more use of direct payments, so that service users have the resources to buy their own care packages, where social workers act as 'care navigators' for clients – assisting and advising about the purchase of services (Leece and Bornat 2006). In children and young people's services, their participation is required by legislation and policy guidance (see e.g. Children Act 1989, Section 1 (3) (a), and Section 22 (5) (c), Children Act 2004, Section 53 (1), (2) and (3) (DoH 2004a) and the UN Convention on the Rights of the Child; the various National Service Frameworks for different client groups also emphasise this approach (see the DoH website www.dh.gov.uk). This now must be seen as a defining factor in how assessments are undertaken, and reviewed, with clients and, indeed, their carers.

Dolan (2006) proposes the use of the Social Provision Scale (SPS) in assessments of families and individuals, as it measures the support that they have access to, and makes reference to examples of how the approach is effective in identifying the area of concern, and therefore areas for intervention arising from the assessment, in collaborative working between the social worker and the client, by way of a co-authored practice style.

Including people with disabilities will often mean ensuring that there are proper interpretation facilities and, where necessary, advocates for the person. This is seen to be important for children and young people when they are looked after, and also for people with learning difficulties, for example (Thompson 2006).

Models of risk assessment decision-making

Risk assessment is now a key element in most social work assessments. Such assessments are often based on actuarial approaches, as used by insurance companies. Such methods for determining risks in providing insurance for groups of people do not try to predict which individuals within those groups will have an accident in their car – they just spread the risks to the insurer across a number of individuals within identified categories; a significant difference from trying to predict risks for an individual, as social workers try to do.

Such methods in relation to the social and medical professional worlds cannot take into account the many and complex areas that intertwine to determine how a particular person will act or feel on a particular day, within a particular set of circumstances. For this reason, models have been developed to aid decision-making in assessments.

Normative models of decision-making attempt to help workers make rational, objective decisions that are likely to bring about the desired outcome (Middleton *et al.* 1999). Some of these models employ complex computational modelling and mathematical techniques (Yoon and Hwang 1995).

While it would be seen as best practice to take into account every aspect of the situation in order to assess that situation properly, it is recognised that this is not possible in all circumstances. In addition, having too much information can actually confuse the assessment, especially if this is combined with too much pressure on the worker in relation to the number of assessments and other pieces of work that they are having to complete at any one time. Therefore Baron (1994) talks of 'satisficing', which is taking into account certain elements of information that are most likely to pertain to the situation we are assessing. Baron argues, as does Parsloe (1999), that there has to be a mix between actuarial risk assessment and clinical professional judgement in the human sciences. This is a point also made by Canton (2005), that social workers do need to have guidelines that can take into account the key known areas of risk from research; these should not be merely mechanistic, but aids to professional, structured decision-making, based upon which workers can justify their decisions. Within such use of tools, however, we need to make sure we do not lose sight of the importance of the social work relationship in formulating assessments; Langan and Lindlow (2004) found staff's assessment of risk by way of risk tools in mental health work very inconsistent, and that the most helpful way of approaching risk assessment was to engage with the service user over time, giving a far more balanced assessment over systems involving tick boxes. This sense of relationship, and the use of it in assessing with clients their needs, is, we suggest, crucial to the nature, and effectiveness, of social work assessments.

Cultural sensitivity versus cultural relativity

Issues of anti-oppressive practice are vital to take into account at the beginning of the assessment process, and as the assessment is enhanced and changed over the period of work with service users (Thompson 2006). While it is important to take cultural sensitivity into account and the way in which people will view their world and act within it, from within their own cultures and learning, cultural relativity is seen as problematic in that all competing views of the world are deemed to be equal. Dingwall, Eekelaar and Murray (1983) found that child protection professionals made prejudiced judgements based on what they thought was normal parenting practice on certain housing estates within their area, or within certain faith or cultural groups. Connolly *et al.* (2006) examine how social work professionals' assessments and decision-making can be affected by how they think, act and feel in relation to the diverse cultural backgrounds of those for whom they are providing a service, particularly in areas of child protection. This affects how child abuse might be defined among different groups of families with varying cultural, religious and ethnic backgrounds, and how, if there is not an individual sensitivity in the social worker and understanding concerning cultural backgrounds, there can be problematic automated responses, which are the result of bureaucratic arrangements for assessment, rather than a focus on the problems and needs of the individual family within their cultural context.

Conclusion

This chapter has examined a number of important principles for assessment within social work processes and values. Consideration has been given to a number of important areas for social workers to take into account in providing ethically sound and knowledge-based practice that can aid the profession in carrying out assessments that take into account the values of social work.

Because social workers are analysing information constantly it is important to be fully aware of this process and the knowledge base on which they draw. This knowledge base will include the range of research available – for example, on risk, protection and factors essential to good outcomes in care. Social workers should be able to cite the knowledge base on which they are structuring their assessments and decisions. There are of course limitations to the empirical knowledge base and in some areas it is still in its infancy; however, workers need to make explicit the basis of their judgements and be prepared to share this with service users.

Furthermore, the concept of 'meaning' should not be ignored in the assessment process. Social workers need to be able to collect and record not only accurate accounts of events, but the feelings associated with and impact of those events, and many of the current, standardised pro formas pay little or no attention to this. To simply record on a form that physical chastisement is used as a form of punishment leaves the situation open to subjective interpretation. It is important to record the exact nature of the form of physical chastisement, in what circumstances, and what meanings are attached to it by all those involved in the situation.

In summary, the important areas to consider in assessment are as follows.

- Take into account government and local agency guidelines and checklists, while still employing the social work skills and knowledge base, in order to ensure that a structured, holistic and relation-based assessment takes place and does justice to service users' (and carers') overall experiences, views and needs, including in situations where social workers are having to act in their control modes.

- In line with the GSCC Codes of Practice, social workers should be constantly updating their own knowledge in relation to important elements in how to approach assessments, as well as what to include within them, but ensuring that this generalised knowledge is utilised in order to consider areas of need that are focused on the individual needs of the client and any carers involved, on an individual basis.

- Be aware of personal biases and prejudices that might affect assessments; take these into account in order to develop capabilities from training, supervision and consultation, as required within the GSCC Codes of Practice.

- Social workers should pay particular regard to areas of cultural competence and knowledge, and ensure that they challenge themselves on their assumptions in these areas with all client groups.

Acknowledgement

To John Corden, for his thoughts and wisdom in helping James Reid in the preparation of this chapter.

Recommended reading

Connolly, M., Crichton-Hill Y. and Ward, T. (2006) *Culture and Child Protection: Reflexive Responses.* London: Jessica Kingsley Publishers.

Dolan, P., Canvan, J. and Pinkerton, J. (eds) (2006) *Domestic Violence and Child Protection: Directions for Good Practice.* London: Jessica Kingsley Publishers.

Humphreys, C. and Stanley, N. (eds) (2006) *Domestic Violence and Child Protection: Directions for Good Practice*. London: Jessica Kingsley Publishers.

Milner, J. and O'Byrne, P. (1998) *Assessment in Social Work*. Basingstoke: Macmillan.

Parsloe, P. (ed.) (1999) *Risk Assessment in Social Care and Social Work*. London: Jessica Kingsley Publishers.

CHAPTER 14

'I just don't want to go there': Sexuality in Social Work Education and Practice

Joy Trotter, Mary Crawley, Lesley Duggan, Emma Foster and Jo Levie

This chapter addresses the ongoing need to re-examine anti-discriminatory learning and practice through looking at sexuality. The title of this chapter includes a quote from an experienced practitioner and post-qualifying (PQ) candidate who had been asked how she addressed sexuality in her practice. Her reply, 'I just don't want to go there', suggests some of the feelings of disquiet this issue raises. It also implies that the subject may not have been studied before. These responses are especially relevant when homophobia and heterosexism continue in society and pervade social work education and practice. This chapter focuses on sexuality and, using personal reflections and narratives alongside three practice examples, provides a range of ideas for analysis and discussion. It highlights the discomfort and silence surrounding lesbian and gay issues, as well as the privileging of heterosexuality. For qualified and experienced practitioners approaching further studies in PQ education and training, this may well be the time to 'go there', to face the feelings of disquiet around sexualities and to explore this under-scrutinised area.

Post-qualifying work has many levels and layers of competence and context, and spans complex and contentious ethical, legal and political arenas.

Recent government developments have been widely disseminated and much is expected of post-registered and post-qualified social workers (GSCC 2006b). One of the numerous and varied vehicles advocated as useful for continuing learning in this and many other government documents, training materials, research papers and academic texts is 'reflection' (Adams, Chapter 2 of this volume; Gould and Baldwin 2004; Graham and Megarry 2005; Leech and Trotter 2006; Moon 2004). However, despite such extensive encouragement to be reflective, little is said about reflecting on one's own personal characteristics, and almost nothing is mentioned about sexuality (the identification or expression of sex through lifestyle, behaviour and appearance).

Although it may be argued that recent legal changes and liberal attitudes towards lesbian and gay people and lifestyles mean that the UK has developed a more relaxed and tolerant approach to different sexualities, discrimination and stereotyping continue in subtle, and frighteningly un-subtle, ways (Cowan and Valentine 2006; Maley 2006). This chapter attempts to explore whether sexuality is relevant to good post-qualifying practice, and where and how this might be addressed. It is written by five qualified social workers from different settings in social work and academia, whose sexual identities and experiences are also different, but who hold a shared commitment to improving social work practice by addressing sexuality issues in post-qualifying social work education.

The chapter provides an introduction to some of the current research literature around sexuality in social work and considers a number of areas of relevance and interest to post-qualifying students in academic and practice settings. Using an amalgamation of personal narratives and practice reflections, which highlight some of the UK's recent legislative reforms, the authors present a case example for analysis and discussion. Combining this with evidence from the literature, they will examine some key issues for more experienced practitioners and students of post-qualifying courses. Furthermore, by including heterosexual issues alongside gay and lesbian ones, this chapter minimises the pathologies and patronising perspectives often adopted in social work practice, and provides a broader understanding of sexualities in social work.

Evidence base

The existing literature that social workers can use in this area is limited and usually focused on lesbian and gay sexuality (which, although overdue for attention, can imply that other sexualities, and especially heterosexuality, do not require scrutiny). Much of the current work is from the United States (for example, *Journal of Gay and Lesbian Social Services*; Martin and Hunter 2001) or found in British texts from other disciplines or professions (Allen 2003; Davies and Neal 1996; Deverell 2001; Wilton 2000). With only a few notable exceptions (Brown 1998; Buckley and Head 2000; Hicks and McDermott 1999; Logan *et al.* 1996), most of the British social work material is limited to occasional, dispersed chapters and articles. However, some of these are extremely useful as they highlight professionals' continued exclusion of gay people and the marginalisation of gay and heterosexual issues in 'everyday' education and practice.

For example, Manthorpe and Price (2006) showed how lesbian parents, lesbian carers and lesbians working in the care sector continue to face discrimination and inequality, and how practitioners can be affected by proactive but piecemeal government policies. In relation to learning disabled people, Abbott and Howarth (2005) found that 'virtually every person' in their study had been harassed or bullied because of their sexuality. Pugh (2005) suggested that older lesbians and gay men are, on the whole, invisible to social care agencies and asserted that practice is failing to reflect diversity or respond to individual need. Others have highlighted differences among minority sexual groups (Hicks 2005; Poon 2004; Schope 2005; Vaughan 2000), showing that social workers need to avoid stereotypes and assumptions.

Many authors have identified Rich's concept of compulsory heterosexuality as an interpretive framework for analysing how people talk about relationships (Perry 2000; Rich 1983; Tolman *et al.* 2003; Trotter 2000) and begun to question some of the consequences, challenging the 'ethnic identity model' of sexuality (Hicks 2006). This can be particularly relevant for work with children and young people – for example, as they negotiate their way through school or try to access mental health services (Ciro *et al.* 2005; Trotter 2006). Leech and Trotter (2005) suggest that social workers fail to recognise their own inner psychological struggles and desires for inclusion and exclusion, which result in homophobic feelings, preventing them from talking about sexuality with service users. The authors of this chapter have shown elsewhere (Trotter *et al.* 2006) that social workers hold differing opinions about what is regarded as an acceptable level of disclosure about sexual identity, and disagree about the use and meaning of key terms. They also found significant discomfort and defensiveness among social work educators, practitioners and students when addressing sexuality.

In relation to social work education, even less has been written in recent years, and it is difficult to judge what social work students are learning. Authors from the United States suggest that heterosexist and homophobic behaviours and attitudes continue in educational settings and practice placements (Hylton 2005; Messinger 2004), much of which is mirrored in the UK (Maldonaldo *et al.* 2006). Studies in the past have shown that, in the UK, despite proscribed

attention to anti-discriminatory issues for some years, homophobia (the irratio-
nal fear or hatred of lesbians or gay men, often resulting in discrimination
and/or abuse) and heterosexism (assumptions and practices that serve to promote and reward the heterosexual, shoring up the legal sanctions and social
structures that 'institutionalise' heterosexuality) continue to feature in students'
work (Burgess *et al.* 1997; Hardman 1997; Logan *et al.* 1996; Trotter and
Gilchrist 1996) and Canadian writers (Brownlee *et al.* 2005) found that the significant level of heterosexism among their social work students did not seem to
be moderated by their education. However, Camilleri and Ryan (2006) argue
that, although social work students in Australia are exposed to only minimal
input about sexuality in their educational programmes, they hold liberal and
supportive attitudes towards lesbian and gay sexuality and lesbian and gay
parenting.

In order to make sense of some of this evidence from the literature, and to
test its relevance to their own experiences, the authors met together,
tape-recorded and transcribed their discussions. These personal narratives,
reflections and practice experiences are summarised here.

Personal narratives and practice reflections

In order to prepare for this chapter, the authors set themselves two questions:
what is PQ about (or what should it be about), and does it address sexuality? As
we attempted to answer these, two additional questions were raised: does (or
should) practice address sexuality and is sexuality addressed in qualifying
education?

As an established group of practitioner-researchers, the authors were able
to begin sharing their experiences and expectations of the PQ award without
prolonged introductions or preparations. As a group, two had completed PQ1
and subsequent PQ modules, one had taught on it and two were current students. All of us knew many other colleagues and friends who had completed or
were currently involved in a number of different PQ programmes. In general
terms, it was felt that the PQ award should show that social workers are continuing to learn and develop, and PQ training should be a way of helping social
workers to face the dilemmas they encounter in practice.

The authors found it less straightforward to consider whether PQ education addressed sexuality. On the whole it was felt that this was not likely,
especially for social workers who were not interested in the issue as, in our
experience, most assessments appeared to be based on self-selected practice
experiences and the production of portfolios. However, despite the authors

themselves being very interested in the subject of sexuality, none had addressed it in their PQ assignments or portfolios:

> I did a massive self-profile for my Practice Teacher's [course], but I didn't talk about my sexuality once in that. It was skirted round. Other people talk about their relationships with their practice teachers...I didn't feel like I needed to.

> And you wouldn't want it written down there. I mean the worry of that, having that written down on paper.

It seemed that heterosexuality was sometimes alluded to by colleagues, in terms of family relationships and responsibilities, but that homosexuality was too risky for discussion with mentors or assessors, or for inclusion in assignments.

It was also thought that social workers usually had so many other requirements and distractions that sexuality could easily be overlooked.

> I think as well, in social work practice, sexuality very rarely comes into it. There are so many other things that are a priority.

It was agreed that most social workers were aware of other, more pressing matters to address in practice and those undertaking PQ assessments would be aware of the importance of reflecting their grasp of such priorities. This led the authors to question whether practice addressed sexuality, and how it did this.

Some of our discussion explored terminology and, as we have done before, debated the merits and reservations around various terms (Trotter *et al.* 2006). For example, the words 'lesbian' and 'dyke' were deemed to be unacceptable in practice and, similarly, 'non-gay', 'straight' and 'heterosexual' appeared to be rarely used. 'Same-sex couples' was acknowledged as a term that was increasingly acceptable in UK practice, particularly since the Civil Partnership Act 2004; however, it has limitations and anomalies. Grammatically, the term cannot be applied to individuals (a 'same-sex person') and the corollary 'opposite-sex couples' is not used. It appeared to the authors that social workers may feel constrained by notions of political correctness:

> ...the best way to be completely correct is to never mention it – just don't say anything and then you're always correct. So it never gets said, so it never gets talked about.

Further conversation about sexuality in social work practice seemed to suggest that occasionally things worked well. For example, when a gay social worker works with gay foster carers, sexuality is not regarded as an issue:

> ...someone who might *not* be gay or lesbian might have an issue with that. But for me its just...I don't have an issue at all with it and I'm quite comfortable, and, you know, able to understand some of their needs.

The authors agreed that there would be occasions in practice when a person's sexuality would be deemed to be part of 'the problem' quite erroneously, and assessments and practice decisions could potentially be flawed because of this. This was felt to be worse in some services than in others:

> I think in some services there's a lot of discrimination around sexuality.

The authors also asked themselves about their experience of sexuality in social work education and agreed that it wasn't particularly addressed in qualifying programmes. It also seemed that university tutors were unwilling, or unable, to help as they seem very wary of 'outing' themselves. For one person, the only occasion when sexuality was addressed was a very negative experience:

> …that was the most oppressive experience I've ever had on that social work course, because people that I was in a class with, and people from other classes on the social work course, were saying really discriminatory stuff.

It was a similar experience for others:

> I just was totally appalled at people's…people's attitudes…how could I ever feel comfortable in this group?

In an attempt to explore and address some of these negative experiences, the authors devised a number of case examples, with accompanying questions, to highlight possibilities and explore the potential for learning and teaching, as well as for good practice. For the purposes of this chapter only three have been included, but the authors believe these illustrate many useful ideas and concepts.

Practice examples and discussion

Practice example 1

Varsha, a PQ candidate, has growing concerns about her colleague John, an older, experienced practitioner. John is working with Grace, a 16-year-old care-leaver who, despite spending most of her life in different foster homes and children's establishments, is a confident and intelligent young woman. John has been her social worker for 14 years but their relationship appears to have changed. John has begun to speak disparagingly about Grace's recalcitrance and sullen attitude (though Varsha has seen no evidence of this). John is also spending more time with Grace, and Varsha is concerned about the necessity of this.

> Another service user has told Varsha that she saw Grace and John at the local takeaway on Saturday evening.

This example focuses on a shifting service user–worker relationship, which might hold a number of possible explanations; child sexual abuse is clearly implied and John's professional behaviour and judgement is questionable. However, this example also highlights the otherwise unspoken sexuality issues in service user–worker and colleague relationships, which conflate assumptions about gender and age, as well as about sexualities. Is John's sexuality relevant here? In what ways might Varsha's sexuality affect her relationship with John, and might this influence her ability to address her concerns about him? If it is not safe for 'middle-aged' heterosexual men to work with young women, whom might they be 'safe' to work with?

Practice example 2

Jackie is a white, married social worker who is based in a multi-disciplinary team attached to a psychiatric hospital. She has been asked to work with Selima, an African woman who has been experiencing a lot of abuse in the local community and has become depressed. Selima is also bisexual and HIV-positive. Jackie had suggested that it would be more appropriate for Selima to be referred to someone with knowledge of HIV/AIDS and preferably a lesbian or bisexual practitioner. No one else was available.

After a brief initial meeting, Jackie learns that the abuse Selima is experiencing relates not to her sexuality nor her HIV status, but to the fact that she is a refugee.

This practice example again demonstrates assumptions and judgements about sexualities and about what might be appropriate in professional practice. It suggests how ignorance, inexperience or prejudices influence some social workers' decisions and illustrates that sexuality (and ill health) should not be constructed as 'issues' or regarded as 'problems' to be addressed. It also shows how mainstream work might be designated, and subsequently sidelined, as specialist. How might Jackie's sexuality affect her work with Selima? What resources might be most helpful to her in this work? What does the research tell us about race, sexuality and gender in relation to depression, and how might this inform practice?

Practice example 3

Diane is a practice teacher. Jane, the student placed with her, is competent and efficient, and gets on well with service users and colleagues. Recently Jane asked Diane for advice about confidentiality as clients frequently ask her whether she is married or has a boyfriend. Jane confided to Diane that she is gay, but does not want to be 'out' about her sexuality on this placement.

At this morning's 'mid-placement' assessment meeting with Ray (the university tutor), Jane was horrified when Diane raised the issue and 'outed' her to her tutor.

This example is about good practice around sharing personal information with service users, colleagues and assessors, but also highlights one of the most important issues for lesbian and gay people about privacy and safety. It emphasises the need for practitioners to be sensitive to the prejudice and discrimination that exists in society (as well as in social work and higher education), and to be more circumspect about protecting others' privacy. There are clearly a number of points worth considering here, and many could (should) be reflected upon in PQ programmes. How should students, practice teachers and tutors 'manage' the information they have about others' sexuality? Should agencies and universities monitor sexualities and, if so, how might this influence people's awareness or behaviours? Might it be useful if heterosexual staff and students were more reticent about their own sexuality?

One of the most interesting things to come out of these personal narratives and practice reflections was the very different ways the authors managed their own sexualities at work. Their discussions revealed conflicts and inconsistencies in approach, but seemed to imply that the sexualities (and attitudes to sexuality) of service users raised far fewer dilemmas and difficulties than those of colleagues.

Sexualities and colleagues

Although writing almost ten years ago, it seems that little has changed since Helen Cosis Brown wrote about social workers (1998): 'There is still considerable fear and anxiety among lesbian and gay social workers about their agencies' responses to lesbians and gay men generally and towards lesbian and gay social work employees specifically' (p.43).

According to UNISON (2005), lesbian, gay and bisexual workers continue to face prejudice and discrimination when seeking work and once they are in a job, and 52 per cent of members responding to a recent UNISON survey had experienced harassment or other discrimination because of their sexual orientation. UNISON points out that many lesbian, gay and bisexual workers seek to avoid discrimination by concealing their sexual orientation.

One of the authors suggested that heterosexual colleagues should be prepared to be more reticent about their own sexuality, leaving this aspect of their identity undisclosed, in a gesture of solidarity and support to their gay colleagues. Such ambiguity might result in misguided associations or stereotypical assumptions being made about them, which could be neither accepted nor denied – further reducing the taken-for-granted heterosexual power base.

Despite having worked for some time in the same team, one of the authors, who is bisexual, claimed not to have a sexuality at work, saying, 'I don't, I just don't deal with it.' This seemed to revolve around issues of trust and confidentiality, and the fear that personal information would be 'out there somewhere', with no security and beyond safeguards:

> I don't trust anyone in my team, I love them to bits my team members, but I just wouldn't…how can you control that? You can't. You might trust them, but how can you control who they tell and then who they tell, and then who…I mean – I just don't want to go there.

Conclusion

This chapter has shown that there is very little written, researched, practised or taught about sexuality in social work, and that although PQ education offers an excellent opportunity to address this, there is little evidence that it will. However, for many practitioners and students, it may offer a way to begin. If PQ students are encouraged (or required) to reflect on their own practice in relation to sexualities, they might do two things: first, in general terms, they might increase their knowledge and be more willing to raise sexuality as a topic, challenge homophobia and heterosexism, and discuss sexuality issues in their work and their studies; second, on an individual and personal level, they might support their colleagues and service users by being more circumspect about their own sexuality, and respecting the privacy of others.

Recommended reading

Brown, H.C. (1998) *Social Work and Sexuality: Working with Lesbians and Gay Men*. Basingstoke: Macmillan.

Buckley, K. and Head, P. (eds) (2000) *Myths, Risks and Sexuality: The Role of Sexuality in Working with People*. Lyme Regis: Russell House Publishing.

Fish, J. (2006) *Heterosexism in Health and Social Care*. Basingstoke: Palgrave.

Hicks, S. (2005) 'Sexuality: Social Work Theories and Practice.' In R. Adams, L. Dominelli and M. Payne (eds) *Social Work Futures: Crossing Boundaries, Transforming Practice.* Basingstoke: Palgrave.

Logan, J., Kershaw, S., Karban, K., Mills, S., Trotter, J. and Sinclair, M. (1996) *Confronting Prejudice: Lesbian and Gay Issues in Social Work Education.* Aldershot: Arena.

Myers, S. and Milner, J. (2007) *Sexual Issues in Social Work.* Bristol: Policy Press.

Wilton, T. (2000) *Sexualities in Health and Social Care: A Textbook.* Buckingham: Open University Press.

CHAPTER 15

Thinking about Loss to Make Sense of Our Self

Maggie Jackson

Introduction

In this chapter I offer a way of using the concept of loss as a reflective tool for social workers to think about how their life experience impacts on their practice. The chapter considers a way of thinking about how we may have experienced and been changed by the many losses that occur in the course of our lives, and using these as the basis for a reflective exercise through which to consider what this might mean for our practice and the interactions we have with service users. I use my own experience as the basis for the exercise to illustrate how this might be done, and offer this as an example so that the reader can then try this for themselves.

First, I will consider further the relevance of reflection to social work practice (see also Chapter 2), then explain the aforementioned exercise and give my example. I will connect this to theories that may help to make sense of the example and then offer some conclusions about how it might help in working with service users.

The chapter also considers the notion of loss in its broadest of meanings. Although it is helpful to be aware of the major and recent work on loss, which focuses predominantly on bereavement through the death of a loved one, it is important not to dismiss its relevance to the work of the social worker by assuming that loss is only about death. Loss is part of all of our lives and the lives of our service users. It comes in many forms, such as unemployment, disability, sickness, divorce, being taken into care, adoption, having to move into a nursing home, and so on. As I will illustrate, it is also important for us to consider how the person who experiences the event regards it – not all loss is felt in the same way and we should avoid considering hierarchies of loss. Each experience is individual and often the reaction to it can surprise us. For this reason an awareness of how we interpret loss in our own lives can help us understand the impact, and the complex and diverse reactions of those with whom we work.

Reflection as a tool in social work

It has become commonplace for us to hear about and be expected to behave as 'reflective practitioner'; often it can feel as if this is something that we should be able to do somehow, perhaps merely by talking to others with whom we work, through supervision or some other nebulous manner that will 'come upon us' as we practise. Being reflective is not a passive activity, but it is not one that is always made clear within our training and education, nor in our daily working lives. What value does it have, and why should it be important to our work? If we have understood theoretical concepts, and we work within the ethical framework and practise within policy guidelines, surely our work will be effective? No; because the nature of social work is complex and changing we need effective ways to help us make sense of the work we do. As Bolton (2005, p.15) has said, 'An effective reflective practitioner attempts to understand the heart of their practice.' It is important that the work we do as social workers goes beyond the 'what and how', and tries to understand the interaction of all aspects of the lives of those with whom we work, and of how we as individuals impact on and are involved with their story. It helps us to avoid merely acting 'on' people:

> Effective reflective practice can enable care…which is alert and alive to the client's…needs and wants, whether professed or not. It can enable the practitioner to use their skill, knowledge and experience creatively and lovingly, and look forward with a greater confidence. (Bolton 2005, p.15)

Although looking back at the facts of a case, seeing what we did and considering how we might improve or change our actions and interventions is an important part of what we should consider, this is only a partial exploration and restricts what might be explored by excluding the thoughts and feelings associated with the work. Our own story and that of the service user interact and impact on every intervention we make; so having an understanding of our own story is imperative for effective practice. We are not robots that perform each task the same way each time we come across it, nor are we unchanged by those with whom we come into contact. We each have our own life story, and using that life and making it available by telling the story can impact on our work directly and show us what may otherwise have remained hidden and unconsidered: 'Stories do social and political work. A story is never just a story – it is a statement of belief, of morality, it speaks about value.' (Goodson 1998, p.12).

So, by exploring and considering our own story, we can make explicit some of the reasons and assumptions that lie behind our actions – we may like to think they are based on good practice learned from experience and study, but they will be mediated by our own personal experience and interpreted through that; if that remains hidden and unavailable for question then we risk slipping into routine and, perhaps even dangerous, practice.

Loss

I choose here to focus on loss as the basis for the exercise as it is sometimes easier to see what once mattered to us and is no longer there than to consider what we value in our lives. The fault lines, if you will, are easier to identify, and often associated with pain or transformations that we may not have anticipated, and can therefore be more memorable. Sometimes it is harder to think about what makes us happy than what makes us sad or annoys us. When we think of loss we often assume that we are talking particularly about death, and reduce the concept to certain specific situations where one has been bereaved by the loss of a loved one; or the death of someone with whom one has been working has occurred and acknowledging the impact of that death is important. These things *are* important, and not always recognised as significant as we hide under the cloak of being 'professional', which sometimes seems to be used to mean that we should have no emotions, and certainly that we should not display them. But in this chapter I want to broaden the concept so that we can begin to see how our life is shaped by losses (and certainly by change), and that the way in which we deal with loss has a direct and significant impact on the way we work with our service users and how we approach their losses. When looking at loss, however, it is often useful to refer to theories of grieving and bereavement as they offer a clearer model, having a finite point from which to measure behaviour and reactions. Other losses may happen over a period of time.

It is not uncommon to hear or read that all change involves loss and so we can consider that, as change is what we strive to effect within the work we do as social workers (or what we try to help people cope with), then it is useful for us also to consider how we have dealt with change, and how we think about change and its impact within our own lives and careers. Any change means giving up old ways of being, things that were good but we have no choice about losing, or things that are not so good and we are perhaps glad to be rid of.

Some losses may not be apparent because the positive outcome is the focus of our endeavours, but nonetheless our ability to cope and our attitude towards these losses and changes is useful in helping make sense of the way we work and live. It is therefore useful and relevant to have a clear and well thought through understanding of how we interpret loss as a significant part of our own lives if we are not to merely apply theories and interventions in a uniform and poorly understood manner.

Reviewing one's career is a useful and helpful exercise as it helps to make sense of how we have got to where we are now; this is important because it can help to make explicit some of our personal values and constructs, which we may tend to pass off as common sense or 'just the way we are'. It is not uncommon to consider the notion of using some sort of 'map' to set out significant moments and events in our life story, and that is the exercise offered here. I will briefly consider the manner in which it can be carried out and then illustrate it using my own experience. In the exercise I will outline how we might think about the losses experienced over our lifetime. It can be helpful to go back as far as one can remember in order to make sense of one's attitude to loss, as early experience often informs our later actions. This is also apparent when working with our service users and helps us to make sense of their story. This was highlighted for me in an experience with a student as part of an option module on loss and death, which I teach. I take the students around a cemetery (for a full explanation see Jackson 2004) and on one particular occasion a student asked me what my family's attitude towards cemeteries and loss was. It hadn't really occurred to me that there had been any particular attitude at all until I began to think about this question in more depth and realised that in fact I had probably always thought they were just places where some of my relatives were, and that perhaps not having thought about it told me something significant about my own attitude to loss.

The exercise

This exercise is by no means original and the reader may well be familiar with the concept in a variety of forms, such as a life line, a life map or a life snake (Oko and Jackson 2007), but despite the fact that it is a well-known tool, used on many social work courses, I feel that it is helpful to consider and use it here to focus on losses in order to make explicit the theories and values that impact upon and shape our own thinking.

To begin this work you will need to draw a life line, snake or map, starting with your birth and continuing to the present day. Along the line you should mark in significant experiences of loss that have occurred in your life. Then you should go back over the life line and consider any other events where there were changes that may not have come to mind at first – for example, changes of school or of house that may not at first have appeared as significant events, or a friend moving away.

It is important to begin to think about these events in terms of losses – what was lost to you in a particular event (perhaps also what was gained, but focus mostly on the things that were given up)? Was it a relief, an event looked forward to with anticipation or one that was dreaded and that remained with you for some time?

It may well be quite hard to think of any events in terms of loss – or it may be that there are some events that feel too overwhelming and thinking about loss at all is something we might try to avoid.

My story of loss

My earliest memory of a 'loss', as far as I can tell, is that of my paternal grandfather, who was buried in the churchyard opposite the house where my grandmother lived. I recall looking at his grave, reading the name on it (he had a slightly unusual middle name, 'Fittis') and playing with the little green stones that were on top of it. It was just ordinary, not frightening or sad. Nor was I told not to go there by any adults. It was simply where grandpa was. I know that I must have been less than five years old as my grandmother died when I was six.

I thought about other losses in my early childhood and remembered that in the reception class of my primary school the headmaster had told us about one of the girls in our class who had died from measles and that a child's coffin was the saddest thing he had ever seen. I have a clear memory of him coming into our classroom – we were all about five years old – and telling us about the little girl who had died of an illness that, at the time, it was not uncommon for children to get. He told us that she was now dead and that he had been to her funeral; he spoke of his own sadness at seeing her small coffin in the church. I don't remember this as being frightening, but I do remember the words about his sadness.

Before going to that school I had attended two other schools, one term at each, as we moved house shortly after I started full-time education. Leaving the town we lived in meant that I had to say goodbye to my best friend Andrew, who I never saw again, and a neighbour of whom I was very fond but whom I did see again from time to time.

Tracking the experience of loss as an everyday part of my young experience then followed, and I considered that at my primary school (the third one!) it was quite usual for children to come and go as the school was the nearest one to the local Army Apprentices' college. Their parents stayed nearby for a while before being posted to Cyprus, Germany or Hong Kong; you might have a friend for a year and then they would leave – it was normal. Sometimes the friendships would continue by letter, but more often than not they would just be part of the friendships made and then lost during the course of a year – not through falling out, but because they were no longer part of my world.

Also during my time at primary school my paternal grandmother died. As was quite common then, children did not attend the funeral. I knew that she was dead and had been ill before (she died at our house), but although it must have been sad I don't remember it as such. We didn't stop talking about her and it was only some 20 or 30 years later that I discovered she had died just before Christmas. My grandmother was a very godly woman and her death was seen as preparation for her resurrection to eternal life. Hers was not an ending.

Throughout this time my cousins would come to visit us every two years or so (they lived in Hong Kong). I suppose I got used to people coming and going as an ordinary event, which might be sad but didn't mean they could not be talked about or were not part of my life, whether physically present or not. When I was 11 they stopped coming to see us because their father (my uncle, my father's brother) died and they stayed in Hong Kong with their mother. We continued to write to one another, but have not seen each other since – it's a bit difficult when you do not live on the same continent!

A few years later my own father died – when I was 14. Obviously this was a sad and tremendously painful thing, and it still feels painful despite the length of time since it happened. Yet I think of him as part of my life, my story.

I had worked in a therapeutic setting for many years before I began lecturing, and had often worked with children and adults who had been bereaved in a variety of ways and, although the work was often about terribly sad stories, I found myself able to hear those stories in ways that other colleagues could not always do.

Many people who knew me and knew of my interest in loss (see Jackson 2004; Jackson and Colwell 2001a, 2001b), suggested that this was because I had experienced the death of my father during my adolescence and, therefore, that would explain why I did not feel so uncomfortable listening to others. This has never felt like a sufficient explanation to me and, although it seems from my experience that many people who work and research in the area of loss and death have experienced the death of one of their parents in childhood, the same is surely true for many who have not. The experience is not of itself enough to explain the capacity to listen to others, or to feel sufficiently comfortable with the pain of others.

Making sense of the story

Trying to consider how loss has played a part in my making sense of the world made me realise that it was an ordinary experience in my early life and one that was dealt with in a fairly open way. I began to see that understanding one's own early attitude towards loss was important in shaping how we are able to hear and deal with the losses experienced by our service users as social workers, particularly because it can give us an insight into the coping strategies and strengths of individuals.

It is now important to consider a possible theoretical understanding of my experience of loss (which I should add is ordinary, but written out might appear a catalogue of misery to some). Making this explicit helps me to understand how I see loss and its function in my life, and also highlights for me where it contrasts with the way in which others may make sense of their own losses.

What theories of loss are useful here?

In order to use the life line as anything other than mere information or story it is important to look at what theory can add to help us make sense of what my experience might mean. What might this tell me about my expectations of how I, and perhaps others, might react to difficult circumstances? I will consider three major theories of loss and grief, and show how they apply to my case; I will also consider why it is important to have an awareness of competing theories in order not to dismiss what we hear from our service users.

Let us start with one of the more popular theories of loss – that of Elisabeth Kubler-Ross (2001).

Stage-based theory: Elisabeth Kubler-Ross (2001)

The stage-based theory of grieving of Kubler-Ross is perhaps the best known of the theories of grieving. It suggests that healthy grief goes through a series of stages (usually five) and ends when one reaches acceptance, which tends to be read as 'letting go' or 'moving on'. This comes from a Freudian understanding of the purpose of grief, which is to feel the pain of the experience but then to gradually decathect and disengage from the lost one, and be ready to emotionally invest in life and others anew. Understanding loss in this way presupposes that, unless we move on, we are somehow not OK. We are maintaining an unhealthy relationship to the past which must be let go of if we are to function as healthy human beings. This is certainly how I understood grief for many years – having no awareness of other theories – but I felt that it made no sense to me as I have no sense that I have let go of any of the many people who have been part of my life, and even feel profound sadness about their loss from time to time even 30 years after the event. And yet to all intents and purposes my life appears to be functioning well. A simplistic and unthought-through understanding would cause me to offer myself counselling (were I my own client) to help me to move on. Some people find the notion of moving through loss to a resolution helpful, but for many this is not their experience. Because the stage-based theory of Kubler-Ross is very well known it can be seen as the 'right' way to react to loss and so cause us to try to fit the theory to the person rather than listen to them and notice their life. We must see, then, if there are other possible theories.

Since the mid- to late 1980s there has been an increasing interest in theories of grief and grieving. These challenge the dominant models of Freud (2005), Kubler-Ross (2001) and Worden (1991), which all contain the notion of grief work and decathexis. The newer models do not offer themselves as the only way to grieve, but try to recognise the variety of coping mechanisms people use, to greater or lesser effect.

'Continuing bonds' theory: Klass, Silverman and Nickman (1996)

The 'continuing bonds' theory suggested by Klass, Silverman and Nickman (1996) even from its name would suggest that it may be useful in my particular case. We feel loss profoundly, as one would expect, and although the pain does reduce over time in intensity, the connection to the loved is not felt to diminish. Conversations with the deceased may continue for many years, consultation or referral to them as a role model may occur. It is a sort of carrying the loved one with you in your head or your heart, and if it is a useful coping mechanism the sense that although they are no longer alive they continue to be part of your life in some way is comforting and reassuring. However, a constant preoccupation with the dead that does not reassure may be a continuing bond but is clearly unhelpful, and if it interferes with our daily functioning it may be one that should concern us. This model is one that can be helpful in considering how adolescents grieve or in understanding parents who have lost a child.

Meaning making: Robert Neimeyer (2000)

Robert Neimeyer (2000) suggests that we strive to make sense of our shattered assumptive world after a serious loss by searching for a meaning from that loss. He talks about 'meaning making'. If our world can be reconstructed to include the sense of loss and devastation yet still offers the possibility that there is some point to it, then we can continue to live our lives in a functional way. A senseless loss, which continues to be senseless to us, may cause us to withdraw from the world. If we can make some sense of the loss, whether that be via a religious or spiritual belief, or by focusing on the good things we gained from the relationship rather than the things we will never experience, then we can attribute some meaning to it. Sometimes this will also include what Neimeyer calls 'benefit finding'. The loss may cause us to campaign in some way, or to join a support group that gives us new friendships and so forth. This is not always possible or desirable, but shows us how the story we tell ourselves about the loss has a direct impact on our life. In my case this might be that having known these people is important in and of itself, and that to have known them has given me much, so that my life is better for having known all these people even though that means I risk losing them too.

Clearly, for me, benefit finding is also relevant as I have been able to use my early experience of loss in my work. It has enabled me to feel comfortable listening to others and has even driven me to study and research the subject further. It is important, though, not to consider that this *must* happen but to notice that personal experience impacts on the way we listen to what we hear, and may act as either a helpful tool or a hindrance if we have expectations that a person should react or behave in a particular way because that is how we reacted – or because we have no understanding of the concept due to lack of reading.

What I have tried to show here, by considering my own reactions to losses throughout my life, is that I have made sense of my reactions by choosing the theories that made sense to me. This is inevitably biased. However, the reason for the exercise is to reveal that attitude and to help demonstrate how I, as a worker, make sense of the world. What is also important here is that I should understand that, for me, loss is an ordinary, if distressing, part of life. Perhaps it might be distilled into an attitude of 'life goes on'. So when I encounter others who are having difficulty coping with loss, or talking about losses, it becomes even more important that I understand that my coping strategy is only one of many healthy coping strategies.

Without first making sense of ourselves we may take on board theories we are taught without testing them or questioning their use.

By doing this we are able to sort out our own responses from those of our service users. It can help us to be more effective in our approach to our work with them. If our expectations are that there is a 'proper' way to react to any loss we will inevitably fail to help.

Conclusion

What I hope to have shown is that it is important to look at our selves in an open and honest way, and to try to make sense of our own lives by reference to theory so that we can really see how and why it is valid and of use or not. I suggest that difficulties are more accessible through reflection and, because they can be uncomfortable, may cause us to see the 'fault lines' more easily. If we are happy we may not always know why but usually we know what is making us sad – even if we don't want to admit it. I offer the exercise in this chapter as a way of provoking thinking.

Recommended reading

It may be useful to have some awareness of the wealth of new writing on loss that has become available since the 1980s and the following is a short list of some useful works.

Currer, C. (2007) *Loss and Social Work*. Exeter: Learning Matters.

Dyregrov, A. (1998) *Children in Grief: A Handbook for Adults*. London: Jessica Kingsley Publishers.

Holland, J. (2001) *Understanding Children's Experience of Parental Bereavement*. London: Jessica Kingsley Publishers.

Klass, D., Silverman, P. and Nickman, S.L. (1996) *Continuing Bonds: New Understandings in Grief*. London: Taylor & Francis.

Neimeyer, R. (2002) 'Making Sense of Loss.' In K. Doka (ed.) *Loss in Later Life*. Washington: HFA.

Stroebe, M. and Schut, H. (1999) 'The dual process model of coping with bereavement: rationale and description.' *Death Studies 23*, 197–224.

CHAPTER 16

The Challenges of Practice Learning Today

Jackie Gilchrist

In teaching over 50 students in practice placements it was not the failing students that caused me the most worry – it was the few borderline students who exercised my skill in evaluating the evidence generated by their practice. If not for the training and structure provided by the Practice Teaching Award I think I would still be weighing the evidence yet! For the past decade and a half the Practice Teaching Award programmes have provided depth as well as breadth, and enabled practitioners to retrieve and articulate their knowledge of theory and its application to practice. In this chapter, I examine some of the challenges and changes of practice education today. Social work is a dynamic and contested area and requires well-educated and well-trained practitioners. A crucial component in producing future practitioners comes from current practitioners who know how to pass on to their future colleagues the knowledge and enthusiasm needed to be successful in their practice. I hope that this chapter will encourage you to do just that.

Why become involved in helping people to learn in social work?

As a practitioner I began practice teaching social work students on placement before the competence approach was introduced. At that time what is now known as the 'sitting next to Nellie' approach was extant, and student social workers were sent to sit next to someone who knew how to do the job but did not necessarily have any expertise in teaching someone else how to do it. The forerunner of the General Social Care Council (GSCC), the Central Council for Education and Training in Social Work (CCETSW), produced Paper 26.3 in 1989, which set out new and more demanding competence-based requirements for practice teachers who supervised social work students (from the former DipSW programme). This mirrored the competence-based approach to the assessment of student social workers. Paper 26.3 was revised in 1998 and published as *Assuring Quality for Practice Teaching* (CCETSW 1998). The resulting Practice Teacher Award (PT Award) programmes based on this competence approach provided depth, breadth and practicality, and did assure quality more than similar courses in the health and social care sector. In my supervision work with social work students from a variety of higher education institutions, referral to these documents allowed me to have the confidence that I provided relevant, ethical and well-structured teaching in the practice environment. The placements I dealt with were in the statutory sector, where I was often on-site, or in small voluntary/independent agencies where I was off-site but went in to assess and support. Values, Management, Teaching, Assessment and Reflective Practice were the units in this framework, and I used them to ask myself the essential questions necessary to provide a good practice learning experience for someone who is essentially a future colleague in practice. For example:

- Have I provided the opportunity for the student to reflect on whether their personal values affect their observance of professional ethics?

- Have I planned the student's learning opportunities in a way that will facilitate them to integrate theory with practice and allow them a breadth of opportunity to learn?

- Do the learning opportunities I provide offer the student enough scope to develop, both personally and professionally?

- Is my assessment of the student based on a range of evidence from different sources in different ways in order that the student's learning strengths are recognised, as well as their apparent weaknesses?

- Have I made use of current research and literature in order to reflect on the experience of teaching this student in order to improve my practice?

These are not exhaustive but do give an idea of how those units stimulated constructive thought in a practitioner beyond what I would normally engage in in my day-to-day work.

The ripple effect of well-trained practice teachers

A key aim of the units was to help practitioners retrieve and articulate their knowledge of theory (see also Chapter 5: Integrating Theory and Practice at Post-Qualifying Level), and its application to practice, to help students make the connections between university (theory) and placement (practice). Later, in teaching on the PT Award programme, it was interesting that some practitioners swore they had never thought of a theory at all while in practice. In fact the average social worker will have a grasp of theories of sociology, social policy, psychology, politics and demographics, and they will apply these on a daily basis to real situations in order to obtain the best results. They do this while taking heed of professional ethics (see also Chapter 3: Ethics and Values in Theory and Practice), and resisting the tendency for process to dictate content. Social workers in practice develop the ability to synthesise knowledge and skills from their own and others' practice and apply it to their current work. This knowledge, and the ability to synthesise it, is internalised to the point that they appear to be working on an intuitive level and no longer articulate or even describe this process/practice. I liken this to learning to drive a car: as a new driver one is aware of all the different actions one needs to take to keep the vehicle on the road without danger, as well as being aware of the Highway Code and the meaning of the different signs; after a while, however, the actual process of driving is internalised and, if asked how to drive to a location, the experienced driver will give geographical directions rather than describe the process of pedals, gear levers and signals. The action of driving appears intuitive. If the driver then becomes involved in an advanced driving programme, however, they will be asked to articulate the process of driving while giving reasons for their actions ('I checked my mirror and there is a motorbike behind me, a junction coming up, therefore I am slowing, showing brake lights, changing down', and so on). This analogy can be taken only so far but it has been helpful to candidate practice teachers struggling to audit their own theoretical base, while helping students to do so too. Chris Jones (1998) puts the challenges of articulating one's theoretical base down to anti-intellectualism in social work education and the removal of social science disciplines from the social work curriculum in favour of 'a mish-mash of methods, skills and values teaching', concluding that 'The domain of social work is compelling, important and contested. It demands and requires integrity, enquiry, debate and research' (Jones 1998, p.210).

Osmond and O'Connor (2004) take the view that you, as a social worker, do form theories and work with bodies of knowledge but that knowledge is not always communicated in formal academic ways; rather case examples, stories and metaphors are used to communicate your knowledge. In addition to this, social workers reformulate or synthesise knowledge in a way that 'appear[s] to result from some level of critical appraisal of an understanding and the recognition that no "one" type of knowledge could be regarded as eminent' (Osmond and O'Connor 2004, p.686). Thus, in merging divergent ideas, the knowledge titles (such as psychodynamic theory, ecological theories, motivational theories) become 'silenced within the new understanding'. This creates a superficial impression that theory, because it is not specifically named, is not being used. Fook (2002) discusses the role of critical reflection in articulating the theoretical base, recognising that this is not only necessary for those involved in practice education but that 'Knowledge creation, through ongoing reflection on experience, is something which never stops in a committed practising professional at any level.' (Fook 2007, p.372).

If there is a perception that theory is not being used by social workers on a day-to-day basis it makes it much more difficult for these professionals to have their opinion taken as a considered and well-founded piece of knowledge. If we undervalue social workers' professional opinion in this way it follows that all 'evidence-based practice' will be more of a quantitative than a qualitative nature, and this is counter to the whole ethos of social work. Lishman (2007) provides an interesting and well-informed discussion on how practitioners can contribute to evidence-based practice in a real way. This includes not only qualitative and quantitative research and evaluation of effectiveness, but also 'theories of meaning (tested with users) and user perceptions' (Lishman 2007, p.386). With this reasoning I would posit that the PT Award, like PQ in general, helps to keep practitioner opinion central to the development of social work in a managerial atmosphere that increasingly values process over content and promotes the one-size-fits-all assessment.

Since 2003, and the advent of an honours degree in social work as the professional requirement, there has been a need to develop more placements and you may well have been asked to 'take a student' on placement. There are two reasons for this. First, there are more students, but second, there are more placement days too (the requirement has increased from 130 to 200 days per student). Many social work programmes decided that first-year students would undertake a short placement in which they could undertake small pieces of work while being observed by a practitioner, as well as observing the practitioner completing their own more complex pieces of work. In order to help develop such placements, universities, in conjunction with other social work organisations, sought to widen the provision of placements in order to, both in number as well as nature, broaden students' learning. The Training Organisation for Personal Social Services (now Skills for Care) commissioned the

Salford Centre for Social Work Research to produce a work-based assessors' course, which has proved popular and which I have delivered[1] The workbook for prospective assessors is specifically designed to use as the basis of a two-day course for those organisations and personnel new to teaching students (i.e. as an induction to work-based learning and assessment in support of the social work degree). It was aimed primarily at voluntary and private social care organisations, although it is also useful for those social workers in the statutory sector who are contemplating taking students. This course (revised in 2005/6) is still available on the Skills for Care website (http://www.skillsforcare.com). I welcomed this move to widen the placement opportunities beyond the statutory sector because it acknowledges the increasing emphasis on public–private partnership in health and social care, and will widen the base of social work. Although social workers have always worked outside the statutory sector, their numbers are increasing with social workers finding employment not only in large voluntary bodies such as NCH Action For Children, Barnardo's and Marie Curie, but also in government schemes such as Surestart, E2E and Connexions.

The mixture of social workers and social care workers I have met in delivering these courses has been interesting and challenging, and we have learned much from each other. After each course I am often confronted by a social work student at the university who tells me that their practice teacher, who had attended the course, is now making them work a lot harder on placement! Usually conversation with the student elicits that they have become more engaged in their placement as a result of their 'extra' work, and understand better how to gather more evidence of their own proficiency in concert with the practice teacher. In turn I have often seen workers who have undertaken the two-day course who want to further develop their skills and knowledge by embarking on the more demanding PT Award.

From practice teaching to practice education and beyond

Under the GSCC requirements for the new degree, all qualified social workers can 'take a student' on and act as practice assessors. However, there is a requirement for a qualified social worker only for the final placement. The GSCC

---

1   It is worth noting here that 'practice teacher' has generally been the term used to denote those practitioners who take on the teaching of a student in practice as it encompasses all the roles undertaken by the practitioners who both teach and assess. The Salford Centre for Social Work Research used the phrase 'work-based assessors' and there are advocates for the title 'practice assessor' or 'practice educator'.

expects that social workers will undertake a Specialist-level qualification that has an element of practice education, representing a rather lower standard than the PT Award. This qualification (effectively replacing the PT Award) will assist in preparing social workers to become involved in the teaching and assessing of students on placement, but also in more general workforce development in the form of the mentoring of colleagues. There will be a Higher Specialist level (corresponding to postgraduate and master's-level study) for practice education, but this will require more time so it will have even more challenges as agencies, particularly the statutory, are as ever working with continuous staff shortages and increasingly difficult targets.

Several questions arise from this reorganisation of the way in which social workers are trained to mentor and assess students in the workplace. I shall look at two of these. First, will it become mandatory for all social workers who have completed a Specialist-level qualification to take part in mentoring and assessing just because they are qualified to do so? Second, will this move to embed practice education skills in the social work post-qualifying framework result in the voluntary, not for profit and growing independent sector becoming the 'poor relation' in practice education terms?

The answer to the first question requires some analysis of what has been stated, and some exploration of how the way in which students are taught on placement may change. That practice education will represent a very small fraction of the Specialist-level post-qualifying study or a complete course of study at Higher Specialist level could mean that practice teachers will be either under-qualified or over-qualified to take singleton students on placement, as has been the case hitherto. The practice education teaching in the Specialist-level post-qualifying framework is not of the same breadth and depth as was required by the previous PT Award, cutting the amount of study needed in half, which marks a definite diminution of standards. On the other hand, it represents a rise in standards if one accepts that many practice teachers currently have no training at all. It could be that this will result in the demise of the practice teacher who worked with the student on a one-to-one basis throughout the placement, and a move towards a placement supervisor who oversees the totality of the student's placement by placing them with different work-based assessors throughout – in other words, a less well-trained work-based assessor who will model and direct the practice. A more worrying thought is that social workers who are qualified at Specialist level to mentor and assess may continue to resist taking students as there is little incentive to do so, bar their own commitment to the future workforce, the income provided by the GSCC and the fact that, in the statutory sector, students on placement improve performance indicators.

The second question asks how these recent changes will affect the independent sector. This is an important issue, trying as we are to expand the placement base, as mentioned above. *Assuring Quality for Practice Teaching* included suitably experienced but not social work-qualified workers as candidate practice teachers, whereas the recent changes mean that only those workers with the protected title of social worker will be able to gain a GSCC-recognised qualification in practice education. Non-social work staff working in the voluntary and independent sectors will be able to study the same modules as Specialist-level post-qualifying social workers and gain university credits for their studies, as under the PT Award, but their competence in practice education will not be acknowledged or certificated by the GSCC in the way it previously was with the practice teacher programmes. It could be argued that we will be seeing more qualified and registered social workers employed by the voluntary and independent sector, which increasingly provides commissioned services to support the statutory sector, and many would argue provides more effective services and expertise.

Conclusion

The changes in post-qualifying training provide challenges for those in practice who facilitate learning and assess students. There should be more opportunities to involve ordinary practitioners in programmes and it is to be hoped that the Specialist award will help to stimulate social workers to analyse and reflect on their practice to the point that they are able to contribute to the development of students who will become future colleagues. This is especially important as the 'traditional' large statutory Social Services Departments are fragmenting into adults and children's services where social workers may not be the lead professionals. Social work is a practice-based profession and we need well-trained practitioners in the workplace to mentor and assess students, and to determine their suitability to enter the profession to which we are so committed.

Recommended reading

Banks, S. (2003) *Ethics and Accountability in the Social Professions.* Basingstoke: Palgrave.
Doel, M. and Shardlow, S. (2005) *Modern Social Work Practice: Teaching and Learning in Practice Settings.* Aldershot: Ashgate.
Parker, J. (2004) *Effective Practice Learning in Social Work.* Exeter: Learning Matters.
Trevithick, P. (2006) *Social Work Skills: A Practice Handbook* (2nd edn). Buckingham: Open University Press.

CHAPTER 17

Users' and Carers' Involvement in Education and Service Delivery

Wade Tovey

We need to ask the question 'What is the relevance to PQ of participation by carers and people who use services?' I hope this chapter affirms its relevance and highlights the need for much further work in this area.

Consultation, involvement and participation of 'service users and carers' have become increasingly familiar terms in social work. However, to some the terms are a government mantra that must be followed, to others they represent a form of political correctness, and to others again a way of working that can be empowering and rewarding to all concerned. This approach is promoted often in social work and social care, but is also ever present, in different forms and terminology, in health and other public services. A number of questions need to be tackled at this point:

- Why is there such a diversity of views among professionals and among the service users and carers themselves?

- What resources and evidence are there to support the ideal?

- How can it be practical?

- Is the approach tokenistic, and ultimately flawed and frustrating for service users, patients and others?

This chapter will provide an insight into these terms and a view of the future.

Background

The ideas behind consultation, and particularly involvement and participation, are founded on ideas of empowerment that have their origins much earlier, in the work of, for example, Mayer and Timms (1970) in *The Client Speaks*. Here one sees the idea that the client (the term used then but we shall return to this later) has a voice that can be heard – something that was rather alien to the concept that the 'professional' knew best. Anti-oppressive practice played a huge part in this movement by challenging where power lay in society and seeking to balance that power. The focus on anti-racist practice had grown, along with anti-sexist practice, disability awareness, anti-ageism and sexuality awareness, into the all-embracing notion that these, and other, groups were powerless and that the balance between service users and professionals needed to change.

Adams developed a framework for involving and empowering service users and carers as long ago as 1990 (Adams 1990). He emphasises that empowerment is an ongoing dynamic process between those wanting greater control and the professionals who work with them.

The idea of empowerment has grown and been used to a point where a Conservative administration used a consumerist belief in user involvement, with consultation initiatives and market research in social care (Beresford and Croft 1993). New Labour has taken this forward into notions of the purchaser/provider split and the 'consumer', to the point of Tony Blair introducing the idea of the 'Third Way' and the emphasis on modernisation and improved service delivery (Heffernan 2006).

New Public Management (NPM) is a term used by many to reflect these new approaches to public service management, and the idea that it empowers those it employs and those it seeks to serve (Dent and Barry 2004, cited in Heffernan 2006).

This general approach of wanting to empower citizens and patients to have a voice in shaping services has led to a number of pieces of legislation. This started with the National Health Service and Community Care Act 1990, which made consultation with service users a duty for local authorities, which as we shall see has not always been realised.

Citizens, service users and carers

The government, in a statement from the Minister of State in November 2006, said that it was committed to empowering citizens to give them more confidence and more opportunities to influence public services in ways that were meaningful to them, and in a way that will make a real difference to services. People have very different ideas about the meaning of words, however, and any attempt to produce an outright definition is doomed to failure. The key issue here is what the people to whom these labels are applied think and believe. In conversations they will often express their views about how professionals label them and their problems. The term 'service user' is examined first, but carers must be considered too, as carer organisations emphasise, for they also have needs and these are different to those of the people for whom they care. One in eight people is a carer, according to Carers UK (a campaigning organisation run by carers for carers), and does 'work' that saves the economy £57 billion per year; they 'give so much to society yet as a consequence of caring, they experience ill health, poverty and discrimination' (Carers UK 2007). Crucially, Carers UK says that 'carers provide *unpaid care* by looking after an ill, frail or disabled family member, friend or partner'.

Beresford (2001, p.509) used the terms 'service user' and 'welfare service user' to describe 'people who receive or are eligible to receive social care and welfare services'. He described the term 'service user' as 'problematic' as it defines them due to their use of services. At that time he could find no other 'umbrella term' and indeed recognised its inadequacies.

Adams (2006) describes the service user simply as a person who uses services, but recognises the many terms used by people (based on a national consultation to devise strategies for user and carer participation for Skills for Care (SfC) in 2005 (Adams *et al.*, 2005, 2006)) and provides a list: client; consultant; contributor; customer; consumer; member; partner; service adviser; service consultant; service member; service user; supporter.

During that consultation other terms arose but were firmly rejected by those consulted, centring on 'user', which had a connotation of using drugs, and 'client', due to the way that word has become associated with prostitution. These terms are also rejected in the literature – the former defined in this way by Herxheimer and Goodare (1999) and the latter due to its 'overtones of professionalism and expertise and social control' (Heffernan 2006, p.140).

The Parliamentary Under Secretary of State for Community, Stephen Ladyman (2004), seems to acknowledge the implications of the term service user:

> If you are a man of 65 retiring today you can expect to live until you are 82; 84 if you are a woman. That's wonderful and we should be celebrating it not worrying in case the loss of mental faculties or physical abilities should mean your wishes should be disregarded and you will be transformed from a citizen to a 'service user'.

The term 'service user', then, still has connotations of negativity and loss of power, but it is hard to achieve consensus on a satisfactory alternative. In a Skills for Care consultation (Hartlepool Partners and University of Teesside: Skills for Care Strategy for participation of people who use services, October 2005), many people's views were heard and there was no clear consensus, but the term 'people who use services' emerged and was welcomed by many as it put people first. This term was used, too, in Scotland in the Executive response to the '21st Century Social Work Review' in February 2006.

The term 'carers' is potentially more challenging than appears at first sight. There have been paid carers or care assistants in social care for a long time. In recent years, with the advent of direct payments, the term 'personal assistant' has been used to describe those people paid to provide care on a paid basis to service users living in the community. As indicated earlier, these are not the unpaid carers whom Carers UK views as discriminated against.

So terminology is a challenge with regard both to people who use services and carers. I have heard some service users suggest that we should simply use the term 'people', so they are treated as individual people with the context providing the appropriate meaning. People may use services from different agencies and bodies at different times, but they and their carers are still people who need to be treated with respect and their needs and diversity acknowledged from the outset. On the other hand, not distinguishing them reduces their power if they are seen as many individuals.

There are many different organisations and movements around different aspects of being a carer (for example, Carers UK, the Princess Royal Trust, Crossroads) or being a service user (for example, People First, the British Council of Disabled People, MENCAP, the Mental Health Foundation), but these lists are very long with many local, regional and national bodies and charities. Shaping Our Lives describes itself as a National User Network that is independent and user controlled. It gives a voice to service users at a national level, but does not provide the national voice for all service users and carers. There are many who question whether or not such organisations can truly 'represent' their own membership, but is that more questionable than the idea that a Member of Parliament represents all the people in their constituency?

Of course, there are many service users and carers who are in no such representative group. In some of the literature they are described as 'hard to reach' and elsewhere as 'seldom heard'. There could be many reasons for this, including a lack of knowledge or lack of access and opportunity, but also some people would not be identified as part of a service user group. Mullender and Hague (2006) want to give a voice to women survivors of domestic violence through recognition as a service user group. Domestic violence, like HIV/AIDS and mental health, say, is not an issue that individual victims would want to share publicly, perhaps not even with people like themselves.

Consultation, involvement and participation

The government's modernisation agenda has a key component, namely that service users and carers need to be seriously involved in considering the quality and development of practice with practitioners. Serious involvement surely means participation rather than tokenism, but it is a challenge to apply a blanket prescription for this. Circumstances differ and with them the level of participation that is most appropriate differs too. Adams and Tovey (2007) draws upon the idea of a ladder of participation, as suggested by Arnstein (1969), which shows the hierarchy between workers and the community from the most controlling to the most manipulative.

Consultation means asking for advice, which – even if given by service users and carers – can be ignored. The *Chambers Dictionary* defines 'to involve' as to make (oneself) emotionally concerned (in or with), whereas the *Longman Dictionary* says it is 'to engage as a participant'. It is the emotional component of the former that perhaps makes involvement uncomfortable for both those becoming involved and those who want or are required to have some form of 'involvement' with their work. The latter definition is more powerful again, as to participate is to have a share in or to take part. It is arguably the relative weight of power that creates the tension in reducing the workers' and agency power, or frustrating the people who receive a service. (Adams, Tovey *et al.* 2007) use the following definition:

> *Involvement* refers to the entire continuum from consultation of carers, through participation by carers to control by carers.

They then go on to differentiate involvement from participation:

> *Participation* refers to a level of involvement which empowers carers to exercise a meaningful and significant level of power to affect the particular area of their participation in the organisation.

Hafford-Letchfield (2006) refers to the Kings Fund model of a service user continuum that goes from information (giving or responding to request), through consultation (user surveys, focus groups or consultation meetings), through partnership (where some representation takes place on committees and the like), through to delegated control. She adds that there are 'no right or wrong levels' (2006, p.61) and emphasises that the pace and level of involvement or participation should be as they wish and as their circumstances allow, even with support.

Furthermore, on a point that will be returned to later, as Carr (2004) says (citing Barnes, Mercer and Din 2003, p.15), the various professions individually assume 'a language, a set of values and practices that privilege the practitioners', so certain types of service user may struggle even further when there is a range of different professional languages. Consequently, the use of plain English or easy-to-understand texts, translations, Braille, tape, signing and so on become a prerequisite of discourse for various service users. Such approaches require extra expense and, crucially, more time, both of which often frustrate those wishing to facilitate the process of participation.

Some service user and carer groups also create their own language to represent their own feelings more fully and this can in turn create challenges for the 'professionals'.

There are more pitfalls too; Carr (2004, citing Danso *et al.* 2003, p.18) refers to work on disabled people and mental health service users leading to a trend she terms the 'technology of legitimisation', in which managers of services seek user approval for their decisions and indeed exploit it using the weight of the service user argument when convenient. Putting the alternative view, Hasler (2003, p.40) refers to the opposite of 'contested representativeness' where there is a tendency to dismiss those who an agency or service does not want to hear as they don't represent service users' views, some even inserting the word 'real' to question their validity. Some refer to the professionalisation of service user representatives who are used by many different organisations as they are prepared to speak out yet are able to maintain a pragmatic approach.

Compensation and expenses payments for participation

The issue of payments and expenses for different levels of participation raises other issues. The various social care regulatory bodies (in England, the Social Care Institute for Excellence (SCIE), SfC, and General Social Care Council (GSCC)) pay different rates of expenses and varying rates of payment for time engaged in participation, some for payment in preparation, and some for the travel needed to be able to get to a venue to participate in meetings. These organisations do tend to regard meetings, and the associated preparation, as the main focus of participation activities, and of course the accessibility of venues becomes critical, not only due to access within and at the venue but also the ability to be able to get to it in the first place. These organisations have, however, got together in a Joint Participation Strategy Group and agreed eight principles of participation; they have worked together to tackle the issue of the payments, and expenses, affecting the benefits of many service users, whose views are crucial. However, even if that issue is resolved with the Department of Work and Pensions, the market economy and the short-term nature of many projects will tend to give vary variable rates of payments and expenses anyway.

Healthcare participation

There is much to be learned from the NHS experience. There were clear strategies and widespread investment made in giving patients a voice, originally in the former Community Health Councils and from 2003 with Patient and Public Involvement (PPI) in Health Forums and the Patient Advice and Liaison Service (PALS). The PPI Forums were to involve some 5000 volunteers in local communities who were 'enthusiastic about helping patients and members of the public to influence the way that local healthcare is organised and delivered' (http://www.cppih.org/). These bodies had the right to conduct a form of inspection of their local Trust but are to be abolished in 2007. This may be because the national network, officers and Executive cost over £200 million, with the volunteers receiving very little for their participation. It may be that the outright expense, and patients' and public frustration at this expense, which many feel could have been spent on 'real' services, may have contributed to the fact that this network is about to be replaced in 2007 with LINks – the Local Involvement Networks. This move to LINks came from the paper 'A Stronger Local Voice' (July 2006), which made clear that the government apparently wants to 'create a system where more people are empowered to be active partners in their health and social care rather than passive recipients'. This aim is laudable but confused and confusing in relation to what has gone before, and it will require a campaign in order to get service users, carers, patients and the public involved.

Social care participation

The social care sector is disparate in comparison to the NHS, as there is no national overarching equivalent in social care, but the creation of the new post of Director General of Social Care at the Department of Health in June 2006 may begin to help. It is therefore not possible for the voices of service users and carers to be heard in the same way as the PPI Forums tried to bring about locally and then nationally. However, the advent of *Every Child Matters* (DfES 2004), the Children Act 2004 (DoH 2004a) and *Our Health, Our Care, Our Say* (January 2006; based on substantial consultation with over 140,000 people) has caused realignment in local authorities of services work in children and families into Children's Trusts, with close links with education, while work with adults is more closely linked to health. This 'division' may well make it harder for service users' voices to be heard, though LINks may in time provide this opportunity. In Scotland, the response to the '21st Century Social Work Review' has been for the Executive to set out a five-year plan, 'Changing Lives', via which it will 'ensure that people who use services and their carers have ever greater involvement in decisions about their own care and the design and delivery of services through new approaches to the co-production of services'.

National social work/care organisations

Despite striving for similar aims, and agreeing a set of principles for participation, these organisations themselves have set about participation in different ways, and they use different terminology that is indicative of divergent perspectives; consequently, taken together, they present a somewhat confusing picture for service users and carers in particular. Furthermore these organisations have varying degrees of regional links. SfC, and soon the Children's Workforce Development Council (CWDC), has national structures with strong regional presence also. Service users and carers have growing opportunities to participate in their work at regional level and thus influence the nature and training of the social care workforce in their region, and perhaps nationally too. The Commission for Social Care Inspection (CSCI), early in 2006, appointed regional consultants to set up 'experts by experience' panels of service users to assist in up to 5 per cent of their inspections of care homes and care services.

The local perspective

At a local level there are many different models of participation but, fundamentally, busy qualified social workers will continue to hear the individual views of service users and carers. However, despite the notion of evidence-based practice in their qualifying training, there will be pressures, perhaps from management systems and associated forms, to provide services from those that are available rather than those that service users and their carers may quite reasonably want and need. Their own agency may well have adopted some notion of service user involvement, which should have had some bearing on their work in the agency. Such involvement may well be varied from the notion of customer service and thus comments on the service through a complaints (and sometimes thankfully, for balance, a compliments) approach, through consultation events, to funded participation through, for example, 'Partners in Policy Making' (http://www.mncdd.org/pipm/classroom.html) training, to give service users and carers the skills and confidence needed to take part in the planning and delivery of services.

Sometimes, though, the practitioner needs to focus on what organisations and studies tell them, with perhaps less concern for complexity of demand and more on fulfilling basic expectations more consistently. This view, set out in the

Reform Focus Groups carried out in 2002 for the GSCC, to determine what people expect from social workers, was for the purposes of thinking about the forthcoming new social work degree. The key points of such expectations from social workers centred on words like availability, respectful, patient, committed, punctual, knowledgeable, practical and not being afraid to tell people their views. These are not complex wishes and they have become absorbed into the GSCC Code of Practice with which all practising social workers nowadays are obliged to comply.

'User involvement' in the new qualifying programmes

In completing a qualification to become a social worker, the GSCC and DoH stated requirements for 'user involvement'. This was closely defined to include all aspects of the new SW degree defined in a DoH matrix with only the staff delivering programmes, and service users being the only parties involved in all parts of the new course.

A small amount of funding has been made available to support service user participation, but the limits of this budget and the competing demands of service user participation have contributed to a whole series of challenges that face the achievement of the ideal sought by all. It is therefore unsurprising that a report for the GSCC, *Working Towards Full Participation* (2005d) concludes that, some three years after the degree started, this 'involvement' varies considerably, with little evidence of how effective this process can be, and, more importantly, the impact that the demands of such involvement can have upon service users and carers themselves. SCIE has provided many materials and resources to assist the process (see http://www.scie.org.uk) and Skills for Care has played a part by providing money and materials for 'Getting Involved' training that allows service users and carers to be involved in the degree.

How does participation work in PQ?

The GSCC has made service user participation in post-qualifying training a requirement on a broadly similar basis to the degree. In Scotland, the User and Carer Forum is an integral part of the changes being considered over the next five years. However, much less funding is available for PQ in England than was made available for the new degree in social work. However, participation may well become more challenging if it is to necessitate service users being representative of the areas of work that post-qualifying social workers will be carrying out in, for example, mental health, child protection, adoption and family placement. Service users from all sectors have been used in research on different and demanding types, and it may be that those studying for PQ can draw upon this work.

Participation – the reality and the challenges

The key for service users and carers to participate centres on them having a confidence that their voices are heard and that there is subsequent feedback to them. Consultation is often tokenistic and based on formulated plans being tested out rather than asking for ideas to inform such plans. A service user with mobility problems recently informed me of the progress he felt that had been made when he was asked by an NHS Trust to look at the plans for a new building with regard to access, rather than looking at the completed building. Perhaps the next logical step is that service users consider the need for the building and then plan it with the architect before a design is started. Ideally, on this principle, service users and carers could be proactive and not reactive when considering the future, for after all it is their future that will be affected by new plans.

Service users may want services that do not currently exist or they may want elements of services provided by different professions. Skills for Care has gone as far as to look at New Types of Worker, and engage service users and carers in debates about the mixture of skills, knowledge and values they need to improve their lives. Indeed, there is a question about whether the existing professions are always the right ones to do what is required and whether it is cost effective and appropriate to have two or more professions going to the same service user to provide elements of services.

As we have already seen, the costs involved in participation through the PPI model are very high in the NHS, but perhaps the price is worth paying if through it service users and carers will ultimately receive better-quality services and achieve a greater level of satisfaction. This surely is the aim of participation, with the added bonus that the social workers or other professionals also have greater job satisfaction. The danger is that some councils and funding, as some have already done, see participation as not a service and therefore dispensable to a greater or lesser degree, which is inevitably a short-term political expedient.

Conclusion

The exploration of users' involvement in education and service delivery has many challenging facets. However, there are many opportunities that should encourage the social work practitioner to consider ways in which they, and their organisation, can make service users' and carers' views count in the development of better practice and better service delivery, with an overall higher level of satisfaction for all parties.

Carr (2004) makes the point that, to date, sustained participation is infrequent and so studies of its effectiveness may take some time to complete. There is no doubt that there are many service users and carers who will welcome the day when such evidence gives a real momentum to their wishes to change the nature and quality of service delivery in all levels of practice, and particularly in the more complex work the qualified social worker will face in the future.

Recommended reading

Adams, R. (2007) *Social Work and Empowerment* (4th edn). Basingstoke: Palgrave.

Carr, S. (2004) *Has Service User Participation Made a Difference to Social Care Services?* London: Social Care Institute for Excellence Position Paper Number 3.

Hasler, F. (2003) *Users at the Heart: User Participation in the Governance and Operations of Social Care Regulatory Bodies.* Social Care Institute for Excellence Report Number 5.

Part 4

Doing PQ

Introduction

Part 4 provides a set of resources for the busy practitioner and those employing, managing, supporting or mentoring them. The GSCC requirements are set out in an accessible format, with illustrations of different workers. It enables all of these involved in PQ to readily draw upon information and tools that will help to develop the evidence needed in order to achieve a PQ award at Specialist level and beyond.

There is some very useful guidance on a strategic approach to the whole process of being successful in PQ. There is further guidance on the construction of the portfolios of evidence that are used on many programmes as the vehicle for demonstrating how knowledge, values and skills have been applied to achieve the appropriate level of practice and critical reflection.

The appendices provide various pieces of guidance for the different people who work with social workers undertaking PQ, and details of various websites from which even further resources and guidance can be obtained, depending on the country in which you work.

CHAPTER 18

The PQ Framework in England from 2007

Vicki Lawson-Brown

Introduction

The new framework provides an exciting opportunity for registered social workers (RSWs) to develop their skills and expertise within a chosen specialism, or indeed within several specialisms during a lifetime's career. The new standard for professional qualification, leading to registration, is successful completion of an approved generic social work degree. Social work graduates may be starting their careers at the age of 21, so in effect they may be looking at a career in social work spanning some 45 years or more.

This raises the issue of currency of knowledge and qualification over such a lengthy period, but there are a number of other factors that will also have an impact, including ongoing professional development (linked to ongoing registration), staff fulfilment, retention of the workforce, competence and performance issues and, not least, ensuring high-quality person-centred provision to those stakeholders who use social work services. The new post- qualifying (PQ) framework allows people with busy lives to study for relevant work-based qualifications in a flexible, bite-sized way. This chapter will summarise and simplify the new PQ framework and the new specialist standards and requirements for PQ social work education in England, published by the General Social Care Council (GSCC) in 2005 and 2006 (GSCC 2005a–e, 2006a–d). This synopsis will then be illustrated with examples of the potential PQ routes practitioners might choose to follow, relating to academic qualifications already held, current post or position, ambition and interest.

How PQ links with post-registration teaching and learning (PRTL)

All registered social workers (RSWs) must demonstrate an element of continuing professional development in order to re-register after the initial three-year period of registration. *The GSCC Registration Rules* (2003, amended 2005) state that, in order to fulfil this requirement, each registrant should complete 'either 90 hours or 15 days of study, training, courses, seminars, reading, teaching or other activities which could reasonably be expected to advance the social worker's professional development, or contribute to the development of the profession as a whole' (p.36, schedule 3).

At the time of writing, there is no GSCC requirement for RSWs to undertake formal PQ training leading to recognised awards. However, by studying for a PQ award, registrants should be able to evidence very easily 90 hours of study within three years. PQ is therefore an excellent way of meeting the PRTL criteria. In addition, many employers will have their own progression criteria, which may be linked with PQ qualifications, but this will vary between employing agencies.

Generic PQ requirements within the new framework

The Post-Qualifying Framework for Social Work Education and Training (GSCC 2005a) defines the general requirements for all new PQ programmes. A key principle is that user and carer involvement is at the heart of all PQ education. Programmes must also be relevant, efficient and effective, meaningful and easily understood, accessible, modular, flexible, and linked to the university credit accumulation and transfer system (CATS). The focus will be on assessment of competence in practice and will enhance the maintenance of national standards. Programmes must also be linked to the *National Occupational Standards for Social Work* (Topss 2002), the *GSCC Codes of Practice* (2002a) and the *Guidance on the Assessment of Practice in the Workplace* (GSCC and Topss 2002), and have strong inter-professional elements. Academic and professional learning must be integrated, with significant workplace learning, and programmes must be linked into Regional Planning Networks (RPNs), which will be responsible for identifying regional workforce needs. PQ awards will be offered to professionally qualified social workers at the three levels (as indicated in Table 1 in the Introduction, p.11).

The GSCC has prescribed generic level criteria across all awards, regardless of the social work specialism in which they are studied. Table 18.1 presents a very brief summary of expectations for the different levels of award.

Table 18.1 Summary of generic expectations at PQ levels (adapted from GSCC 2005a)

Specialist level	Higher Specialist level	Advanced level
Meet the academic standards for this level	Meet the academic standards for this level	Meet the academic standards for this level
Think critically about practice	Use independent critical judgement including inter-professional work	Take a leading role in systematically developing own practice
Consolidate in direct work the full range of competences within relevant National Occupational Standards		
Promote service users' rights, choice, independence	Use critical knowledge of service users' issues to develop rights, choice, independence	Use critical knowledge to actively promote service users' rights, choice, independence
Reflect on and analyse practice, including inter-professional contexts, and draw upon theory and research	Demonstrate fully developed capacity to reflect using up-to-date research	Demonstrate fully developed capacity to take responsibility for the use of reflection applying relevant up-to-date research
Develop in-depth competence	Demonstrate enhanced competence at a higher level	Demonstrate a substantially enhanced level of competence and take a leading role in promoting good practice

Continued on next page

Table 18.1 continued

Specialist level	Higher Specialist level	Advanced level
Work effectively in context of risk, conflict, contradiction	Work effectively and make judgements in a context of risk, conflict and contradiction where there are complex challenges	Work creatively, make judgements and take a leading role in the context of risk, conflict and contradiction where there are complex challenges
Teach and assess the practice of social work students and mentor	Support, supervise and mentor others	Support, supervise, mentor and manage others, exercising leadership
Take responsibility for effective use of supervision		Undertake research in professional practice
Effectively manage own work and respond to organisational context	Take responsibility for managing complex change	Take a lead/ responsibility for managing key aspects of complex change including other agencies
Develop networking, multi-agency working to deliver integrated person-centred services	Develop effective ways of networking, multi-agency working and resolving complex issues to deliver integrated person-centred services	Take a leading role in the development of networking across sectoral boundaries to ensure integrated person-centred services

Requirements for social work specialisms within the new framework

As well as the generic PQ level requirements mentioned above, the GSCC has published specific requirements associated with particular areas of social work specialism for:

- Children and Young People, their Families and Carers
- Social Work with Adults
- Social Work in Mental Health Services
- Leadership and Management
- Practice Education.

These specialism requirements apply to all the levels described in Table 18.1. In other words, the GSCC has not published requirements for each level of award; the progression from Specialist level through to Advanced level is demonstrated in Table 18.1. Social work specialisms develop and progress as social workers acquire new skills through consolidation of their practice, through a continuum of in-depth competence in complex situations and, finally, through taking leading roles and demonstrating leadership in areas of specialism.

At the Specialist level, consolidation of competence must be successfully completed before any other module can be started; this will include assessed competence in the relevant National Occupational Standards. Core Practice Education must also be included in the Specialist-level award. The three domains described in *Guidance on the Assessment of Practice in the Workplace* (Topss/GSCC 2002) contain details of the relevant competences.

Approved Social Worker training can be found within the Specialist level of Social Work in Mental Health Services.

In addition to the generic requirements found in Table 18.1, a summary of the requirements for social work specialisms can be found in Table 18.2.

How the new PQ framework might work in practice

The new PQ framework very clearly builds on the professional social work degree and, in future, it is envisaged that graduates will consolidate their practice and move through the PQ levels over a period of time. However, the vast majority of the current social work workforce in England consists of practitioners who qualified with a Diploma in Social Work (DipSW), a Certificate of Qualification in Social Work (CQSW) or a Certificate in Social Services (CSS).

A few social workers hold other GSCC (formerly CCETSW) recognised awards and international social workers also hold GSCC-recognised awards or their equivalents. A number of social workers will be graduates in social work (other than the GSCC-approved degree) and allied or non-allied subjects, but their degrees will not be classed as professional qualifications for the purposes of registration. Others hold master's degrees and doctorates in a variety of subjects.

It is stated very specifically within the new PQ framework that social workers at all levels and with the full spectrum of qualifications must have access to relevant PQ programmes. DipSW and CQSW were the equivalents of the first two years of a university degree; the PQ Specialist level is set at honours level, the equivalent of a third year leading to an honours degree; this will allow graduates to study for a graduate diploma; non-graduates will be able to study for a 'top-up' degree at this level. Some universities may be approved to offer

Table 18.2 A summary of the requirements for social work specialisms

Specialism	Underpinning	Consolidation	Content and competence	Embedded values
Children, Young People, their Families and Carers	Outcomes defined in *Every Child Matters* (DfES 2004), the National Services Framework for Children, Young People and Maternity Services and relevant Occupational Standards. Promote the development of children and young people and help meet additional or complex needs. Develop knowledge and skills in relation to family functioning. Develop knowledge and skills in relation to the impact of traumatic issues or events such as war, genocide and forced migration on the development of children and young people.	Communication and engagement (including direct work). Child and Young Person Development. Safeguarding and Promoting Welfare. Supporting transitions. Multi-agency working, including accountability in a multi-agency context. Sharing information, including recording and sharing information effectively with other organisations.	Working in partnership including effective communication, support, advocacy and involvement of children and young people in decision-making. Application of assessment models associated with physical and mental health needs, impact of drug and alcohol misuse, physical impairment and learning disability, youth and family justice systems, asylum seekers, looked after children, legal issues in private fostering. Presenting professional views. Promoting positive change including in divorce and separation. Empowering those who have been discriminated against including poverty, bullying, homelessness, homophobia, racism. Working with parental mental health issues, alcohol and drug misuse, domestic violence. Core practice education (see below).	Engaging with others to develop trust. Exploring ways to share control over decision-making with young people and their families. Respect for others, including respect for difference. Honesty and openness. Ability and willingness to look at needs holistically and appreciation of diversity.

Continued on next page

Table 18.2 continued

Specialism	Underpinning	Consolidation	Content and competence	Embedded values
Social Work with Adults	Outcomes defined in *Independence, Wellbeing and Choice* (DoH 2005b) and *Our Health, Our Care, Our Say* (DoH 2006b), NOS for Social Work. Principles of human rights and concern with well-being of individuals. Person-centred. Inter-professional.	Human growth and development. Mental health. Disability. Assessment. Planning intervention. Review. Partnership working. Information sharing. Common Induction Standards.	Legislation, social policy and social welfare. Adulthood, development (physical, intellectual, psychological, emotional, sexual, social and cultural) and transitions. Communication and engagement. Assessment, independence, risk vulnerability and protection. Inter-professional, multi-agency working, networking, community-based services, accountability. Knowledge and skills sets linked to specific service user group. Core practice education (see below).	Service users and carers as experts through experience. Critical reflection on professional power and enabling partnership. Capability rather than limitation, inclusion, social model of disability. Understanding of issues of exclusion. Person-centred philosophy of care. Inter-professional working.

| Social Work in Mental Health Services | Promote the social work contribution to mental health services.

Wider than statutory role, but Approved Social Worker training found within broader programmes.

Will be suitable for proposed Approved Mental Health Professional.

Unique sociological and empowerment ethic.

Ten Essential Capabilities Framework and New Ways of Working (NIMHE), outcomes defined in *Independence, Wellbeing and Choice* (DoH 2005b), *Our Health, Our Care, Our Say* (DoH 2006b), NOS for Social Work, National Service Framework for Mental Health (DoH 2001b), other NOS if working with younger people.

Holistic approach, centrality of user.

Specific Approved Social Worker Training under the Mental Health Act 1983. | Signs, symptoms and assessment of mental disorders.

Understanding experience of mental distress from perspective of service users and families.

Social, physical and development factors.

Legal policy and context.

Evidence and value-based interventions.

Working together in promoting non-discriminatory practice.

Writing accurate reports, understanding power issues. | Assessment of multi-layered and complex needs and resources in a mental health context.

Applying knowledge and skill in legal and policy frameworks including mental health, children and young people, community care, disability, race and equality, mental capacity, vulnerable adults, criminal justice, welfare rights, human rights.

Working with carers to promote well-being, safety and recovery.

Promote social inclusion through networks including housing, employment, brokering care.

Understanding consequences of abuse, trauma and discrimination, and challenging oppression.

Proactive with service users, valuing diversity.

Working collaboratively with other professions in multi-disciplinary settings.

Working in a person-centred way.

Understanding mental health issues in relation to health, disability, dual diagnosis, drugs and alcohol.

Using research and evidence-based practice.

Influencing and supporting communities and organisations to promote positive mental health.

Apply understanding of cross-cultural perspectives.

Core practice education (see below). | Identify, challenge and where possible redress discrimination and inequality.

Respect individuals' qualities, abilities and diverse backgrounds, enabling contributions to decisions that might affect liberty.

Promote rights, dignity and self-determination.

Sensitivity to individuals' needs for personal respect, choice, dignity and privacy. |

Continued on next page

Table 18.2 continued

Specialism	Underpinning	Consolidation	Content and competence	Embedded values
Leadership and Management	Inspire staff. Promote and meet service aims and goals. Develop joint working and partnerships. Ensure equality for staff and service users. Challenge discrimination and harassment. Empower staff and service users. Value people, recognise and actively develop potential. Develop and maintain awareness. Provide an environment to develop reflective practice. Take responsibility for continuing professional development of self and others. *10 Principles of Social Care Management* (Topss 2004).	There is no Specialist level for Leadership and Management. It is very likely that practitioners will have consolidated their practice in a specialist area such as Adults, Mental Health or Children, Young People, their Families and Carers.	Ability to mentor and develop staff and plan organisational strategies for workforce development. Managing self and personal skills, mentoring, managing and supporting staff. Provide direction. Facilitate change. Work with people. Use resources and achieve results. Promote cross-professional working and accountability through multi-agency networks. Expertise in quality assurance and quality enhancement including an understanding of internal and external regulators and the role of service users and carers. Selective use of research and other evidence to support decision-making. Risk-management strategies.	*10 Principles of Social Care Management* (Topss 2004). Demonstrate how learning outcomes will affect service outcomes. Should not be seen in isolation and may be linked to leadership within other specialisms.

Practice Education			
• Supporting, mentoring and supervising others, enabling identification and exploration of issues and improving practice. • Exercising practice, research, management or educational leadership to identify and explore issues and improve own practice. • In-depth understanding of discipline of teaching and assessment and growing awareness of student learning experience.	There is no Specialist level for Practice Education. Within the PQ Specialist level for Children, Young People, their Families and Carers, Adults and Mental Health, practitioners need to complete an element of core practice education and demonstrate competence in the three domains:	• The teaching, mentoring and assessment of practitioners undertaking core practice education component within specialist award. • Teaching, mentoring and assessing other senior practitioners. • Managing contribution of other people in the learning and assessment processes and systematically working with groups of learners. • Contributing to teaching in partner universities and colleges. • For both the social work degree and the PQ awards, direct practitioner input to formal teaching to ensure exchange of theory and practice. • Coordinating or managing practice learning and assessment support systems, delivering and quality-assuring training programmes, across teams, within departments and between organisations and universities or colleges.	All other PQ award provision will require suitably experienced and qualified personnel to mentor and assess qualified social workers undergoing PQ training. For any PQ award approved by the GSCC, practice competence must be systematically and comprehensively assessed to an appropriate standard and level. Principles of pedagogy and adult learning to be located within the workplace.

Continued on next page

Table 18.2 continued

Specialism	Underpinning	Consolidation	Content and competence	Embedded values
	Promote and enhance adult learning experience, located within the workplace.	1. Organise opportunities for the demonstration of assessed competence in practice. 2. Enable learning and professional development in practice. 3. Manage the assessment of learners in practice.	Designing and planning learning activities and study programmes. Assessment and feedback to learners. Developing effective environments, student guidance and support systems. Knowledge and understanding of the subject area. Appropriate methods for teaching and learning. Understand how students learn, both generally and in their specialism. The use of appropriate learning technologies. Methods for evaluating the effectiveness of teaching. Commitment to evidence-based practice and the application of research in teaching. Development of work-based learning communities. Knowledge of the principles of the learning organisation and how these will promote critical understanding. Ability to deliver, contribute significantly to or plan and implement organisational strategies for workforce training and development.	The linkage with the assessment of practice in the workplace must remain paramount. Therefore, at the two higher PQ levels practice education providers will need to show how candidates will engage with their local and regional training and development frameworks as champions of the learning organisation. Respect for individual learners, encouraging participation, diversity and promotion of equal opportunities in learning.

the PQ Specialist level at postgraduate level, but only if practitioners have access to graduate programmes within their regions, a process coordinated by the Regional Planning Networks.

It is also very clear that universities must give recognition for previous study and experience through Accreditation of Prior Learning (APL), which may be evidenced through certificates and awards or through experience, demonstrated by means of a portfolio or other work. Universities will have their own systems for this but individual cases will be considered on their own merit. Holders of the current PQ1 (part of the old framework) will receive some or full APL towards the consolidation module as long as they can evidence relevant competences and have successfully met all learning outcomes. It is by no means automatic that PQ1 holders will be exempt from the consolidation module; it will depend in part how universities have structured that module. Likewise, holders of the Practice Teachers Award will be eligible for APL. Practitioners who have completed a full PQSW will be considered to have completed the equivalent of a PQ Specialist award.

Experienced practitioners with or without PQ awards may wish to enter at PQ Higher Specialist or PQ Advanced levels; this is possible as long as they can demonstrate to the university that they have met the outcomes at PQ Specialist level. This should not be dealt with as an application for credit, nor should it be linked to APL, and there should be fast-track routes for experienced social workers to demonstrate their skills in other ways, such as a portfolio route.

The programmes need to be flexible and practitioners should be able to choose from a basket of modules offered at different universities in their regions, subject to university regulations. Employers, however, could specify particular routes, for certain roles and funding streams might follow only certain routes, narrowing choices for individuals. It is hoped that employers will be flexible and will make full use of the opportunities for practitioners to study at higher levels.

How will practitioners decide which routes to follow?

The reality may be that employers, funding or resource issues and availability of regional courses may determine the routes practitioners are able to follow. Having said that, there will be a number of options to consider. Table 18.3 presents examples of the potential routes that might be appropriate for practitioners; the list is not exclusive.

Examples of possible career journeys

Example 1

A DipSW qualified Approved Social Worker has been working for the local authority for eight years. His ASW course awarded him with PQ1–PQ6, which is a full PQSW award under the current framework. He has been a mental health team leader for four years and is keen to move on. He chooses to register on a Higher Specialist award combining some leadership and management modules with mental health modules. Having greatly enjoyed the programme, he continues on the PQ Advanced award which also awards him a master's degree.

Example 2

A social worker holding CQSW worked in adult services for eight years before taking time out to have a family. While working, she found there were no appropriate adult services courses, but she started to do a PQSW by portfolio route. There was not much support and no workload relief, and she dropped out. During this time, she had an interest in practice teaching and practice-supervised several CQSW students. When she returned to work eight years ago she did a week's course in practice teaching and this led to her registering on the Practice Teachers Award. She successfully completed the components for the award but did not do the additional work to complete PQ1 or the full PQSW. Recently she has decided that she wants to work part-time and pursue further study, but the PQ Specialist award does not appear to be appropriate as she has adequately consolidated her practice and holds the Practice Teachers Award. She registers on the PQ Higher Specialist award in Social Work with Adults and intends to take at least three years completing it. She will contact the universities in her region to see which modules can be combined to make the programme of most relevance to her work.

Example 3

A newly qualified graduate from a generic social work degree is employed by the Social Services Department where she completed her final practice learning placement. After six months she and her employer agree that she is ready to register on a PQ Specialist award and she chooses a postgraduate Children and Young People, their Families and Carers award. She spends nine months completing the consolidation module and 18 months finishing the award, including the core practice education component. She feels ready to support

Table 18.3 Potential PQ routes for practitioners

	Specialist	Higher Specialist	Advanced
Children and Young People, their Families and Carers	Recently qualified social worker working in this specialism Experienced social worker who has no PQ qualification or holds PQ1 Social worker holding PQ award in a different specialism	PQSW holder in Child Care or another specialism wishing to change specialism PQ Specialist level holder in Children and Young People Experienced Children and Families social worker who can evidence they have met the Specialist level outcomes Children and Young People, their Families and Carers social worker in a specialist setting	PQSW holder in Child Care PQ Specialist level holder in Children and Young People AASW in Child Care Very experienced Children and Families social worker who can evidence they have met the Specialist level outcomes and who has the ability to study at Master's level Experienced Children and Young People, their Families and Carers Social Worker in a specialist setting
Social Work with Adults	Recently qualified social worker working in this specialism Experienced social worker who has no PQ qualification or holds PQ1 Social worker holding PQ award in a different specialism	PQSW holder in adults SW or another specialism wishing to change specialism PQ Specialist level holder in Social Work with Adults Experienced adults social worker who can evidence they have met the Specialist level outcomes Adults social worker in a specialist setting	PQSW holder in adults SW PQ Specialist level holder in adults SW AASW in adult SW Very experienced adults social worker who can evidence they have met the Specialist level outcomes and who has the ability to study at Master's level Experienced adults SW in a specialist setting

Continued on next page

Table 18.3 continued

	Specialist	Higher Specialist	Advanced
Social Work in Mental Health Services	Recently qualified social worker working in this specialism	ASW or PQSW holder in another specialism wishing to change career	ASW or PQSW holder in Mental Health SW
	Experienced social worker who has no PQ qualification or PQ1	PQ Specialist level holder in Social Work in Mental Health Settings	PQ Specialist level holder in SW in a Mental Health setting
	Social worker holding PQ award in a different specialism	Experienced ASW or Mental Health social worker who can evidence they have met the Specialist level outcomes	AASW in Mental Health SW
	SW who wants to become an ASW (but the course will be available to a wider audience of mental health professionals)	Mental Health social worker in a specialist setting	Very experienced Mental Health SW, who can evidence they have met the Specialist level outcomes and who has the ability to study at master's level
	The impending reform of mental health legislation proposes the role of an Approved Mental Health Professional (AMHP). Specific training requirements for AMHPs will be established when appropriate and will be linked to the generic requirements of the GSCC's PQ framework as well as the Mental Health Specialist requirements.		Experienced ASW or Mental Health SW in a specialist setting

Leadership and Management	The Leadership and Management awards will be at Higher Specialist and Advanced levels. The *only* exception to this will be for social workers who are managers of registered services, for whom awards at Specialist level may be offered	Newly appointed, first-line, junior or middle managers who may or may not hold PQ awards or other management awards Senior practitioners who may wish to combine another specialism with leadership and management modules Inspectors and regulators of social care	Senior managers who hold strategic positions who may or may not hold PQ awards or other management awards Managers in inspection and regulation
Practice Education	Core practice education within specialisms above	Experienced mentors and practice teachers who may or may not hold the Practice Teachers Award or another teaching qualification Experienced senior practitioners who may wish to combine another specialism with practice education modules	Very experienced practice teachers who may or may not hold other qualifications Experienced senior practitioners who may wish to combine another specialism with practice education modules Social work educators

others in the workplace and, over the next two years, supervises two social work degree students.

After five years in practice, she is recruited to a CAMHS team as a senior social work practitioner in a multi-disciplinary setting. In order to consolidate her new experience in mental health she opts to do the PQ Specialist level in Mental Health, finding a university in the region that can offer one specialist module in Child and Adolescent Mental Health alongside other mental health modules. She is exempt from the practice education component. Because of her previous experience, she completes the consolidation module in three months and the rest of the course in one year. She continues to act as a practice teacher for social work students and increasingly for PQ Specialist Children and Young People, their Families and Carers students.

After seven years she is promoted to team leader in the same team and, within another year, has been appointed as a senior manager in a statutory organisation. The agency requires her to complete a leadership and management qualification. She registers on a PQ Advanced award, combining leadership and management modules with some practice education modules, leading to a master's degree, which she completes in three years; articles from her dissertation are published. After a brief secondment to one of the social care regulators, she accepts a senior lecturer post at a leading social work university. She continues to publish work and completes a professional doctorate.

Example 4

A DipSW qualified social worker with a degree in law has been working in an adoption and fostering team for three years. His agency feels that the PQ Specialist level is not relevant to his work and supports him in applying to a university that runs PQ Higher Specialist Children and Young People, their Families and Carers with modules in adoption through open learning. To meet the entry requirements he has to present a portfolio of evidence. He successfully completes the award over two years. After three years he makes a sideways move to adult services, choosing to work with asylum seekers and their families in an independent organisation. His agency does not have the resources to sponsor him in completing PQ Higher Specialist Social Work with Adults but he chooses to sponsor himself on the programme and his employer agrees to give him study time. He has no interest in becoming a manager but moves to a training department, where he develops an interest in teaching. His agency supports him in applying for the PQ Higher Specialist Award in Practice Education, which he successfully completes. He is now supervising students from a number of PQ Specialist and PQ Higher Specialist awards and hopes to become a freelance supervisor in the future. These are purely illustrations and a number of combinations can be considered, from sideways moves to progression from PQ Specialist through to Advanced. Practitioners do not need to start at PQ Specialist level if they can demonstrate their ability to start at PQ Higher Specialist or Advanced levels. Likewise, some universities will allow PQ Advanced students who choose not to complete a master's degree to exit with a PQ Higher Specialist award, as long as they have fulfilled the criteria.

Potential links to health and other workforce frameworks

A recent discussion paper (Readhead and Mather 2006) expands upon dialogue between the Care Services Improvement Partnership (CSIP) and the North East Teaching Public Health Network. The suggestion is to apply the NHS career framework, the skills escalator developed in 2004, to the wider workforce in local authorities. Their model has been adapted and is shown here as Table 18.4.

This model appears to fit well with the new PQ framework. The concept of pitching levels of practice to qualifications is not new, but in social work has been less well defined. The outgoing PQ structure was developed in a piecemeal way, hence the need for revision. The new PQ framework gives a clearer structure for social workers, a clearer road map; it may make the concept of the skills escalator more relevant, certainly to social work if not to the public sector as a whole.

Conclusion

This chapter gives a very summarised and simplified version of the new PQ framework and of the specialist levels. It is recommended that, before embarking on any PQ course, practitioners refer to the recommended reading below and do not rely on the scant information presented here. However, this chapter is designed to give a flavour of what the possibilities might be, and a taster of what might be in store. Whether the new framework will prove to be more attractive than the outgoing one remains to be tried and tested. It can certainly be argued that it provides a more coherent structure and progression route, which fits well with graduate social workers and compares favourably with the continuous professional development models for other professions. Perhaps in future, social work will be perceived as having the high status it deserves. In that sense, the new framework will reach the parts that historical models have failed to reach.

Table 18.4 Potential skills escalator for local authorities

Job title	Generic criteria	Academic requirement	NHS role	Public-sector role
Practitioner	Work without direct supervision, take accountability for actions	Professional qualification	RGN Associate practitioner	Environmental Health Officer Social Worker
Senior/specialist practitioner	Higher degree of autonomy, expertise in one area, may be managing services	Degree Postgraduate	Clinical care practitioner Liaison Nurse	Healthy Schools Coordinator Social Work Team Manager
Advanced practitioner	Contribution to planning and development of services	Master's degree in specialism	First contact practitioner	Home Manager Senior Researcher Senior Manager
Consultant practitioner	High level of expertise and responsibility	Professional doctorate Master's	Matron Nurse Consultant	Assistant Director of Specialist Service
Professional lead	Professional lead with corporate and strategic responsibility	PhD Professional doctorate Master's	Consultant	Director

Source: adapted from Readhead and Mather (2006)

Recommended reading

The GSCC website contains all the details about standards and requirements concerning the different awards. You are advised to look at those specific to your interest and you can start at: http://www.gscc.org.uk/Training+and+ learning/Continuing+your+training/.

Relevant national occupational standards and other sector skill council endorsed standards: please refer to the appropriate websites listed in Appendix 2 for the sector skills council relevant to you.

CHAPTER 19

Adopting a Strategic Approach to Post-Qualifying Learning

Paula Sobiechowska

Introduction

However they are designed, most post-qualifying (PQ) awards will require you to take the lead in identifying and pursuing areas of learning and professional competence development. In this it is likely you will be supported by workplace and/or university-based mentors, peers, your line manager and work colleagues. Nonetheless, following a course of study alongside everyday work is very demanding and the challenge is probably best met when you take control of the process. With that assertion in mind, this chapter recommends and promotes a strategic approach to undertaking PQ programmes.

Research (Entwistle and Peterson 2004; Heikkilä and Lonka 2006; Ley and Young 1999; Stavenga de Jong and Wierstra 2006) indicates that learners who adopt strategic and self-regulating approaches to their studies (i.e. who take control of the learning experience) tend to achieve successful and meaningful outcomes for themselves. The three sections of this chapter embody a strategic approach encompassed in:

1. pre-programme self-evaluation

2. managing your learning experience

3. monitoring and self-evaluation.

The strategy emerges from the literature of educational psychology, as noted, and the accompanying discussion points, suggestions and examples emerge from many years of experience as a PQ programme manager, tutor, mentor and assessor.

Pre-programme self-evaluation

Before embarking on a course of study it is advisable to undertake a little self-analysis. Our motivations, self-concept, conceptions of learning and pre-ferred learning approaches greatly influence our capacity for, and engagement with, learning.

Motivation

It is perhaps self-evident that a lack of, or an ambivalent sense of, motivation will impede progress. However, motivation is more complicated in that we are driven by internal and external factors as well as a variety of life goals. Beatty, Gibbs and Morgan (1997, p.75) have extended the discussion about motiva-tion in terms of 'learning orientations'. A learning orientation is described as 'all those attitudes and aims which express the student's individual relationship with a course of study' (Taylor *et al.* 1981, cited in Beaty, Gibbs and Morgan 1997, p.76)… It is the collection of purposes which form the personal context for the individual student's learning.'

The grid presented here as Table 19.1 is adapted from a version in the work of Entwistle and Peterson (2004), in which they contrast learning orientations. This checklist is intended to prompt you to think about your motivation to undertake a PQ award – the categories are indeed contrasting but not mutually exclusive; your motivation may arise out of a complex mix of incentives. A clear understanding of your motivation will help you plan your way forward – for example, in determining what sort of award might be best suited to your pur-poses (e.g. a short CPD course, a postgraduate diploma or a full master's-level programme).

Self-concept

Of course, our self-concept is shaped by both current and past experience, and how we regard ourselves will influence the nature of our relationship with for-mal learning. It is useful to reflect upon yourself as a learner before beginning to study – for example:

- Do you expect to struggle with the content of the course, or do you welcome the challenge it might offer?

- Are you confident in your writing skills, or are you anxious about putting pen to paper?

- Are you able to share your reflections on experience with others, or would you mostly prefer others to do the talking?

- Do you actively seek out feedback on your work, or do you resist or avoid it?

Table 19.1 Motivation checklist

My reasons for undertaking a post-qualifying award are:		Only	Mostly	Include	Are not
Vocational					
Extrinsic:	To obtain a qualification of recognised worth	☐	☐	☐	☐
	To secure future career progression	☐	☐	☐	☐
	An expectation of my employment contract	☐	☐	☐	☐
	An expectation of my professional body	☐	☐	☐	☐
Intrinsic:	To seek effective and relevant training for a career	☐	☐	☐	☐
	To become a better practitioner	☐	☐	☐	☐
	To develop a greater understanding of those with whom I work	☐	☐	☐	☐
Academic					
Extrinsic:	To progress further up the academic ladder	☐	☐	☐	☐
	To demonstrate my intellectual capacity	☐	☐	☐	☐
Intrinsic:	To pursue a subject for its own sake	☐	☐	☐	☐
	To pursue an intellectual interest	☐	☐	☐	☐

Continued on next page

Table 19.1 continued

My reasons for undertaking a postqualifying award are:		Only	Mostly	Include	Are not
Personal					
Extrinsic:	To compensate for past failure	☐	☐	☐	☐
	To demonstrate my intellectual capacity	☐	☐	☐	☐
	To be a role model for others	☐	☐	☐	☐
Intrinsic:	To broaden my personal horizon	☐	☐	☐	☐
	To meet the challenge of new learning	☐	☐	☐	☐
	To challenge and test my current theories, beliefs and assumptions	☐	☐	☐	☐
Social					
Extrinsic:	To meet and enjoy the company of new people	☐	☐	☐	☐
	To extend my professional network	☐	☐	☐	☐
	To influence public debate	☐	☐	☐	☐
Intrinsic:	To contribute to the development of a local group/faith	☐	☐	☐	☐
	community/community of interest	☐	☐	☐	☐
	To contribute to society generally	☐	☐	☐	☐

Obviously, these prompts represent distinctive positions but it is important to think about whether you have a more or less positive view of yourself as a learner. Your outlook is likely to affect your capacity to make the most of the learning opportunities on offer.

As the work of Bandura (1994) illustrates, low self-esteem or a limited sense of personal efficacy is likely to predispose us to under-achievement, or even failure. This may be because a lack of confidence distracts us into avoidant or irrelevant tasks that do not support our actual learning needs; just think of all those interesting but not always relevant books you have read from cover to cover, while the assignment remains unwritten! A lack of confidence is also likely to focus our attention on the parts of the curriculum we can manage and perhaps reproduce (Stavenga de Jong and Wierstra 2006, p.156), rather than inspiring us to take risks with material that is unfamiliar and seemingly difficult; this approach limits our potential. Heikkilä and Lonka (2006) describe these approaches as 'self-handicapping' and contrast them with an 'optimistic strategy' that encompasses the expectation of 'managing' new situations at the very least. Their work indicates that those with positive, self-confident mindsets orientated towards success are more likely to achieve their goals. This is not just because such learners are 'happy' but because, in aiming to succeed, they consciously adopt appropriate and purposeful learning strategies, thereby taking responsibility for regulating their learning. Their success, in effect, is not particularly dependent on others but is largely the consequence of their personal efficacy.

Conceptions of learning

Entwistle and Peterson (2004) make the argument that we have individual *conceptions* of learning – that is, varying ways of understanding the generally shared concept of 'learning'. They cite the work of Marton, Dall'Alba and Beaty (1993) in identifying six conceptions of learning:

1. acquiring factual information

2. memorising what has to be learned

3. applying and using knowledge

4. understanding what has been learned

5. seeing things in a different way

6. changing as a person/sense of identity.

In the first two conceptions learning can be seen as a reproducing process, essentially an exercise in memory and recall – there is no sense that what is learnt means anything or is even understood. It is in applying and understanding what has been learnt that learning becomes conceived of as a meaning-making activity. The last two conceptions of learning – as a process where the worldview of the individual begins to change, and ultimately where the person changes – require considerable critical and reflexive effort on behalf of the learner to make sense of information in terms of what they already know.

Essentially this framework suggests that 'learning' can be understood in a number of different ways. This is important because *how* we understand what learning is can determine how we approach it; if we understand learning to be about the acquisition of facts then we might only memorise and 'learn by rote'. There is no 'right' or 'wrong' conception or approach here; however, an awareness of the range of conceptions enables us to 'pick and choose' appropriate processes dependent on the learning task. For example, an assignment focusing on mental health provision is likely to require us to *apply and understand* what has been learnt, demonstrating that a knowledge only of basic factual information will probably not be enough. Entwistle and Peterson (2004, p.411) note that 'context also means that students have to develop ways of learning appropriate to the particular subject they are studying'.

The majority of PQ awards will require learners to apply and use knowledge, to understand what has been learnt and to be able to see things in different ways. There will be few occasions where memorising and reproducing information will be sufficient.

Approaches to learning

As the preceding commentary argues, the way we approach learning is influenced by our motivations, concept of self and how we understand 'learning'. In a groundbreaking study, Marton and Säljö (1976) identified two predominant approaches to learning: *deep* and *surface* levels of engagement with, and processing of, material. As Entwistle and Peterson (2004) explain, a deep or surface approach is not reflective of student ability but of the learner's intent with regard to the material – that is, what the material represents to the learner, how the learner values it and the use to which they intend to put it. As you will be aware, if you are not interested or cannot see the relevance of a text, lecture or assessment task you are not likely to invest much time and effort. However, evidence generally indicates that those who adopt a deep approach to their learning achieve well academically. Table 19.2, adapted and reproduced from Entwistle and Peterson (2004), may help you think about your own approaches to learning. Which of the statements would you tick for yourself?

Self-regulated learners are increasingly identified in the educational literature, and the general description of such a learner fits very neatly with the strategic approach characterised by Entwistle and Peterson (2004). For example, Heikkilä and Lonka (2006, p.101) describe the self-regulated learner as:

> a student who is...able to set task-related, reasonable goals, take responsibility for his or her learning, and maintain motivation... These students are able to vary their strategies to accomplish academic tasks...student's management and control of their effort is shown to be an

important component of self-regulation: Pintrich and De Groot (1990) reported that self-regulating students are able to maintain their cognitive engagement in the task even if there are distractions.

Undoubtedly these are qualities and characteristics to be developed and honed on a PQ award, which will expect you to be an active participant in your own learning.

Managing your learning experience

Let us assume that you would describe yourself as a well-motivated learner who wants to develop as a practitioner, that you are determined to succeed in getting your PQ award and that, in the short time available, you want to learn as much as possible from the course. It might be useful to think about: how to organise time, space and other people; how to make the most of what you know; and how to use feedback.

Organising time, space and other people

Time will be very precious as you try to manage home life, work and study; in order to take the stress out of the situation you need to take charge of time. From the outset, 'action plan' your way through the PQ course of study; think of undertaking and completing the award as your personal project so 'project plan' it as if you were the managing director of Oxfam. As soon as you start the programme put all the relevant dates into your diary or onto a wall-planner (these are times when you will not be available for work). Include:

- all course dates – account for university attendance, tutorials and personal study time

- all practice mentor supervision dates (if appropriate)

- assessment submission dates – with sufficient study time booked into the two weeks prior to submission; this should be time enough to incorporate last-minute insights and revisions, final editing, the tidying-up of references, double-checking the bibliography, printing and presentation (e.g. reprographics and comb-binding).

Once the dates are in your diary they should be seen as 'fixed' by you and others; experience suggests that when they become negotiable the strategy can start to unravel. Ad hoc arrangements tend to drift: if study time is in the diary it is more likely to happen; set dates are helpful to family and friends in their support of you, lending both you and them a strong sense of your commitment to the programme and a clear view of your availability for social activities. It is also

Table 19.2 Approaches to learning: a personal checklist

I adopt a:		Always	Mostly	Never
Deep approach – seeking meaning – analytical				
Holistic:	relating ideas to previous knowledge and experience	☐	☐	☐
	looking for patterns and underlying principles	☐	☐	☐
Logical:	tracing connections between ideas	☐	☐	☐
	examining evidence, logic and argument critically	☐	☐	☐
	checking evidence and relating it to conclusions	☐	☐	☐
	Awareness of learning process: monitoring personal understanding as learning progresses	☐	☐	☐
	enjoying the intellectual challenge	☐	☐	☐
Surface approach – reproducing content – descriptive				
Tech-nocratic:	treating the course as unrelated bits of knowledge	☐	☐	☐
	routinely memorising facts and carrying out procedures	☐	☐	☐
	focusing on the minimum syllabus requirements	☐	☐	☐
Awareness of learning process:	regarding the course of little worth	☐	☐	☐
	finding little meaning in the materials, tasks, processes of the course	☐	☐	☐
	unreflective with regard to content, purpose of course	☐	☐	☐
	or own personal strategy	☐	☐	☐
	feeling undue pressure and anxiety about the work involved	☐	☐	☐

Continued on next page

Table 19.2 continued

I adopt a:		Always	Mostly	Never
Strategic approach – self-regulated learning – *organised*				
Awareness of learning process	organises study thoughtfully, logically and progressively, in accordance with course requirements and own goals	☐	☐	☐
	takes responsibility for managing time and effort effectively	☐	☐	☐
	concentrates on work and minimises opportunities for disruption	☐	☐	☐
	alert to assessment requirements and criteria	☐	☐	☐
	self-monitoring of own progress, adapting study strategy as appropriate	☐	☐	☐
	sense of 'moral duty', responsibility for 'doing best' consistently	☐	☐	☐

helpful for family and friends to know when you will complete your study, thereby putting your current unavailability in perspective! The same messages apply with regard to the workplace: if your line manager can see from the beginning the demands of PQ study they will be in a better position to organise their own and team time to be supportive of you. It is much easier for your manager to plan ahead, or around your agreed diary, than on an 'as and when' basis.

Physical space is as important as temporal space for effective learning. Ley and Young (1999) emphasise the need to find a quiet, comfortable place to study where the distractions are minimal (e.g. no TV, radio, telephone, cats/dogs, family members). If you are to study at home it is quite important that the space you use is seen as yours; having to clear everything away for supper and set up again later is very disruptive for everyone. On the other hand, a 'study time' – when everyone sits down and does their 'homework' after supper – rather than a 'study place' may prove a useful tactic. With relatively easy access to the Internet and university libraries' extensive catalogues of e-journals and e-books, learning at home is more of a viable option (indeed you may find yourself on an e-learning programme) than in the past. However, if a busy or space-limited home is a constraint be sure to decamp to a university or college library, where you will find private study carrels, study rooms and a degree of quietness.

Other people who will be involved with your learning are likely to be an assigned mentor or tutor, your line manager or work supervisor, as well as your peers on the programme. Primarily the tutor/mentor will support you with the academic and/or portfolio requirements of the programme. Within the PQ award tutors/mentors occupy an assessor role; in this they need to be assured that the practice experience and evidence you present and develop is in accordance with, or exceeds, the standards of the programme of study, the GSCC Codes of Practice and the National Occupational Standards for Social Work.

It is in your best interests that the role and influence of the workplace – with regard to your PQ award – are explicitly acknowledged and negotiated to some degree. The spectrum of involvement ranges from the marginal and peripheral to over-involvement; you are best advised to aim for a middle way of constructive interest and flexibility. Having your line manager/work supervisor on-side is hugely advantageous: mutually beneficial work projects can be agreed (thus ensuring the material generated for the award is part of your workload, not an extra add-on); best practice approaches can be reviewed and reinvigorated; the line manager's direct contributions, such as observations, recordings of supervision or appraisal sessions, can be secured; and study time mapped out.

Whether meeting with an academic tutor, mentor, peer group or work-based supervisor, always turn up to a supervision session with an agenda or some kind of material for discussion, even if it is a problem. Concept maps, diagrams, a list of words, a questionnaire, a training plan, observation report, journal entry or a photocopy of the piece of text for discussion all provide good starting points for analysis, debate, reflection and learning. Abstract discussions about what you *could do* will usually prove to be of little use and not particularly inspiring. Worse, without material to work on, both you and others are likely to lose focus and motivation; this means that you may leave the session not knowing how to progress. From your point of view, as a student, it is critical that you leave a supervision or tutorial session knowing what you need to do next and by when. This next step will provide the material for future tutorial/supervision sessions and, ultimately, for assignments.

Making the most of what you know

Modular learning programmes and professional frameworks are made up of competency statements and/or learning outcomes that can present compartmentalised views of the world. Arguably the design of many programmes lends itself to a surface approach to learning, appearing to require us to 'fit' our knowledge into particular boxes and not obviously necessitating the holistic connections described in the deep learning process. Given this apparent atomisation of knowledge and learning, experience indicates that learners respond with a sense of having to absorb a new area of knowledge for each new competence or module undertaken. This looks like a gloomy analysis; however, there are ways of 'making the most of what you know' by adopting a deep and strategic approach to navigate the learning required. For example:

- build your PQ award on the foundations of your current knowledge and experience, thereby deepening and extending that knowledge, becoming expert in your field

- approach the entire programme of learning thematically – this could be in terms of race or gender, sexuality and/or gender politics, ageism, disability and/or poverty, systems theory or attachment theory – over and above the specifics of the competence statements or modules; again, the value-added of this approach is that you may develop an expertise in the field of disability, for example

- maintain a learning journal in which you jot down random thoughts and ideas, cross-referencing to where you have had a similar insight in the past or where your thoughts echo those of published writers; this will help you build up a sense of your progress in learning and remind you of the things you do know and that you might use in assessment tasks; the learning journal can be developed to incorporate clippings from newspapers and periodicals, which you can annotate to make connections with your own thinking and experience

- remember that books read in one context can be used in another; knowledge is not discrete – it overlaps with itself as intimated in the notion of a deep, holistic approach to learning

- think about how your leisure interests can inform your learning; art (i.e. cinema, music, lyrics, theatre, opera productions, visual and plastic arts), for example, can be understood as a hall of mirrors reflecting and refracting aspects of the world, expressing particular and collective knowledge and experience.

These suggestions offer a way of approaching learning that is both pragmatic and holistic, an approach to learning that is about understanding and making meaning rather than simply reproducing others' points of view. It is an approach primarily informed by strong intrinsic motivations such as becoming an effective practitioner, developing an understanding of service user groups, pursuing intellectual interests (and demonstrating intellectual capacity), and challenging personally established theories, beliefs and assumptions.

Monitoring and self-evaluation

As outlined, the strategic and self-regulated learner is concerned to keep track of progress during a course of study, adopting the most effective approaches in order to achieve their aims. This monitoring and self-evaluative activity can be managed through a learning journal, through the supervisory process in the workplace, through feedback from service users and/or carers and, of course, through academic feedback. You will find that feedback on your work is an integral aspect of the PQ experience; the critical question centres on what you will do with it.

How to use feedback

Feedback is usually described as being 'formative' or 'summative'. Formative feedback is offered as you progress through a course; it might be built into the design of the course or you may exercise your initiative and ask for it. Formative feedback is intended to provide you with ideas and advice as to how to develop and progress your work. Both you, your supervisors and your peers need to remember that your practice and assignment material will never be perfect, exactly right, but it needs to be of a good enough standard. Feedback is always meant to be helpful rather than obstructive and, difficult though it may be, keeping an open mind to others' opinions will help you make best use of their comments.

Summative feedback is the final, formal response to the work you submit for assessment. Fundamentally, the assessor's comments will focus on whether or not you have passed the required task. Additionally the assessor might comment on where and how your work could be improved, note general improvements for the future, and might engage in a brief debate with the content of your submission. It is imperative to pay attention to the comments made in this summative, concluding assessment. The feedback is usually written to support your future learning or to help you recoup a failure and so should be taken seriously. Be sure that you understand what the comments mean; check them out with a supervisor or the assessor so that you can really make the best use of them. Should your work be deemed 'not yet ready' or a 'fail', be absolutely sure you understand the attendant feedback; assuming you wish to continue on the course, do not ignore it and try to avoid becoming defensive (difficult though this is). In these circumstances the tendency is to manage failure quietly in private – this is not a good strategic response; it is advisable to seek the support of your tutor/mentor in order to get back on track as quickly as possible.

Conclusion

This chapter has drawn on research evidence from the field of educational psychology, and the author's experience, to promote a proactive and strategic approach to post-qualifying and continuing professional learning in social work. In terms of preparing to learn and managing learning experiences it asks the reader to seriously consider their personal motivations, their concept of themselves as a learner and the meaning they attach to learning. Managing learning is explored in practical terms with regard to planning study time, creating physical learning spaces and maintaining positive, supportive relationships with others. It also suggests that, as learners, we should ensure that we 'make the most of what we (already) know', slowly building up knowledge and skills bases. The chapter encourages a strategic approach to assessment feedback, using it as information that can support successful academic achievement and professional competence.

Recommended reading

Boud, D. and Miller, N. (1996) *Working with Experience: Animating Learning*. London: Routledge.

General Social Care Council (2005) *Post-Qualifying Framework for Social Work Education and Training*. London: GSCC.

Heikkilä, A. and Lonka, K. (2006) 'Studying in higher education: students' approaches to learning, self-regulation, and cognitive strategies.' *Studies in Higher Education 31*, 1, 99–117.

Schon, D. (1987) *Educating the Reflective Practitioner*. San Francisco, CA: Jossey-Bass.

CHAPTER 20

The Use of Portfolios in Social Work Education

Maire Maisch

Introduction

Portfolios are used in a range of professional education programmes and are well established at all levels in social work education (Taylor, Thomas and Sage 1999). They have been integral to social work post-qualifying (PQ) education since the early 1990s and the new PQ framework (GSCC 2005a) will continue to require evidence of competence in Specialist, Higher Specialist and Advanced practice, thus furthering the potential of the portfolio as a tool of practice development, learning and assessment. 'Practice competence is at the heart of the revised PQ framework and all approved programmes will be expected to incorporate significant amounts of workplace learning' (GSCC 2005a, p.10).

In this Chapter, I review pertinent literature and draw extensively from my own and colleagues' experience over the past ten years of working in a university department, developing and implementing a work-based, competence-led, degree-level, post-qualifing award in social work that has made extensive use of prtfolios. Latterly a master's degree and Advanced Award in social work were also validated by the university. This Award and the degree were achieved largely through assessment of individual portfolios, which documented learning from the workplace accompanied by critical, reflective commentaries that met the core and general requirements of the Advanced and PQ awards. The Advanced award portfolios allowed students to exercise more autonomy through individual learning agreements and were less prescriptive than portfolios undertaken by degree-level students.

In this chapter, I will discuss portfolio construction within the social work PQ framework. It will address the potential of portfolio usage and some of the tensions of the portfolio process. I will consider five main aspects of portfolio compilation and explore each of them in turn. In order, the five sections consider: the meaning of the term 'portfolio' and its application to social work; the different types and models of portfolios; the appropriateness of evidence for portfolios; guidelines on the presentation of the portfolio; and, finally, assessment issues.

The portfolio: what do we mean?

Portfolios may be used in almost any discipline and are generally fashioned to represent a collection of one's work for a particular purpose. Artists, photographers and architects use portfolios in order to display their best work: 'People in the visual arts regularly create portfolios of their work to demonstrate knowledge, skills, and accomplishments' (Montgomery and Wiley 2004, p.4). In social work, portfolios have been used in a continuum of both qualifying and post-qualifying education, and have been pioneered as learning tools for competence development and to compile evidence about performance in practice. When we consider the portfolio in social work, Taylor *et al.* (1999) observe that 'given its widespread use there is surprisingly little critical analysis of its application' (p.148).

There are many definitions of educational portfolios, which reflect their different purposes and uses: 'A portfolio is a purposeful and selective collection of work showing reflection and progress or achievement over a period of time' (Montgomery and Wiley 2004, p.4); similarly, 'A purposeful collection of products and criteria that demonstrates students' growth in knowledge and skill over time' (Solomon and Campbell 2002, p.147) and 'A portfolio may be tailored to fit the needs of many different learning outcomes and may be in various formats, for example, electronic portfolios are becoming more common' (White 2004, p.37). Doel and Shardlow (1995) suggest that the portfolio 'is a collection of material which shows practical abilities…a good social work portfolio depicts a range of skills and competences and is designed around the materials it has to accommodate' (p.5). The following features of a portfolio emerge from these and other, similar definitions.

The portfolio contains work/evidence/items/artefacts that are:

•   purposefully selected by the student

- varied and in different formats

- demonstrative of knowledge and skills

- illustrative of a learner's progress over time

- designed to meet learning outcomes or competences (goal driven)

- individual and student centred

- drawn from practice situations.

Social workers undertaking PQ programmes have encountered the use of portfolios as an assessment tool to evidence capability, achievement and learning within a course of study. Historically this has been variously 'in-house', self-directed, or following a course or programme of study at an institute of higher education. Most notably, portfolio compilation has been used to demonstrate the first part of the PQ framework (PQ1), which has required practitioners to show 'that they have improved and extended the level of competence acquired by the point of qualification' (GSCC 2001, p.4). The consoli- dation stage of the new PQ framework, to be fully implemented by September 2008, replaces PQ1. The focus of the first, or Specialist, level is on consolidating, extending and deepening initial professional competence in a specialist context.

The portfolio: what type of model?

Within the current PQ framework there are various interpretations of the portfolio ranging from anything that has been produced during the learning process or practice experience to material/evidence that has to meet a series of competence statements or learning outcomes or, alternatively, that documents professional development over a period of time. Under the outgoing PQ framework, portfolios may earn professional but not academic credits. This is particularly the case where local authorities have developed their own in-house programmes. The new framework will require all PQ programmes to be academically credit-rated within a pathway validated by an academic institution. Portfolios will continue to be used to assess the practice or work-based learning component of a particular pathway. Professional body requirements and/or occupational standards will be embedded within the aims and outcomes of the academic award.

A search of the literature identifies many different types/models of portfolios. Orland-Barak (2005, p.25) differentiates between a 'process portfolio' and 'product portfolio'. The product portfolio (as the name suggests) emphasises the use of the portfolio as a tool for representing 'the products of learning' of identified educational objectives and is structured accordingly. Items are selected to focus on particular educational experiences or goals. In contrast, the content of the 'process portfolio' is left to the discretion of the participants, who give feedback to one another in the process of 'constructing, analysing and evaluating the entries' (p.30). The 'process portfolio' documents the facets or phases of the learning process and shows integration of specific knowledge or skills, and progress towards the overall aim.

A portfolio that contains the student's completed best work, often determined through a combination of student and teacher selection, is sometimes known as a 'showcase portfolio' (Benson 2005). It may include audio-visual artefacts and photographs, in fact any documents of accomplishments. This type of professional portfolio may be used not only to demonstrate the meeting of competences or outcomes but also as evidence for a change or advancement of career.

Doel, Sawdon and Morrison (2002) describe the development of 'the signposted portfolio' as a model of learning and assessment. This model of a portfolio has three organising principles: first, overall content, which is divided into sections and subsections of learning and assessment reflecting aspects of practice and curriculum content; second, constructive questioning designed to describe, analyse and reflect on an experience; and, third, anti-oppressive practice to consider issues of power and oppression.

Construction of portfolios within the PQ framework for social work may be seen as a hybrid of process and product. The end product is assessed as meeting the outcomes of courses or modules mapped to professional body requirements or standards, while a developmental approach is used either through peer groups facilitated by experienced tutors (Winter and Maisch 1996) or through individual contact with a mentor. In meeting competences, outcomes or requirements, learners will select the best evidence available, as in the 'showcase' portfolio.

The use of portfolios to demonstrate competence at one of the three levels (Specialist, Higher Specialist or Advanced) in the new PQ framework will be variously structured according to the requirements of the particular academic pathway, but will undoubtedly have the following characteristics:

- evidence of critical thinking skills, including the ability to formulate, analyse and assess (Mumm and Kersting 1997)

- carefully selected evidence to show how the outcomes of a course or module have been met through integration of theory and practice

- demonstration of progress, process and product linked with critical thinking and reflective learning

- inclusion of service user feedback, self-evaluation and opportunities for comment from peers, colleagues and/or supervisors, mentors and managers.

In essence, portfolios in the social work PQ framework will include at least the following four elements:

1. description and analysis of a practice experience

2. reflection and demonstration of theoretical understandings of the practice experience

3. an account of the intervention pertaining to the practice experience

4. a representation of service users' views and perceptions of the intervention.

The portfolio: what kind of evidence?

All portfolios within the social work PQ framework require both the gathering and presentation of evidence, accompanied by critical thinking, reflection or commentary. This may either be integrated within other elements of the portfolio or be a separate element in its own right, in which the student 'draws the evidence together into a coherent tale of learning, of sense made, of new ideas developed, tested and sometimes discarded' (Baume 2001, p.8).

Portfolio-based learning thus tends to draw heavily on experiential learning theory, particularly Kolb's (1984) concept of the 'learning cycle' (see also Maughan and Webb 1996). This recognises that experience by itself is just a starting point. Learning takes place only if students reflect on that experience, conceptualise new 'rules' for action based on their experience and reflection, and then test those rules in another concrete situation.

Portfolios make heavy demands for evidence (Taylor *et al.* 1999). As previously stated, a social work portfolio will typically include a variety of evidence drawn from practice, with accompanying reflective and critical commentaries. It is a requirement of current PQ and Advanced awards in social work that examples and observation of a candidate's practice are produced as evidence. This will continue to be the case in the new PQ framework. The increasing amount of official documentation being used as evidence in portfolios, and the involvement of service users, have implications for confidentiality. It is therefore important that only material that is relevant to evidencing a particular requirement is used, and all identifying features and facts should be changed or deleted.

Practice evidence will be understood and explained through relevant theo-retical constructs and critical reflection. Whether the portfolio can be described as 'process' or 'product', or both, it will be essential to think carefully about what constitutes evidence, and the nature and volume of the evidence required. Taylor *et al.* (1999) have identified the following key questions in relation to the use of evidence in portfolios:

- What constitutes evidence and how can it be verified?

- How much, how often and what range of evidence should be demonstrated?

- How is confidentiality managed for the learner in terms of personal reflection, service users and agencies?

It is true to say that individual portfolios differ enormously, as do the systems that underpin them. The amount of support given via a mentor or line manager varies considerably, as does the availability of written and verbal guidance from those delivering the programmes. Some will ask for little more than written tasks, while others ask for a comprehensive portfolio of materials that could include audio-tape, video, flipchart, collage, case studies, letters, questionnaires and more. So what do portfolios have in common given the enormous variety of evidence that is available? The following questions are generally relevant in considering the collation of evidence for the portfolio:

- What existing experience and knowledge do I already have that I can use as evidence?

- What practice examples do I have that demonstrate my skills and competence?

- What theoretical sources can I draw upon to inform and support this piece of evidence?

- How can I demonstrate best practice to use as evidence?

- What further development do I need in order to provide the necessary evidence?

- How will I demonstrate the authenticity and validity of the evidence I use?

As previously stated, the identity of sources of evidence must be protected and issues of confidentiality considered, including the question of whether material in the portfolio could be used as evidence in court (Hull and Redfern 1996).

Presenting the portfolio

In social work, the theoretical basis of portfolio compilation is underpinned by theories of adult learning (Knowles 1975). The learner is self-directed, past experiences are a rich resource for learning, there is a readiness to learn from life's experiences, and the learner is self-motivated to grow and achieve. The portfolio approach in social work is based on experiential learning where the learner is actively involved in constructing the portfolio. The aim is to enable the learner to be in control of the collection process, receiving feedback to accomplish professional targets/learning goals (Boud 1995).

Portfolios need to be accessible to the reader and should have an introduction containing both the purpose and a statement about how the portfolio is organised. The conclusion should contain a summary of the student's reflections on learning. Each item in the portfolio must have an annotation to the educational objectives and evidence of self-reflection. The materials selected should be based on the work the student believes best demonstrates attainment of programme competences or outcomes. Academic content, enhanced by student reflections, shows how students have synthesised the meaning of experiences, learnt from mistakes, built on what is deemed successful, and how past knowledge has been modified or built upon (Coleman, Rogers and King 2002).

The following guidelines will assist in the presentation of the portfolio.

- The essential arrangements of the portfolio should be clear, well articulated and structured.

- A contents page, together with a clear outline of the portfolio and exactly where to find relevant evidence, is crucial.

- Clearly articulated reasons must be provided to justify anything put into the portfolio.

- There should be an indication of word limits or equivalence.

- Specified learning outcomes, competences, course or programme guidelines and marking criteria should be taken into account and/or addressed.

- Overall, the portfolio should be descriptive, critically reflective, analytical, realistic and discerning.

Taylor et al. (1999, p.156) ask 'to what extent should the responsibility for structuring the presentation lie with the individual learners or assessors?' They suggest that 'presenting material in a clear and concise fashion should be part of the explicit assessment criteria for portfolios'. They identify that, on the one hand, there is the fear that standardisation will cramp the individual learner's style but, on the other hand, there is the learner's own anxiety about not knowing what is expected and their obsessions with the mechanics of the portfolio. The paradox is that giving learners a structure for the portfolio is likely to encourage rather than constrain innovation. Hull and Redfern state their views:

> Portfolios should then be structured as required by the assessors but the structure must not be so constraining that learners are unable to speak with their own voice, nor should they be so smart that learners are apprehensive about writing in them for fear of making them look untidy. (Hull and Redfern 1996, p.9)

In social work there is a need to capture the complex, multiple dimensions of practice. Schon (1987) describes this as the 'swampy lowlands'. Fish (1998) talks about the hidden dimensions of professional practice. Product portfolios based on meeting competences or outcomes in the workplace have been contested by a number of academic theorists, most notably Barnett (1990, 1994). Professional education is not considered as being reducible to a set of competence statements or outcomes that could realistically encapsulate the holistic and dynamic complexity of social work (Hodkinson and Issitt 1995). Reflective, critical, interrogatory commentaries are essential in ensuring that evidence-based portfolios maintain standards of rigour and excellence. There is not 'one way' to compile a portfolio, which is being presented for academic and professional credits. Essentially, it must meet the outcomes or requirements of the awarding bodies, it must be accessible and clearly signposted, it must maintain standards of confidentiality, and contain authenticated and reliable evidence of practice accompanied by theoretical, reflective and critical commentaries.

Assessing the portfolio

In professional education, portfolios are widely established as a means of assessing, or accrediting, competence in practice. In social work, at qualifying level, practice placements are normally assessed by means of a portfolio to demonstrate practice competence and at the PQ stage to demonstrate progression beyond qualification and knowledge and skills in Specialist and Higher Specialist practice. Despite the wide and growing use of portfolios, the reliability of portfolio assessments has been little addressed (Baume 2001). As most portfolios in social work are an amalgam of process and product, both formative and summative assessment tools are employed. In the social work PQ degree and master's programmes I have been involved with, participants have consistently evaluated the formative assessment of their portfolios by their peers as both supportive and immensely helpful in providing insights into the generation of evidence from their own practice. In other instances – for example, in-house programmes – a mentor has offered a singleton model of formative assessment. When the formative processes have been undertaken, the portfolio is submitted for summative assessment and usually graded using norm or criterion referencing.

The individual nature of portfolios necessitates a need for explicitness regarding the expectations placed on the assessees, and the need to ensure that all who are party to the assessment practice share an awareness of what is expected (Baume and Yorke 2002). Portfolio assessment needs to take into account the individualism of the work being submitted, which may illuminate a student's personal strengths and skills more than a traditional essay or assignment. In the author's experience it is this individualism that can lead to increased subjectivity in the assessment process. To counteract this possibility, all portfolios should be moderated by an independent assessor (i.e. one who has not been involved with the student) and a mark agreed. Where PQ candidates are providing evidence to meet particular competences or requirements, a decision will have to be made as to whether an overall grade or pass is given or whether each element or requirement is graded or passed individually. Baume and Yorke (2002) provide a useful discussion on this point, describing it as the 'relationship between holism and particularism in assessment' (p.24). Winter and Maisch (1996) uses terms such as 'the development of an expert community' (Chapter 6), and Baume and Yorke (2002) discuss 'communities of practice around assessment'.

In my experience, and that of colleagues, students become more adept at the mechanics of constructing their portfolios for assessment. Social workers who have some experience in their qualifying programmes of designing portfolios of practice can use transferable skills to develop their portfolios in the PQ framework, while those who are new to portfolio construction may struggle with inculcating and implementing the language of the portfolio and the requisite linguistic and literary skills required to describe and evidence their practice.

There is a deficit in the literature on the theoretical underpinnings of assessing portfolios. However, drawing from experience, my view is that assessment of the portfolio is a complex and sometimes contentious task. This can be resolved by the involvement of both assessees and assessors in clarification of what is required while encouraging diversity, innovation and individuality in the compilation of the portfolio.

Conclusion

This chapter provides a brief overview of the main issues in the compilation of a portfolio, in the context of the PQ awards in social work. There are many different uses of portfolios and the limited amount of research is enthusiastic about their potential as a teaching and learning tool. Recently, more mention has been made of the 'e-portfolio' (Montgomery and Wiley 2004) and no doubt this will emerge as a growth area in social work. The new PQ awards will be based in universities, with evidence of competence in Specialist and Higher specialist practice forming a strong component of the award. Coleman *et al.* (2002) are hopeful that, as portfolios in social work are used more extensively, 'portfolios and critical thinking will emerge as partners in education to allow students to become competent social workers' (p.593). Portfolios will doubtless remain as a method of evaluating and assessing practice competence on courses and modules, but further work is needed to address the problems and benefits of their use in social work education, particularly in the PQ arena.

Recommended reading

Boud, D. (1995) *Enhancing Learning Through Self.* London: Kogan Page.

Cournoyer, B. and Stanley, M. (2002) *The Social Work Portfolio: Planning, Assessing and Documenting Lifelong Learning in a Dynamic Profession.* Columbia: OPOE-ABE Books.

General Social Care Council (2005) *Post-Qualifying Framework for Social Work Education and Training.* London: GSCC.

Hull, R., Redfern, L. and Shuttleworth, A. (2004) *Profiles and Portfolios: A Guide for Health and Social Care.* London: Palgrave Macmillan.

Pearce, R. and Smojkis, M. (2003) *Profiles and Portfolios of Evidence.* London: Nelson Thorne.

Afterword

The UK Government has set out a strategy for all to have a commitment to life-long learning – a strategy that is unlikely to change regardless of the country in the UK in which you practise. This need for lifelong learning is greatest in the professions, and that is especially so in social work. Here the public, and especially people who use services and carers, demand changes and improvements all the time. There will therefore always be changes in the available resources and approaches, and social workers will have to possess the skills and knowledge to continually adapt. The social work profession has thankfully moved beyond the 'minimum standard to be a qualifying social worker' as set out by CCETSW in the former Diploma of Social Work (DipSW), and by expecting more of ourselves individually and collectively we must surely contribute to our status and our confidence as a profession.

If you have used this book effectively, and you have been provided with some support, as well as your own motivation for post-registration training and post-qualifying training, then you will find yourself more confidently on the road to a post-qualifying award. As Robert Adams said at the outset: 'the most promising and exciting aspect' of the post-qualifying agenda for practice is that it is 'contested, provisional and incomplete', which 'maximises the potential for creative practice in the future'.

Supporting Roles in PQ
Geoff Owens

Managers of PQ candidates

Change is a reality that has to be addressed in all aspects of the management of social work services. Service structures change, patterns of employment change, the demographic profile of users of services changes and the evidence base for effective social work practice changes.

In such a context the best managers recognise the importance of ensuring the continuing professional development (CPD) of their workforce.

As service structures change and teams become increasingly multi-disciplinary, the inter-professional learning that the new PQ framework emphasises will be increasingly valued. Developing links between the post-qualification frameworks of different professional groups will enable inter-professional learning that leads to further qualifications and a more skilled and knowledgeable workforce. Awards in leadership and management and practice education will be at least as relevant to managers as they are to practitioners (and will contribute to performance indicators for local authority employers).

As employment patterns change, recruitment and retention difficulties will become an increasingly significant concern in social work services and are known to have a major impact on the quality of service provision and to create low morale. In a competitive employment market, potential employees are likely to be attracted by opportunities for professional development and the achievement of further qualifications.

A key principle of the new PQ awards is that they are responsive to employers' needs. This can work only if employers can define the development needs of their workforce. Good workforce planning is part of the answer to this dilemma. It is often the case that workforce information is limited, that such information that does exist is insufficiently analysed and that such analysis is rarely used as a planning tool.

Forward-thinking managers will know the shape of their workforce and how it is changing and developing. They will plan workloads in line with this knowledge and ensure that roles and tasks in teams are appropriately allocated. It is only through such planned processes that reflection and study time are likely to be achievable in a way that is helpful to PQ candidates.

A further reason for managers to facilitate the achievement of PQ awards is that they are a measurable indicator of a commitment to continuing professional development and the creation of 'learning organisations'. It will be increasingly recognised by regulatory and inspectoral bodies that the quality of service provision is improved where CPD is a recognised and supported part of organisations' functioning.

Workforce development staff

Workforce development staff have a number of key roles to play in achieving the aims of the new PQ framework. These include: planning and resourcing participation in the awards; ensuring that workforce development needs are reflected in the awards; ensuring that there is appropriate support for candidates; and facilitating evaluation of the impact of the awards.

Ensuring access to the new awards in a context of limited resources will be an important role for employees in workforce development. This will require planning on the basis of good workforce information, arguing for resources and promoting the benefits of the awards.

Employees in workforce development often provide the interface between programme providers and the strategic managers of their organisations. This is a vital role if the intention of making the new PQ framework responsive to employers' needs is to be achieved. Strong links between operational services and workforce development are essential for this.

There is clear evidence that award achievement rates are improved when candidates feel well supported. In this context support may include the provision of study time, reduced caseload, line manager support, and rewards for achievement (financial rewards, career advancement, etc.). Employees in workforce development should be arguing for the inclusion of such elements in the human resources policies of their organisation.

The *raison d'être* of the new PQ framework is to improve standards of practice. It is this that needs to be measured in order to determine the success of the awards. In the same way that workforce development staff can provide an interface between service managers and universities in planning the awards, they can play the same role in relation to evaluating their impact. Here again workforce development staff will be well aware of how PQ (and practice learning too) contributes significantly to performance indicators.

Mentors of PQ candidates

Mentoring is an increasingly common activity in a range of learning situations. Mentors are defined as guides and supporters through learning and development processes.

Research into the experience of PQ candidates found that mentors were a highly valued source of support in helping candidates find their way through the process of providing evidence that award requirements have been met.

Anyone who has ever completed a portfolio of evidence for an award will remember the difficulties they faced when first addressing that task. They will also remember that this did become a manageable task because the principles, concepts and language eventually made sense.

In the new PQ awards all candidates will be required to provide evidence of their practice in relation to a set of learning outcomes and occupational standards. Good mentors will understand how this process works and what the requirements are.

In essence, the mentor's tasks are to assist the candidate to plan, to guide their work and development, and to provide helpful feedback.

More specifically, the mentor will assist the candidate to identify and make best use of appropriate learning opportunities, support the candidate in taking responsibility for their own learning and advise the candidate on structuring their evidence in line with award requirements.

In carrying out this role, mentors will be contributing to colleagues achieving an award, but will also learn a great deal themselves as they reflect on practice with staff undertaking PQ – often, perhaps, from a slightly different part of the organisation.

Assessors of PQ candidates

The GSCC's requirements for the new PQ framework state that:

- all programmes must ensure that they draw on direct evidence of practice competence in addition to any other types of evidence that might be considered necessary
- all programmes must draw on a range of evidence, including evidence drawn from the workplace

- all programmes must demonstrate that the assessment strategy is based on a partnership between higher education institutions and employers.

The whole purpose of the new PQ framework is to improve the quality of social work practice, so it is vital that practice assessment is part of the awards. However, though the GSCC has set the general requirements, each university may have slightly different approaches to the assessment process and documentation. Some training and support should be available when questions can be answered. The key principles of assessing practice are, however, as follows.

- *Validity:* is the evidence of practice being assessed able to be validated as the practice of the candidate? This is likely to require some witness testimony (from a colleague or someone who uses services) and/or some direct observation of practice (by the assessor or a reliable observer).

- *Reliability:* assessment judgements are agreed and can be seen to be consistent and made against common standards.

- *Sufficiency:* is there sufficient quality, quantity, range and level of evidence of practice at an appropriate standard?

- *Authenticity:* is the evidence presented a true representation of the candidate's practice? This needs to be verified – probably by a manager of the service in which the candidate works.

- *Currency:* is the evidence current? Does it reflect how the candidate practices now? If the evidence is dated then it may be that further work is required to demonstrate that standards of practice have been maintained.

It should be remembered that assessment is part of a learning process. In particular the feedback given by assessors to candidates can be a helpful part of a learning process. In order for this to be true it is important that feedback is given in a helpful manner. The following are some issues to consider.

- Feedback should be targeted to enhancing learning rather than being heavily judgemental.

- Feedback should take account of the feelings of the candidate – who will have put a good deal of time and effort into producing their evidence.

- Feedback should always include positive comments.

- Feedback should include sufficient detail to ensure that the candidate can understand clearly what they have done well and what they have not done so well – and thus to understand and learn what they need to do differently.

- Feedback should be realistic – there is no sense in asking candidates to do things they are unable to do due to factors beyond their own control.

- Feedback should be honest – if there are serious problems the candidate needs to know what they are; difficult issues should not be avoided.

- Feedback should be specific – it should directly refer to the relevant assessment criteria and learning outcomes.

The new PQ framework provides opportunities to develop skills in practice assessment and mentoring, and to have those skills assessed and gain credits towards awards. At the Specialist PQ level all programmes will include a 'practice education' module and at the Higher Specialist PQ level there will be a whole award focused on practice education. In essence, mentoring and assessing will assist in one's own professional development.

Useful Websites

Here is a selection of some of the many useful websites available. If you follow up those you find relevant, you will find further links that apply to your country and area of interest.

Sector Skills Councils, and education and training

General Social Care Council
http://www.gscc.org.uk/

Skills for Care
http://www.skillsforcare.org.uk/

Children's Workforce Development Council
http://www.cwdcouncil.org.uk/

Northern Ireland Social Care Council
http://www.niscc.info/

Scottish Social Services Council
http://www.sssc.uk.com/

Care Council of Wales
http://www.ccwales.org.uk/

Research and information resources

Social Care Institute for Excellence
http://www.scie.org.uk/

Social Care Online (this free service provides ready access to the UK's most complete range of research and information on all aspects of social work and social care)
www.scie-socialcareonline.org.uk/

Barnardo's (major children's charity)
http://www.barnardos.org.uk/resources.htm

Commission for Social Care Inspection
http://www.csci.org.uk/

Help the Aged (major national charity – research into ageing)
http://research.helptheaged.org.uk/_research/default.htm

Joseph Rowntree Foundation (seeking solutions to social problems)
http://www.jrf.org.uk/

National Centre for Social Research
http://www.natcen.ac.uk/index.html

NSPCC (major childrens' charity)
http://www.nspcc.org.uk/helpandadvice/professionals/professionals_wda33449.html

SWAP (social policy and social work subject centre of the Higher Education Academy)
http://www.swap.ac.uk/

Why Employers Should Engage with the Revised PQ Framework
Amanda Hatton

The Options for Excellence: Building the Social Care Workforce of the Future (DfES/ DoH 2006) is a ministerial review report that makes it clear that 80 per cent of expenditure in social care is on the workforce and therefore 'the service provided *is* the workforce, and the relationships workers build with service users and carers are essential' (p.13, 3.18). In order to deliver excellent services in a changing context the workforce needs to be appropriately skilled and qualified, and central to maintaining and developing such skills and knowledge is a good-quality continuing professional development (CPD) system. As a Sector Skills Council, Skills for Care is working with its equivalent, the Children's Workforce Development Council (CWDC), the GSCC and partners, to produce a CPD strategy and framework for the social (work) care sector. The resultant products are designed to help people implement best practice in the CPD of workers within their own organisations, and to enable registered social care workers to meet the Post Registration Teaching and Learning (PRTL) requirement of the GSCC, applicable to their post. They are also designed to enable all those working in social care to reach their full potential and support flexible career pathways leading to a range of opportunities sector-wide.

The Skills for Care Chief Executive Officer, Andrea Rowe, states that:

> People who use social care services have often told us that their care is only as good as the person delivering it. The new CPD strategy aims to move organisations towards a learning culture, where the workforce develops the right human qualities alongside their qualifications. Skills for Care clearly sets out the necessary standards of skills and qualifications to

enable social care workers to develop their roles and keep their practice up to date. A workforce that is well trained and motivated, with appropriate values and behaviours, is crucial to delivering quality social care services in a changing environment.

The strategy also draws on research which demonstrates that good CPD opportunities support better recruitment and retention and, in turn, better services. As part of the CPD programme, Skills for Care is supporting the development of employer-led planning networks to work with universities to develop the number and type of PQ programmes that they need for their workforce for the new PQ framework for social workers.

In order to support employers, Skills for Care, the CWDC and the GSCC have developed an employers PQ guide (see http://www.skillsforcare.org.uk/view.asp?id=854), which includes:

- a business case for PQ
- support with workforce development planning
- inspection drivers
- learning from the current system
- good practice for the involvement of people who use services
- candidates' experiences of PQ study.

The guide is supported by a DVD, which includes candidate experience of PQ and includes candidates talking about how PQ has supported them to feel more confident in working with people who use services and colleagues in a multi-agency setting, more able to support staff that they manage, and to have a more relevant knowledge base.

Post-Qualifying Education and Training for Social Workers

	England	Northern Ireland	Scotland	Wales
Governance	Care Standards Act 2000 Rules: GSCC approval of post-qualifying courses, November 2005	Health and Personal Social Services Act (Northern Ireland) 2001 Rules: Rules for the Approval of PQ Education and Training in Social Work in NI	Regulation of Care (Scotland) Act 2001 Rules/Guidance: all new approved courses will fall under Rules and Requirements for Specialist Training for Social Service Workers in Scotland 2005 The SSSC has developed rules for specialist training courses. The first course to be approved under these Rules will be the Practice Learning Qualification (Social Services)	Care Standards Act 2000 Rules: CCW Council approval in July 2006 (awaiting Welsh Assembly approval) Further development of 'Specified Named Course Requirements' Post-Qualifying Social Work award in mental health (approved social worker) agreed in November 2006
What is the new provision for PQ social work training?	Key document outlining the framework: Post-qualifying framework for social work education and training – February 2005	Northern Ireland Post-Qualifying Education and Training Framework in Social Work 2006	SSSC is introducing a continuum of professional development model, within which social work post-qualifying education can be approved Advanced standards are currently being developed	A 'Modular Framework for PQ Learning and Development in Social Work' agreed by CCW in March 2005

Continued on next page

	England	Northern Ireland	Scotland	Wales
Links to Post-Registration Training and Learning (PRTL)?	At the point of renewing registration, individual registrants are required to produce evidence of post-registration learning achieved. The requirement is 90 hours or 15 days and guidance on this is available on the GSCC website. Learning gained through PQ awards provides positive evidence of PRTL PQ awards are not a specific requirement for PRTL	By 2010, career structures in social work and social care will be linked to agreed accredited training and/or qualifications linked to continuing registration (PSS Development and Training Strategy 2006–2016)	All post-qualification learning and development will be relevant to PRTL. Registered social workers are required to complete 15 days over the three-year period of registration. Five days must focus on working effectively with colleagues and other professionals to identify, assess and manage risk to vulnerable people. Primary responsibility of social workers, e.g. risk assessment interviewing in a suitable manner All newly qualified social workers from summer 2006 will be required to complete 24 days or 144 hours within the first 12 months from date of registration. Re-registration on or before 14-month anniversary	PRTL – and other links under ongoing review – proposal to link to induction. However, it is not expected that PRTL requirements will form part of the new PQ framework

How will training be commissioned?	Skills for Care and the Children's Workforce Development Council are developing employer-driven partnerships with universities, set up as Regional Planning Networks. Arrangements to meet the needs of national organisations are being developed	NI PSS Development and Training Strategy has set priorities. Employers and Higher Education Institutes (HEIs) will develop programmes to meet priorities. Commissioning will move to Regional authority under the Review of Public Administration (RPA)	Any future training will be placed within the Rules and Requirements. Any commissioning process would be agreed in consultation with the Scottish Executive The Sector Skills Agreement and the process re-skills gaps should enhance the potential for employers to commission what they feel are the gaps outwith those courses that the SSSC might approve	Employers in partnership with HEIs will commission, develop and provide training
What closing date has been set for closure of existing arrangements?	31 March 2007 – final registrations with award programmes for all current awards 27 September 2008 – final date for registering awards achievement with the GSCC	Registrations will stop on 31 March 2007, except for PQ1 which will continue for another year. The final date for awards is 30 September 2010	March 2008 No new registration from June 2005	December 2009

Continued on next page

	England	Northern Ireland	Scotland	Wales
Will PQ consortia continue to operate after this date?	No consortia or award programmes will continue after September 2008. It is envisaged that business will cease for many before this date. Action plans to be produced to reflect QA activity after 31 January 2008	Yes. See below	No	No
What form do the new arrangements take?	HEI in partnership with employers and stakeholders through Regional Planning Networks. GSCC approves HEIs to offer awards, sets specialist standards and approves courses that meet the requirements. GSCC annual monitoring and review system is a requirement	NISCC will be the awarding body and the NI PQ Education and Training Partnership (NIPQETP) will determine and manage the PQ arrangements	Employer led, continuum of professional developments. New specialist training courses may be delivered through the Learning Networks. These may become a conduit for provision	Employers in partnership with HEI, programmes approved by CCW

What academic level has been set?	3 levels: PQ Award in Specialist Social Work (Hons degree/Graduate Diploma (H level)); Higher Specialist and Advanced Award Programmes (Post- Graduate Diploma (M level)); PQ Award in Advanced SW Minimum Level (M level – Master's)	The entire framework is at M level. There will be opportunities for both academic and professional awards	Specialist training will be available from SCQF 7– 11 (M level). The SCQF 7 – 11 is relevant to the PL (SS). The levelling of the new MHSWA has still to be determined	Level 6 (Graduate Certificate, Graduate Diploma) and Level 7 Post-Grad Diploma (Equates to H and M levels of England, Wales and Northern Ireland Framework for Higher Education Qualifications – FHEQ)
Is there a module that provides for consolidation of practice?	Yes. Consolidation must be demonstrated against generic and specific award requirements at Specialist Social Work Award level, as a first module	No. This should be covered during the Assessed Year in Employment (AYE) before candidates enter the NI PQ Framework.	No. All courses that are approved under the Rules will need to ensure that all candidates will be assessed in practice in such a way as to demonstrate that they are able to carry out the following to the required level Contribute to the learning and development of others and work in a way that actively promotes and values diversity	Guidance is being produced on first year in employment for both social workers and employers (the latter to be inspected by the Social Services Inspectorate) There is still discussion on entry requirments for some programmes such as approved mental health programmes

Continued on next page

	England	Northern Ireland	Scotland	Wales
Can other social service/care and professional groups access the framework?	Yes. Access is a key principle and modular basis widens access to learning and academic achievement but not to a professional award in social work. IPE is a key principle and joint-courses are likely to take place between professional groups	Enrolment for a PQ award will be restricted to registered social workers. There will be arrangements for the accreditation of multi-disciplinary programmes so the social workers attending those programmes can obtain a PQ award	Any new specialist training courses will encourage access by other social service workers, e.g. the MHSWA will allow modular access for those not pursuing the full award. In the new Practice Learning Qualifications the rules allow for access by other professionals, although the award that they receive will have a different title. This is due to the legislation only allowing the SSSC to approve courses for social service workers who are either registered or for whom the register is open	Yes. This will be encouraged, but the Council will not be approving courses other than for qualified social workers
AP(E)L – Accreditation of Prior (Experience) Learning	Creative and flexible use of AP(E)L is encouraged to promote relevance to practice contexts and access. All current GSCC awards and PQ1 certificates must be fully recognised. PQSW is equivalent to new specialist award for progression to higher level awards	AP(E)L will be an essential element of the NI PQ framework. Guidance has been developed by the PQ Partnership.	As above, the SSSC has no plans to develop a new PQ framework. In Scotland any new developments under the Rules will need to fit within SCQF and also needs to include RPL (Recognition of Prior Learning)	Required by Rules for approval. Link to Credit and Qualification Framework for Wales

What standards will awards be based on?	UK National Occupational Standards for Social Work, Codes of Practice, QAA guidance, nationally agreed standards for specialist areas and specialist standards produced by the GSCC for Practice Education, Mental Health, Adult Social Care, Children, Young People, their Families and Carers, and for Leadership and Management	The NI PQ framework has requirements that must be met for three professional awards. There will be requirements for accreditation of training provision and Standards for the Approval of the PQ Partnership. The rules allow for other standards to be developed	As previously mentioned generic advanced standards are currently being developed. For SSSC-approved awards specialist standards will be written	Generic Rules and Specified Named Course Requirements, National Occupational Standards for Social Work and the Codes of Practice for social care workers
How will UK agreed national occupational standards be used?	NOS for social work underpin learning outcomes and course curriculum building	There is a requirement to develop competence to agreed national, occupational or recognised agency standards	SiSWE based on the NOS form the basis of the social work degree. Reference to NOS will be made where appropriate when approving new specialist training courses	Rules will require indication of which NOS are relevant at modular level

Continued on next page

	England	Northern Ireland	Scotland	Wales
Arrangements for practice assessment?	Assessment must always be based on actual practice. Registered social workers must be part of the overall assessment. GSCC Code of Practice, relevant specialist standards and 'Guidance on the assessment of practice in the workplace' are vital to practice assessment	Practice assessors will be trained to assess at M level	This will be dependent on the course that is being undertaken. We would expect all provision to have a strong emphasis on assessment of practice	Rules will require a statement showing how assessment is relevant to practice modules
Practice education	Practice education and enabling others is integral to the framework and must be demonstrated at all levels of the award	The Practice Teacher Award is being reconfigured to meet the requirements of the NISCC Practice Learning Standards 2006, and the NI PQ Framework		Consultation in autumn 2006
External examiners	PQ programmes must appoint at least one external examiner who has a GSCC-recognised social work qualification. Annual QA monitoring will include scrutiny of external examiners' reports and HEI actions on their recommendations	The External Assessment Model will continue to apply. The PQ Partnership will set criteria for external assessors	As identified in the Rules and Requirements Examiners acceptable to the SSSC will be professionally qualified and have expertise and experience relevant to the course provision	Required as part of HEI and QAA requirements. QA will replicate the requirements established for the social work degree

Making PQ courses relevant – user involvement	integral to regional planning networks, programme design and delivery including teaching, assessment and course planning	Broad statement included in Rules. NISCC accreditation requirements will ensure all programmes include all stakeholders appropriately	All relevant stakeholders will be involved in the design, delivery and evaluation of course provision. The role of service users is particularly important and this can be evidenced in the design of the PLQ that has been structured to enable access and achievement by users of services and carers	Required by Rules
End of course recording – transcripts	Students must be given annual transcripts of learning, and for each module completed. On leaving a programme all students must be provided with a full transcript identifying modules passed and credit acquired. Learning is certified by means of transcripts, essential for mobile workforce	Transcripts will be an important element of the framework. They will record all accredited learning. New database being developed will enable transcripts to be issued	In respect of the Practice Learning Qualification this will be supplied by the provider	Candidates' Learning Plan required at beginning of courses and required at both modular and end of course levels

Continued on next page

	England	Northern Ireland	Scotland	Wales
International recognition of social work qualifications and PQ	The PQ framework is for all registered social workers including holders of SW qualifications gained overseas	IRS equivalency issues will have been considered at the registration stage	Needs to recognise the statutory differences while taking this into account for e.g. MHSWA. IRS equivalency issues will have been considered at the registration stage. Anyone registering for a course approved by the SSSC either needs to be registered or currently eligible for registration in terms of the Regulation of Care (Scotland) Act 2001, section 44	Anyone enrolling for a PQ award must be registered with the Council
Review and redefinition of social work	The government 'Options for Excellence' reported in October 2006, and involves a GSCC-led review of the roles and tasks of social workers – out for consultation in spring 2007	There has been a review of public administration and the Board/Trust structure will be changed fundamentally in 2007. Social workers in HSS Trusts are included in the Agenda for Change and the Knowledge and Skills Framework will apply. PSS Development and Training Strategy 2006–2016 is a key document for social work education and training	The Scottish Executive Changing Lives: Report of the 21st Century Social Work Review identifies future direction under five change programmes: • Performance Improvement • Service Redesign • Practice Governance • Leadership • Workforce Development	Welsh Assembly Government ten-year strategy for social services: 'Fulfilled Lives: Supportive Communities'

Source: Post-Qualifing Education and Training for Social Workers UK Matrix – February 2007 (Education Standards and Information Team, GSCC)

Contacts for PQ in the care councils are:

Bryan Healy
Scottish Social Services Council
email: Bryan.Healy@sssc.uk.com

Ian Thomas
Care Council for Wales
email: ian.thomas@ccwales.org.uk

Alison Kavanagh
Northern Ireland Social Care Council
email: alison.kavanagh@niscc.n-i.nhs.uk

Cyndy Whiffin
General Social Care Council
email: cyndy.whiffin@gscc.org.uk

Cathrine Clarke
General Social Care Council
email: cathrine.clarke@gscc.org.uk

References

Abbott, D. and Howarth, J. (2005) *Secret Loves, Hidden Lives: Exploring Issues for People with Learning Difficulties who are Gay*. Bristol: Policy Press.

Adams, R. (1990) *Self-Help, Social Work and Empowerment*. Basingstoke: BASW/Macmillan.

Adams, R. (1996) *Social Work and Empowerment* (3rd edn). Basingstoke: BASW/Macmillan.

Adams, R. (2006) Personal communication with author.

Adams, R. and Tovey, W. (2007) 'Involving Carers and People Using Services.' In R. Adams (ed.) *Foundations of Health and Social Care*. Basingstoke: Palgrave.

Adams, R., Dixon, G., Henderson, T. Linighan, L. and Tovey, W. (2005) *A Strategy for Bringing About Participation by Service Users in the Work of Skills for Care*. Middlesbrough: University of Teesside.

Adams, R., Dixon, G., Henderson, T., Linighan, L. and Tovey, W. (2006) *A Strategy for Bringing About Participation by Carers in the Work of Skills for Care*. Middlesbrough: University of Teesside.

Adams, R. Dominelli, L. and Payne, M. (eds) (2006b) Critical Practice in Social Work. Basingstoke: Palgrave Macmillan.

Adams, R., Dominelli, L. and Payne, M. (2002a) *Critical Practice in Health and Social Care*. Basingstoke: Palgrave.

Adams, R., Dominelli, L. and Payne, M. (2002b) *Social Work: Themes, Issues and Critical Debates*. Basingstoke: Palgrave.

Adams, R., Dominelli, L. and Payne, M. (2005) 'Engaging with Social Work Futures.' In R. Adams, L. Dominelli and M. and Payne (eds) *Social Work Futures*. Basingstoke: Palgrave Macmillan.

Adzema, M. (1998) 'The emerging perinatal unconscious: consciousness evolution or apocalypse?' *Journal of Psychohistory 25*, 3, 262–273.

Alberg, C., Hatfield, B. and Huxley, P. (1996) *Risk Assessment*. Manchester: University of Manchester.

Allen, J.D. (2003) *Gay, Lesbian, Bisexual and Transgender People with Developmental Disabilities and Mental Retardation*. London: Harrington Park Press.

Allen, R. (2006) 'The Context of Mental Health Social Work in 2006.' Paper given at the New Visions for Mental Health Social Work Conference, Hertfordshire Partnership NHS Mental Health Trust and the University of Hertfordshire.

Arnstein, S. (1969) 'A ladder of citizen participation.' *Journal of the American Institute of Planners 35*, 4, 216–224.

Ashford, M. (2004) *Bologna Declaration 1999*. Available at http://www.swap.ac.uk/quality/bologna.asp (accessed 29 December 2006).

Askeland, G.A. and Payne, M. (2001) 'Broadening the mind: cross-national activities in social work.' *European Journal of Social Work 4*, 3, 263–274.

Association of Directors of Social Services Safeguarding Adults Network (2005) *Safeguarding Adults: A National Framework of Standards for Good Practice and Outcomes in Adult Protection Work*. London:

ADSS. Avilable on http://www.adss.org.uk/publications/guidance/safeguarding.pdf (accessed 11 July 2007).

Association of Social Work Boards (ASWB) (2006) Available at http://www.aswb.org/ (accessed 29 December 2006).

Audit Commission (2004) *Youth Justice 2004: A Review of the Reformed Youth 'Justice System'*. London: The Stationery Office.

Bailey, R. and Brake, M. (eds) (1975) *Radical Social Work*. London: Edward Arnold.

Baker, K., Jones, S., Merrington, S. and Roberts, C. (2005) *Further Development of Asset*. London: Youth Justice Board for England and Wales.

Balloch, S., McLean, J. and Fisher, M. (1999) *Social Services: Working Under Pressure*. Bristol: Policy Press.

Bandura, A. (1994) *Self-Efficacy*. Available at http://www.des.emory.edu/mfp/BanEncy.html (accessed 6 June 2006).

Banks, S. (1995) *Ethics and Values in Social Work* (1st edn). Basingstoke: Palgrave Macmillan.

Banks, S. (2001) *Ethics and Values in Social Work* (2nd edn). Basingstoke: Palgrave Macmillan.

Banks, S. (2006) *Ethics and Values in Social Work* (3rd edn). Basingstoke: Palgrave Macmillan.

Barnes, J. (2002) *Focus on the Future. Key Messages from Focus Groups about the Future of Social Work Training*. London: Department of Health.

Barnes, M. and Bowl, R. (2001) *Taking Over the Asylum: Empowerment and Mental Health*. Basingstoke: Palgrave.

Barnett, R. (1990) *The Idea of Higher Education*. Buckingham: Open University Press.

Barnett, R. (1994) *The Limits of Competence*. Buckingham: Open University Press.

Baron, M. (1994) *Thinking and Deciding*. Cambridge: Cambridge University Press.

Barrett, G., Sellman, D. and Thomas, J. (eds) (2005) *Interprofessional Working in Health and Social Care: Professional Perspectives*. Basingstoke: Palgrave Macmillan.

Barrowclough, C., Tarrier, N., Lewis, S., Sellwood, W., Mainwaring, J., Quinn, J. and Hamlin, C. (1999) 'Randomised controlled effectiveness trial of a needs-based psychosocial intervention service for carers of people with schizophrenia.' *British Journal of Psychiatry 174*, 6, 505–511.

Baume, D. (2001) *A Briefing on Assessment of Portfolios*. Assessment Series, No. 6. York: LTSN.

Baume, D. and Yorke, M. (2002) 'The reliability of assessment by portfolio on a course to develop and accredit teachers in higher education.' *Studies in Higher Education 27*, 7–25.

Bean, P. (2001) *Mental Disorder and Community Safety*. Basingstoke: Palgrave.

Beaty, L., Gibbs, G. and Morgan, A. (1997) 'Learning Orientations and Study Contracts.' In F. Marton, D. Hounsell and N. Entwistle (eds) *The Experience of Learning: Implications for Teaching and Studying in Higher Education* (3rd (Internet) edn). Edinburgh: University of Edinburgh, Centre for Teaching, Learning and Assessment, 72–86.

Beckett, C. and Maynard, A. (2005) *Values and Ethics in Social Work: An Introduction*. London: Sage.

Bellamy, J.L., Bledsoe, S.E. and Traube, D.E. (2006) 'The current state of evidence-based practice in social work: a review of the literature and qualitative analysis of expert interviews.' *Journal of Evidence-Based Social Work 3*, 1, 23–48.

Benson, B. (2005) *Student Led Conferencing Using Showcase Portfolios*. New York: Corwin Press.

Beresford, P. (2001) 'Service users, social policy and the future of welfare.' *Critical Social Policy 21*, 4, 494–512.

Beresford, P. and Croft, S. (1993) *Citizen Involvement: A Practical Guide for Change*. Basingstoke: Macmillan.

Berger, R. (2002) 'Teaching research in practice courses.' *Social Work Education 21*, 3, 347–358.

Bilson, A. and Ross, S. (1999) *Social Work Management and Practice: Systems Principles* (2nd edn). London: Jessica Kingsley Publishers.

Blom-Cooper, L. (1985) *A Child in Trust: The Report of the Panel of Inquiry into the Circumstances Surrounding the Death of Jasmine Beckford*. London: London Borough of Brent.

Bolton, G. (2005) *Reflective Practice: Writing and Professional Development.* London: Sage.

Boud, D. (1995) *Enhancing Learning Through Self Assessment.* London: Routledge.

Bowles, W., Collingridge, M., Curry, S. and Valentine, B. (2006) *Ethical Practice in Social Work: An Applied Approach.* Maidenhead: Open University Press/McGraw-Hill Education.

Braye, S. and Preston-Shoot, M. (2005) 'Emerging from out of the shadows? Service user and carer involvement in systematic reviews.' *Evidence and Policy 1,* 2, 173–193.

Braye, S., Preston-Shoot, M. and Thorpe, A. (2006) *Social Work Law in Practice. A Research Project to Explore Social Work Students' Law Learning on Practice Placement.* Southampton: SWAP (Social Work and Social Policy Subject Centre).

British Association of Social Workers (BASW) (2003) *The Social Work Contribution to Mental Health Social Work.* Birmingham: BASW.

Brookes, I., Munroe, M., O'Donaghue, E., O'Neill, M. and Thompson, M. (eds) (2004) *Chambers Concise Dictionary.* Edinburgh: Chambers Harrap Publishers Ltd.

Brookfield, S. (1987) *Developing Critical Thinkers.* Buckingham: Open University Press.

Brown, H.C. (1998) *Social Work and Sexuality: Working with Lesbians and Gay Men.* Basingstoke: Macmillan.

Brown, K. and Rutter, L. (2006) *Critical Thinking for Social Work.* Exeter: Learning Matters.

Brownlee, K., Sprakes, A., Saini, M., O'Hare, R., Kortes-Miller, K. and Graham, J. (2005) 'Heterosexism among social work students.' *Social Work Education 24,* 5, 485–494.

Bruenlin, D. and Schwartz, R. (1983) 'Why clinicians should bother with research.' *The Family Therapy Networker 7,* 22–27, 57–59.

Buckley, K. and Head, P. (2000) *Myths, Risks and Sexuality: The Role of Sexuality in Working with Young People.* Lyme Regis: Russell House.

Burgess, A. and Ruxton, S. (1997) *Men and Their Children: Proposals for Public Policy.* London: Institute for Public Policy Research.

Burgess, R., Healey, J., Holman, J., Hyde, P., McBride, S., Milburn, H., Millican, K., Nnaji, J., Prest, P., Spence, J., Stainsby, P., Trotter, J. and Turner, K. (1997) 'Guilty by association: challenging assumptions and exploring values around lesbian and gay issues on a DipSW course.' *Social Work Education 16,* 3, 97–108.

Burnett, R. and Appleton, C. (2004) *Joined-Up Youth Justice: Tackling Crime in Partnership.* Lyme Regis: Russell House Publishing.

Cambridge, P. and Carnaby, S. (2005) *Person-Centred Planning and Care Management with People with Learning Disabilities.* London: Jessica Kingsley Publishers.

Camilleri, P. and Ryan, M. (2006) 'Social work students' attitudes toward homosexuality and their knowledge and attitudes toward homosexual parenting as an alternative family unit: an Australian study.' *Social Work Education 25,* 3, 288–304.

Canton, R. (2005) 'Risk Assessment and Compliance in Probation and Mental Health Practice.' In B. Littlechild and D. Fearns (eds) *Mental Disorder and Criminal Justice: Policy and Practice.* Lyme Regis: Russell House Publishing.

Care Services Improvement Partnership (CSIP) (2006) *New Ways of Working in Mental Health.* London: CSIP.

Carers UK (2007) Available at http://www.carersuk.org/ (accessed 11 July 2007).

Carpenter, J. (2005) *Evaluating Outcomes in Social Work Education.* London and Dundee: Social Care Institute for Excellence and Scottish Institute for Excellence in Social Work Education.

Carr, S. (2004) *Has Service User Participation Made a Difference to Social Care Services?* Position Paper Number 3. London: Social Care Institute for Excellence.

CCETSW (1995) *Paper 30: Assuring Quality in The Diploma in Social Work.* London: CCETSW.

CCETSW (1998) *Assuring Quality for Practice Teaching.* London: CCETSW.

Chapman, T. and Hough, M. (1998) *Evidence Based Practice: A Guide to Effective Practice.* London: HM Inspectorate of Probation/Home Office.

Cheetham, J. (1992) 'Evaluating social work effectiveness.' *Research on Social Work Practice 2*, 3, 265–287.

Ciro, D., Surko, M., Bhandarkar, K., Helfgott, N., Peake, K. and Epstein, I. (2005) 'Lesbian, gay, bisexual, sexual-orientation questioning adolescents seeking mental health services: risk factors, worries and desire to talk about them.' *Social Work in Mental Health 3*, 3, 213–234.

Clark, C. (2000) *Social Work Ethics: Politics, Principles and Practice.* London: Macmillan.

Cleaver, H. and Walker, S. with Meadows, P. (2004) *Assessing Children's Needs and Circumstances: The Impact of the Assessment Framework.* London: Jessica Kingsley Publishers.

Coleman, H., Rogers, G. and King, J. (2002) 'Using portfolios to stimulate critical thinking in social work education.' *Social Work Education 21*, 5, 583–595.

Commission for Social Care Inspection (CSCI) (2006a) *The State of Social Care in England 2005–06.* London: CSCI.

Commission for Social Care Inspection (CSCI) (2006b) *Time to Care? An Overview of Home Care Services for Older People in England, 2006.* London: CSCI.

Connolly, M., Crichton-Hill, Y. and Ward, T. (2006) *Culture and Child Protection: Reflexive Responses.* London: Jessica Kingsley Publishers.

Cooper, A. and Lousada, J. (2005) *Borderline Welfare: Feeling and Fear of Feeling in Modern Welfare.* London: Karnac.

Corby, B., Millar, M. and Pope, A. (2002) 'Assessing children in need assessments – a parental perspective.' *Practice 14*, 4, 5–15.

Corcoran, J. (2000) 'Family interventions with child physical abuse and neglect: a critical review.' *Children and Youth Services Review 22*, 7, July, 563–591.

Coulshed, V. (1991) *Social Work Practice, An Introduction.* London: Macmillan Education.

Coulshed, V. and Orme, J. (1998) *Social Work Practice, An Introduction.* Basingstoke: Macmillan.

Coulshed, V. and Orme, J. (2006) *Social Work Practice* (4th edn). Basingstoke: Palgrave Macmillan.

Cowan, K. and Valentine, G. (2006) *Tuned Out: The BBC's Portrayal of Lesbian and Gay People.* London: Stonewall.

Cox, P. and Hardwick, L. (2002) 'Research and critical theory: their contribution to social work education and practice.' *Social Work Education 21*, 1, 35–47.

Crawshaw, M. and Wates, M. (2005) 'Mind the gap: a case study for changing organisational responses to disabled parents and their families using evidence based practice.' *Research Policy and Planning 23*, 2, 111–122.

CSWE (2006) *CSWE Online.* Available at http://www.cswe.org/ (accessed 29 December 2006).

Daniel, B. and Taylor, J. (2001) *Engaging with Fathers: Practice Issues for Health and Social Care.* London: Jessica Kingsley Publishers.

Davies, D. and Neal, C. (eds) (1996) *Pink Therapy: A Guide for Counsellors and Therapists Working with Lesbian, Gay and Bisexual Clients.* Buckingham: Open University Press.

Davies, M. (1995) *The Essential Social Worker* (3rd edn). Hampshire: Ashgate Publishing.

Davis, A. (1996) 'Risk Work and Mental Health.' In H. Kemshall and J. Pritchard (eds) *Good Practice in Risk Assessment and Risk Management.* London: Jessica Kingsley Publishers.

Department for Education and Skills (DfES) (2004) *Every Child Matters: Change for Children.* Nottingham: DfES. Accessed at www.everychildmatters.gov.uk/aims.

Department for Education and Skills (DfES) (2005) *Common Core of Skills and Knowledge for the Children's Workforce.* Nottingham: DfES.

Department for Education and Skills (DfES) (2006) *The Common Assessment Framework for Children and Young People. A Practitioner's Guide.* London: HMSO.

Department for Education and Skills (DfES)/Department of Health (DoH) (2006) *Options for Excellence: Building the Social Care Workforce of the Future.* London: HMSO.

Department of Health (DoH) (1991) *Care Management and Assessment: Practitioner's Guide.* London: HMSO.

Department of Health (DoH) (1994) 'Health service guidelines for the introduction of supervision registers.' *Health Service Guidelines 94*, 5.

Department of Health (DoH) (1998) *Modernising Social Services.* London: The Stationery Office.

Department of Health (DoH) (1999) *Effective Care Co-ordination in Mental Health Services: Modernising the Care Programme Approach.* London: HMSO.

Department of Health (DoH) (1999a) *Caring About Carers: A National Strategy for Carers.* London: The Stationery Office.

Department of Health (DoH) (1999b) *Policy Implementation Guidance: Assertive Outreach.* London: The Stationery Office.

Department of Health (DoH) (1999c) *National Service Framework for Mental Health: Modern Standards and Service Models.* London: HMSO.

Department of Health (DoH) (2000) *Framework for the Assessment of Children in Need and their Families.* London: The Stationery Office.

Department of Health (DoH) (2001a) *Continuing Care: NHS and Local Councils' Responsibilities.* HSC 2001/015, LAC (2001) 18.

Department of Health (DoH) (2001b) *National Service Framework for Mental Health.* London: HMSO.

Department of Health (DoH) (2001c) *National Service Framework for Older People.* London: HMSO.

Department of Health (DoH) (2001d) *Policy Implementation Guidance: Crisis Services.* London: HMSO.

· Department of Health (DoH) (2001e) *Policy Implementation Guidance: Early Intervention in Psychosis.* London: HMSO.

Department of Health (DoH) (2001f) *The Journey to Recovery: The Government's Vision for Mental Health Care.* London: HMSO.

Department of Health (DoH) (2001g) *Valuing People: A New Strategy for Learning Disabilities in the 21st Century.* London: HMSO.

Department of Health (DoH) (2002a) *Developing Services for Carers and Families of People with Mental Illness.* London: HMSO.

Department of Health (DoH) (2002b) *Fair Access to Care Services: Guidance on Eligibility Criteria for Adult Social Care.* LAC (2002) 13.

Department of Health (DoH) (2002c) *Mental Health Policy Implementation Guide: Community Mental Health Teams.* London: HMSO.

Department of Health (DoH) (2002d) *Mental Health Policy Implementation Guide: Dual Diagnosis Good Practice Guide.* London: HMSO.

Department of Health (DoH) (2002e) *The Requirements for Social Work Training.* London: DoH.

Department of Health (DoH) (2003a) *Inside Outside: Improving Mental Health Services for Black and Minority Ethnic Communities.* London. HMSO.

Department of Health (DoH) (2003b) *Women's Mental Health into the Mainstream.* London: HMSO.

Department of Health (DoH) (2004a) *Children Act.* London: HMSO.

Department of Health (DoH) (2004b) *Implementation Plan for Research Governance in Social Care.* London: DoH.

Department of Health (DoH) (2004c) *National Service Framework for Children, Young People and Maternity Services.* London: DoH.

Department of Health (DoH) (2005a) *Carers and Disabled Children Act 2000 and Carers (Equal Opportunities) Act 2004 Combined Policy Guidance.* London: DoH/DfES.

Department of Health (DoH) (2005b) *Independence, Wellbeing and Choice: Our Vision for the Future of Social Care for Adults in England.* London: DoH.

Department of Health (DoH) (2006) *Our Health, Our Care, Our Say.* London: HMSO.

Deverell, K. (2001) *Sex, Work and Professionalism: Working in HIV/AIDS.* London: Routledge.

Dingwall, R., Eekelaar, J. and Murray, T. (1983) *The Protection of Children: State Intervention and Family Life.* Oxford: Blackwell.

Doel, M. and Shardlow, S. (1995) *Preparing Post-qualifying Portfolios.* London: CCETSW.

Doel, M., Sawdon, C. and Morrison, D. (2002) *Learning, Practice and Assessment: Signposting the Portfolio.* London: Jessica Kingsley Publishers.

Dolan, P. (2006) 'Assessment, Intervention and Self Appraisal Tools for Family Support.' In P. Dolan, J. Canavan and J. Pinkerton (eds) *Family Support as Reflective Practice.* London: Jessica Kingsley Publishers.

Dominelli, L. (2005) 'Social Work Research: Contested Knowledge for Practice.' In R. Adams, L. Dominelli and M. Payne (eds) *Social Work Futures: Crossing Boundaries, Transforming Practice.* Basingstoke: Palgrave.

Doyle, M. (1999) 'Organisational Responses to Crisis and Risk: Issues and Implications.' In T. Ryan (ed.) *Managing Crisis and Risk in Mental Health Nursing.* London: Jessica Kingsley Publishers.

Duggan, M., Cooper, A. and Foster, J. (2002) *Modernising the Social Model in Mental Health: A Discussion Paper.* Leeds: Training Organisation for the Personal Social Services.

Dunlap, K.M. (1993) 'A history of research in social work education: 1915–1991.' *Journal of Social Work Education 29,* 3, 293–301.

EASSW (2006) *About EASSW.* Available at http://docweb.khk.be/Jan%20Agten/eassw/html/about/easswEng.html (accessed 29 December 2006).

England, H. (1986) *Social Work as Art: Making Sense for Good Practice.* London: Allen and Unwin.

Entwistle, N.J. and Peterson, E.R. (2004) 'Conceptions of learning and knowledge in higher education: relationships with study behaviour and influences of learning environments.' *International Journal of Educational Research 41,* 407–428.

Epstein, I. (1987) 'Pedagogy of the perturbed: teaching research to the reluctant.' *Journal of Teaching in Social Work 1,* 1, 71–89.

Eraut, M. (1994) *Developing Professional Knowledge and Competence.* London: Routledge Falmer.

Etzioni, A. (1969) *The Semi-Professions and their Organisation: Teachers, Nurses and Social Workers.* New York: Free Press.

European Commission (2006a) *Europa – Gateway to the European Union.* Available at http://europa.eu/index_en.htm (accessed 29 December 2006).

European Commission (2006b) *ECTS – European Credit Transfer and Accumulation System.* Available at http://ec.europa.eu/education/programmes/socrates/ects/index_en.html (accessed 29 December 2006).

European Commission (2006c) *What is SOCRATES–ERASMUS?* Available at http://ec.europa.eu/education/programmes/socrates/erasmus/what_en.html (accessed 29 December 2006).

Ferguson, H. (2005) 'Working with violence, the emotions and the psycho-social dynamics of child protection: reflections on the Victoria Climbié case.' *Social Work Education 24,* 7, 781–795.

Fish, D. (1998) *Developing Professional Judgement in Health Care.* London: Butterworth Heinemann.

Fletcher, R. and Willoughby, P. (2002) *Fatherhood: Legal, Biological and Social Definitions.* Research Paper No. 1. Newcastle: Engaging Fathers Project and University of Newcastle, NSW.

Fook, J. (2002) *Social Work. Critical Theory and Practice.* London: Sage.

Freud, S. (2005) *On Murder, Mourning and Melancholia.* Harmondsworth: Penguin Books.

Gambrill, E. (2003) 'Evidence-based practice: sea change or the emperor's new clothes?' *Journal of Social Work Education 39,* 1, 3–23.

General Social Care Council (GSCC) (2001) *Social Work Education Post-Qualifying Training Handbook.* London: GSCC.

General Social Care Council (GSCC) (2002a) *Codes of Practice for Social Care Workers and Employers.* London: GSCC.

General Social Care Council (GSCC) (2002b) *What are the Codes? GSCC Code of Practice for Social Care Workers.* London: GSCC.

General Social Care Council (GSCC) (2003, amended 2005) *General Social Care Council Registration Rules.* London: GSCC.

General Social Care Council (GSCC) (2005a) *Post-Qualifying Framework for Social Work Education and Training*. London: GSCC.

General Social Care Council (GSCC) (2005b) *Specialist Standards and Requirements for Post-Qualifying Social Work Education and Training: Children and Young People, their Families and Carers*. London: GSCC.

General Social Care Council (GSCC) (2005c) *Specialist Standards and Requirements for Post-Qualifying Social Work Education and Training: Practice Education*. London: GSCC.

General Social Care Council (GSCC) (2005d) *Working Towards Full Participation*. London: GSCC.

General Social Care Council (GSCC) (2005e) *Specialist Standards and Requirements for Post-Qualifying Social Work Education and Training: Leadership and Management*. London: GSCC. London: GSCC.

General Social Care Council (GSCC) (2006a) *Annual Quality-Assurance Report on Social Work Education and Training 2004–05*. London: GSCC.

General Social Care Council (GSCC) (2006b) *Post Registration Training and Learning (PRTL) Requirements for Registered Social Workers: Advice and Guidance on Good Practice*. London: GSCC.

General Social Care Council (GSCC) (2006c) *Specialist Standards and Requirements for Post-Qualifying Social Work Education and Training Social Work with Adults*. London: GSCC.

General Social Care Council (GSCC) (2006d) *Specialist Standards and Requirements for Post-Qualifying Social Work Education and Training Social Work in Mental Health Services*. London: GSCC.

General Social Care Council (GSCC)/Topss (2002) *Guidance on the Assessment of Practice in the Workplace*. London: GSCC/Topss.

Gibbs, G. (1988) *Learning by Doing: A Guide to Teaching and Learning Methods*. Oxford: Further Education Unit.

Gilbert, P. (2003) *The Value of Everything: Social Work and its Importance in the Field of Mental Health*. Lyme Regis: Russell House.

Glasby, J. and Littlechild, R. (2002) *Social Work and Direct Payments*. Bristol: Policy Press.

Glasby, J., Littlechild, R. and Pryce, K. (2004) *Show Me the Way to Go Home: Delayed Discharges and Older People*. Birmingham: Health Services Management Centre, University of Birmingham.

Glover, H. and Kalyanasundaram, V. (2006) *Unpacking Practices that Support Recovery: Workbook One and Two*. Hertford: Hertfordshire County Council.

Goodson, I. (1998) 'Storying the Self.' In W. Pinar (ed.) *Curriculum: Towards New Identities*. New York/London: Taylor and Francis.

Gould, N. (1996) 'Introduction: Social Work Education and the "Crisis Of Professions".' In N. Gould and I. Taylor (eds) *Reflective Learning for Social Work*. Aldershot: Ashgate.

Gould, N. and Baldwin, M. (eds) (2004) *Critical Social Work, Reflection and the Learning Organization*. Aldershot: Ashgate.

Graham, G. and Megarry, B. (2005) 'The social care work portfolio: an aid to integrated learning and reflection in social care training.' *Social Work Education 24*, 7, 769–780.

Hafford-Letchfield, T. (2006) *Management and Organisations in Social Work*. Transforming Social Work Practice Series. Exeter: Learning Matters.

Hallett, C. and Birchall, E. (1992) *Co-ordination and Child Protection*. London: HMSO.

Halmos, P. (1978) *The Personal and the Political in Social Work*. London: Hutchinson.

Halton, W. (1997) 'Some Unconscious Aspects of Organizational Life: Contributions from Psychoanalysis.' In A. Obholzer and V. Roberts (eds) *The Unconscious at Work*. London: Routledge.

Hanson, M. (1995) 'Practice in Organizations.' In C.H. Meyer and M.A. Mattaini (eds) *The Foundations of Social Work Practice*. Washington, DC: NASW Press.

Hardman, K.L.J. (1997) 'Social workers' attitudes to lesbian clients.' *British Journal of Social Work 27*, 545–563.

Hasler, F. (2003) *Users at the Heart: User Participation in the Governance and Operations of Social Care Regulatory Bodies*. Social Care Institute for Excellence Report Number 5. London: Social Care Institute for Excellence.

Hawley, C.J., Littlechild, B., Sivakuumaran, T., Sender, H., Gale, T.M. and Wilson, K.J. (2006) 'Structure and content of risk assessment proformas in mental healthcare.' *Journal of Mental Health 15*, 4, 437–448.

Healy, K. (2005) *Social Work Theories in Context.* Basingstoke: Palgrave Macmillan.

Heclo, H. (1974) *Modern Social Policies in Britain and Sweden.* London: Yale.

Heffernan, K. (2006) 'Social work, new public management and the language of "service user".' *British Journal of Social Work 36*, 139–147.

Heikkilä, A. and Lonka, K. (2006) 'Studying in higher education: students' approaches to learning, self-regulation, and cognitive strategies.' *Studies in Higher Education 31*, 1, 99–117.

Herxheimer, A. and Goodare, H. (1999) 'Who are you, and who are we: looking through some key words.' *Health Expectations 2*, 3–6.

Hicks, S. (2005) 'Lesbian and gay foster care and adoption: a brief UK history.' *Adoption and Fostering 29*, 3, 42–56.

Hicks, S. (2006) 'Thinking Through Sexuality.' Paper presented at the ATSWE conference: Professional – Personal – Practical: Sexuality and Social Work Education, 3 March, York.

Hicks, S. and McDermott, J. (eds) (1999) *Lesbian and Gay Fostering and Adoption: Extraordinary yet Ordinary.* London: Jessica Kingsley Publishers.

Hinshelwood, R. (2001) *Thinking About Institutions: Milieux and Madness.* London: Jessica Kingsley Publishers.

HM Government (2006) *Working Together to Safeguard Children: A Guide to Inter-Agency Working to Safeguard and Promote the Welfare of Children.* London: The Stationery Office. Available at http://www.everychildmatters.gov.uk/ (accessed 9 July 2007).

Hodkinson, P. and Issitt, M. (eds) (1995) *The Challenge of Competence.* London: Cassell.

Hoghughi, M.S. (1980) *Assessing Problem Children.* London: Andre Deutsch.

Holland, S. (1996) 'Developing a Bridge to Women's Social Action.' In T. Heller, J. Reynolds and R. Gomm (eds) *Mental Health Matters.* London: Macmillan.

Hope, R. (2006) 'New Ways of Working in Mental Health'. Paper given at the CSIP/NIMHE Conference: The Social Work Contribution to Mental Health Services – The Future Direction, Northampton.

Horwath, J. (2000) 'Child care with gloves on: protecting children and young people in residential care.' *British Journal of Social Work 30*, 2, 179–191.

Hospice Information (2006) Available at http://www.hospiceinformation.info/ (accessed 29 December 2006).

Hugman, R. (1998) 'Social Work and Deprofessionalisation.' In P. Abbott and L. Meerabeau (eds) *The Sociology of the Caring Professions.* London: UCL Press.

Hull, C. and Redfern, L. (1996) *A Guide for Nurses and Midwives.* Houndmills: Macmillan.

Humphreys, C., Berridge, D., Butler, I. and Ruddick, R. (2003) 'Making research count: the development of "knowledge-based practice".' *Research Policy and Planning 21*, 1, 11–19.

Hunt, J.G. (1983) *Leadership.* Newbury Park, CA: Sage.

Hylton, M.E. (2005) 'Heteronormativity and the experiences of lesbian and bisexual women as social work students.' *Journal of Social Work Education 41*, 1, 67–82.

IASSW (2006) *International Association of Schools of Social Work: Working for Social Work Education Worldwide.* Available at http://www.iassw-aiets.org/ (accessed 29 December 2006).

ICSW (2006) *The International Council on Social Welfare.* Available at http://www.icsw.org/ (accessed 29 December 2006).

IFSW (2006) *Welcome to IFSW.* Available at http://www.ifsw.org/home (accessed 29 December 2006).

Irving, Z. and Payne, M. (2004) 'Globalisation: Implications for Learning and Teaching.' In H. Burgess and I. Taylor (eds) *Effective Learning and Teaching in Social Policy and Social Work* (LTSN series). London: Routledge Falmer.

Jackson, M. (2004) 'Looking Around us to Talk about Death (Using Environmental, Social and Cultural Resources to Teach About Loss and Death to Social Work Students).' Symposia: *Journal for Studies in Ethnology and Anthropology*, 77–86.

Jackson, M. and Colwell, C. (2001a) *A Teacher's Handbook of Death*. London: Jessica Kingsley Publishers.

Jackson, M. and Colwell, C. (2001b) 'Talking to children about death.' *Mortality* 6, 3, 321–325.

Jones, C. (1998) 'Social Work and Society.' In R. Adams, L. Dominelli and M. Payne (eds) *Social Work: Themes, Issues, Critical Debates*. Basingstoke: Macmillan.

Jones, C. (2001) 'Voices from the front line: state social workers and New Labour.' *British Journal of Social Work 31*, 4, 547–562.

Jones, R. (1990) 'Merging basic with practical research to enhance the adolescent experience.' *Journal of Adolescent Research 5*, 2, 254–262.

Jones, R. (ed.) (2004) *Mental Health Act Manual* (9th edn). London: Sweet and Maxwell.

Jordan, B. (1990) *Social Work in an Unjust Society*. Hemel Hempstead: Harvester.

Jordan, B. (2002) *Social Work and the Third Way: Tough Love as Social Policy*. London: Sage.

Karban, K. and Frost, N. (1998) 'Training for residential care: assessing the impact of the Residential Child Care Initiative.' *Social Work Education 17*, 3, 287–300.

Kelly, A., Mabbett, G. and Tome, R. (1998) 'Professions and Community Nursing.' In A. Symonds and A. Kelly (eds) *The Social Construction of Community Care*. Basingstoke: Macmillan.

Kelly, G.A. (1955) *The Psychology of Personal Constructs*. New York: Norton.

Kemshall, H. (2002) *Risk, Social Policy and Welfare*. Buckingham: Open University Press.

Klass, D., Silverman, P. and Nickman, S.L. (1996) *Continuing Bonds: New Understandings in Grief*. London: Taylor and Francis.

Knowles, M. (1975) *Self-Directed Learning: A Guide for Learners and Teachers*. New York: Association Press.

Kolb, D.A. (1984) *Experiential Learning: Experience as the Source of Learning and Development*. Englewood Cliffs, NJ: Prentice-Hall.

Kubler-Ross, E. (2001) *Death and Dying*. London: Routledge.

Ladyman, S. (2004) Speech to the Laing and Buisson Annual Long Term Care for Older People Conference, 17 March. Available at http://www.dh.gov.uk/en/News/Speeches/Speecheslist/DH_4076973. (accessed 9 July 2007).

Lamb, M.E. (1987) *Father's Role*. New Jersey: Lawrence Erlbaum Associates.

Lamb, M.E. (1997) *The Role of the Fathers in Child Development* (3rd edn). Chichester: Wiley.

Laming, Lord (2003) *The Victoria Climbié Inquiry*, Cm 5730. London: The Stationery Office.

Langan, J. and Lindlow, V. (2004) *Living with Risk: Mental Health Service User Involvement in Risk Assessment and Management*. Bristol: Policy Press.

Lawrence, W. (1999) *The Presence of Totalitarian States-of-Mind in Institutions*. Available at http://www.human-nature.com/hraj/lawren.html. (accessed 9 July 2007).

Leathard, L. (ed.) (2003) *Interprofessional Collaboration*. Hove: Routledge.

Lebow, J. (1988) 'Research into practice/practice into research.' *Journal of Family Psychology 1*, 3, 337–351.

Leece, J. and Bornat, J. (eds) (2006) *Developments in Direct Payments*. Bristol: Policy Press.

Leech, N. (1999) 'The individual, society and trauma: coping with abuse in England.' *Tapestry: The Journal of Historical Motivations and the Social Fabric 1*, 3/4, 60–65.

Leech, N. (2002) 'Some ideas on the hidden aspects of care work in present-day society.' *History and Philosophy of Psychology 4*, 2, 49–56.

Leech, N. and Trotter, J. (2005) '"None of them ever asked about sex": some personal thoughts as to why social workers have difficulty discussing sexuality with young people.' *Socio-analysis 7*, 19–36.

Leech, N. and Trotter, J. (2006) 'Alone and together: some thoughts on reflective learning for work with adult survivors of child sexual abuse.' *Journal of Social Work Practice 20*, 2, 175–187.

Leiba, T. (1999) 'Crisis Intervention Theory and Method.' In D. Tomlinson and K. Allen (eds) *Crisis Services and Hospital Crises: Mental Health at a Turning Point.* Aldershot: Ashgate.

Levitas, R. (1998) *The Inclusive Society? Social Exclusion and New Labour.* Basingstoke: Macmillan.

Ley, K. and Young, D.B. (1999) 'Instructional Principles for Self Regulation in Proceedings of Selected Research and Development Papers.' Paper presented at the National Convention of the Association for Educational Communications and Technology (AECT).

Liddle, H.A. (1991) 'Empirical values and the culture of family therapy.' *Journal of Marital and Family Therapy 17*, 4, 327–348.

Lishman, J. (ed.) (1991) *Handbook of Theory for Practice Teachers.* London: Jessica Kingsley Publishers.

Lishman, J. (ed.) (2007) *Handbook for Practice Learning in Social Work and Social Care* (2nd edn). London: Jessica Kingsley Publishers.

Littlechild, B. (2005) 'The stresses arising from violence, threats and aggression against child protection social workers.' *Journal of Social Work 5*, 61–82.

Littlechild, B. and Bourke, C. (2006) 'Men's Use of Violence and Intimidation Against Family Members and Child Protection Workers.' In C. Humphreys and N. Stanley (eds) *Domestic Violence and Child Protection: Directions for Good Practice.* London: Jessica Kingsley Publishers.

Logan, J., Kershaw, S., Karban, K., Mills, S., Trotter, J. and Sinclair, M. (1996) *Confronting Prejudice: Lesbian and Gay Issues in Social Work Education.* Aldershot: Arena.

London Borough of Greenwich and Greenwich Health Authority (1987) *A Child in Mind: Protection of Children in a Responsible Society. The Report of the Commission of Inquiry into the Circumstances Surrounding the Death of Kimberley Carlisle.* London: London Borough of Greenwich.

London Borough of Lambeth (1987) *Whose Child? The Report of the Panel Appointed to Inquire into the Death of Tyra Henry.* London: London Borough of Lambeth.

Loxley, A. (1997) *Collaboration in Health and Welfare: Working with Difference.* London: Jessica Kingsley Publishers.

Lymbery, M. (2005) *Social Work with Older People.* London: Sage.

Machin, S. (1998) 'Swimming Against the Tide: A Social Worker's Experience of a Secure Hospital.' In G. Hunt (ed.) *Whistleblowing in the Social Services: Public Accountability and Professional Practice.* London: Arnold.

Maldonaldo, J., Mall, N., Hafford-Letchfield, T. and Higgins, M. (2006) 'Coming Out in Social Work Education: The Student Experience.' Paper presented at the ATSWE conference: Professional – Personal – Practical: Sexuality and Social Work Education, 3 March, York.

Maley, J. (2006) 'Two face long jail terms for homophobic murder of barman.' *Guardian*, 13 May.

Mallett, R., Power, M., Heslop, P. and Lewis, J. (2003) *All Change – Transition into Adult Life.* Brighton: Pavilion Publishing.

Mandelstam, M. (1999) *Community Care Practice and the Law.* London: Jessica Kingsley Publishers.

Mandelstam, M. (2007) *Betraying the NHS: Health Abandoned.* London: Jessica Kingsley Publishers.

Manthorpe, J. and Price, E. (2006) 'Lesbian carers: personal issues and policy responses.' *Social Policy and Society 5*, 15–26.

Marsh, P. and Triseliotis, J. (1996) *Ready to Practise? Social Workers and Probation Officers: Their Training and First Year in Work.* Aldershot: Avebury.

Martin, J.I. and Hunter, S. (2001) *Lesbian, Gay, Bisexual, and Transgender Issues in Social Work: A Comprehensive Bibliography with Annotations.* Alexandria, VA: Council on Social Work Education.

Marton, F., Dall' Alba, G. and Beaty, E. (1993) 'Conceptions of Learning' *International Journal of Educational Research, 19,* 277–300.

Marton, F. and Säljö, R. (1976) 'On qualitative differences in learning I: outcome and process.' *British Journal of Educational Psychology 46*, 4–11.

Martyn, H. (ed.) (2000) *Developing Reflective Practice. Making Sense of Social Work.* Bristol: Policy Press.

Maughan, C. and Webb, J. (1996) 'Taking Reflection Seriously: How was it for us?' In J. Webb and C. Maughan (eds) *Teaching Lawyers' Skills*. London: Butterworth.

Mayer, J. and Timms, N. (1970) *The Client Speaks*. London: Routledge and Kegan Paul.

McAuliffe, A. (2003) 'Challenging methodological traditions: research by email.' *The Qualitative Report 8*, 1.

McBeath, G. and Webb, S. (2002) 'Virtue, ethics and social work: being lucky, realistic and not doing one's duty.' *British Journal of Social Work 32*, 1015–1036.

McGowan, B. (1995) 'Values and Ethics.' In C.H. Meyer and M.A. Mattaini (eds) *The Foundations of Social Work Practice*. Washington, DC: NASW Press, 28–41.

McGuire, J. (ed.) (1995) *What Works: Reducing Re-offending*. Chichester: Wiley.

McNeill, F. (2001) 'Developing effectiveness: frontline perspectives.' *Social Work Education 20*, 6, 671–687.

Melville, R. (2006) 'Human research ethics committees and ethical review: the changing research culture for social workers.' *Australian Social Work 58*, 4, 370–383.

Mental Health Foundation and the Sainsbury Centre for Mental Health (2003) *Being There in a Crisis: A Report of the Learning from Eight Mental Health Crisis Services*. London: Mental Health Foundation.

Menzies, I. (1984) *The Functioning of Social Systems as a Defence Against Anxiety*. London: Tavistock Institute of Human Relations.

Messinger, L. (2004) 'Out in the field: gay and lesbian social work students' experiences in field placement.' *Journal of Social Work Education 40*, 2, 187–204.

Meyer, C.H. and Palleja, J. (1995) 'Social Work Practice with Individuals.' In C.H. Meyer and M.A. Mattaini (eds) *The Foundations of Social Work Practice*. Washington, DC: NASW Press.

Middleton, W., Clyne, A. and Harris, P. (1999) 'Risk Assessment and Decision Making.' In D. Messer and F. Jones (eds) *Psychology and Social Care*. London: Jessica Kingsley Publishers.

Millar, M. and Corby, B. (2006) 'Children in need and their families – a basis for a "therapeutic" encounter?' *British Journal of Social Work 36*, 6, 887–899.

Milner, J. and O'Byrne, P. (1998) *Assessment in Social Work*. Basingstoke: Macmillan.

Montgomery, K. and Wiley, D. (2004) *Creating E-Portfolios Using PowerPoint: A Guide for Educators*. London: Sage Publications Inc.

Moon, J.A. (2004) *A Handbook of Reflective and Experiential Learning: Theory and Practice*. London: Taylor and Francis.

Mullender, A. and Hague, G. (2006) 'Giving a voice to women survivors of domestic violence.' *British Journal of Social Work 35*, 8, 1321–1339.

Mullender, A. and Perrott, S. (2002) 'Social Work and Organisations.' In R. Adams, L. Dominelli and M. Payne (eds) *Social Work Themes, Issues and Critical Debates*. Basingstoke: Palgrave.

Mumm, A. and Kersting, R. (1997) 'Teaching critical thinking in social work practice courses.' *Journal of Social Work Education 33*, 1, 75–84.

NACRO (2006) *The Dangerousness Pack*. London: NACRO.

Neimeyer, R. (ed.) (2000) *Meaning Reconstruction and the Experience of Loss*. Washington: American Psychological Association.

Nellis, M. (1999) 'A Question of Degree – the Diploma in Probation Studies and Effective Probation Training.' Paper presented to the NPRIE conference, May.

NICE (2004) *Improving Supportive and Palliative Care for Adults with Cancer: The Manual*. London: National Institute for Clinical Excellence.

NIMHE (2004) *The Ten Essential Shared Capabilities – A Framework for the Whole of the Mental Health Workforce*. London: NIMHE.

O'Brien, M. (2004) 'What is social about social work?' *Social Work and Social Sciences Review 11*, 2, 5–19.

O'Connor, I., Hughes, M., Turney, D., Wilson, J. and Setterland, D. (2006) *Social Work and Social Care Practice*. London: Sage.

O'Donnell, J.M., Johnson Jr, W.E., Easley D'Aunno, L. and Thornton, H.L. (2005) 'Fathers in child welfare: caseworkers' perspectives.' *Child Welfare 84*, 3, May/June, 387.

O'Hagan, K. and Dillenburger, K. (1995) *Abuse of Women in Childcare Work*. Milton Keynes: Open University Press.

O'Neill, S. (1999) 'Social work – a profession?' *Journal of Social Work Practice 13*, 1, 9–18.

O'Sullivan, T. (2002) 'Managing Risk and Decision Making.' In R. Adams, L. Dominelli and M. Payne (eds) *Critical Practice in Social Work*. Basingstoke: Palgrave Macmillan.

Obholzer, A. and Roberts, V. (eds) (1997) *The Unconscious at Work*. London: Routledge.

Oko, J. and Jackson, M. (2006) 'Human Growth and Development.' In R. Adams (ed.) *Foundations of Health and Social Care*. Basingstoke: Palgrave.

Onyett, S. (2003) *Team Working in Mental Health*. Bristol: Palgrave.

Orland-Barak, L. (2005) 'Portfolios as evidence of reflective practice: what remains "untold".' *Educational Research 47*, 1, 25–44.

Osmond, J. and O'Connor, I. (2004) 'Formalizing the unformalized: Practitioners' communication of knowledge in practice.' *British Journal of Social Work 34*, 677–692.

Osmond, J. and O'Connor, I. (2006) 'Use of theory and research in social work practice: implications for knowledge-based practice.' *Australian Social Work 59*, 1, 5–19.

Parker, J. (2004) *Effective Practice Learning in Social Work*. Exeter: Learning Matters.

Parsloe, P. (ed.) (1999) *Risk Assessment in Social Care and Social Work*. London: Jessica Kingsley Publishers.

Parton, N. (1994) 'Problematics of government, (post) modernity and social work.' *British Journal of Social Work 24*, 1, 9–32.

Parton, N. (ed.) (1996) *Social Theory, Social Change and Social Work*. London: Routledge.

Parton, N. and Franklin, B. (eds) (1991) *Social Work, the Media and Public Relations*. London: Routledge.

Paugam, S. (1995) 'The Spiral of Precariousness.' In G. Room (ed.) *Beyond the Threshold: The Measurement and Analysis of Social Exclusion*. Bristol: Policy Press.

Payne, M. (1982) *Working in Teams*. London: Macmillan.

Payne, M. (2002a) 'Social Work Theories and Reflective Practice.' In R. Adams, L. Dominelli and M. Payne (eds) *Social Work: Themes, Issues and Critical Perspectives*. Basingstoke: Palgrave.

Payne, M. (2002b) 'Management.' In R. Adams, L. Dominelli and M. Payne (eds) *Critical Practice in Social Work*. London: Palgrave.

Payne, M. (2005) *Modern Social Work Theory*. Basingstoke: Palgrave Macmillan.

Payne, M. and Shardlow, S.M. (eds) (2002) *Social Work in the British Isles*. London: Jessica Kingsley Publishers.

Payne, M., Adams, R. and Dominelli, L. (2002) 'On Being Critical in Social Work.' In R. Adams, L. Dominelli and M. Payne (eds) *Critical Practice in Social Work*. London: Palgrave.

Pearson, G. (1975) *The Deviant Imagination: Psychiatry, Social Work and Social Change*. Basingstoke: Macmillan.

Perkins, R.E. and Repper, J.M. (1996) *Working Alongside People with Long Term Mental Health Problems*. London: Chapman and Hall.

Perry, T. (2000) 'Straight Talking on Sexuality.' In K. Buckley and P. Head (eds) *Myths, Risks and Sexuality: The Role of Sexuality in Working with People*. Lyme Regis: Russell House Publishing.

Personal Social Services Research Unit (2005) *Implementing the Single Assessment Process: Key Findings from the Literature* (PSSRU Report 34, October 2005). Available at http://www.pssru.ac.uk/pdf/rs034.pdf. (accessed 9 July 2007).

Phillipson, C., Allan, G. and Morgan, D. (2004) *Social Networks and Social Exclusion: Sociological and Policy Perspectives*. Aldershot: Ashgate.

Pierson, P. (1994) *Dismantling the Welfare State? Reagan, Thatcher, and the Politics of Retrenchment*. Cambridge: Press Syndicate of the University of Cambridge.

Pilgrim, D. and Rogers, A.E. (1996) 'Two Notions of Risk in Mental Health Debates.' In T. Heller, J. Reynolds and R. Gomm (eds) *Mental Health Matters*. London: Macmillan.

Pincus, A. and Minahan, A. (1973) *Social Work Practice: Model and Method.* Ithaca, NY: Peacock Press.

Pinker, R. (1990) *Social Work in an Enterprise Society.* London: Routledge.

Printich, P. R. and De Groot, E. V. (1990) 'Motivational and self-regulated components of classroom academic performance.' *Journal of Educational Psychology 82,* 33–40.

Pollock, A. (2004) *NHSplc: The Privatisation of Our Health Care.* London: Verso.

Poole, L. (2001) 'Germany: A Conservative Regime in Crisis.' In A. Cochrane, J. Clarke and S. Gewirtz (eds) *Comparing Welfare States: Family Life and Social Policy.* London: Sage, 153–194.

Poon, M.K.-L. (2004) 'A missing voice: Asians in contemporary gay and lesbian social service literature.' *Journal of Gay and Lesbian Social Services 17,* 3, 87–106.

Powell, F. (2001) *The Politics of Social Work.* London: Sage.

Preston-Shoot, M. (2000) 'Making Connections in the Curriculum: Law and Professional Practice.' In R. Pierce and J. Weinstein (eds) *Innovative Education and Training for Care Professionals: A Providers' Guide.* London: Jessica Kingsley Publishers.

Preston-Shoot, M. (2002) 'Why social workers don't read.' *Care and Health 11,* 10–12.

Pugh, S. (2005) 'Assessing the cultural needs of older lesbians and gay men: implications for practice.' *Practice 17,* 3, 207–218.

Quinney, A. (2006) *Collaborative Social Work Practice.* Exeter: Learning Matters.

Randall, J. (2002) 'The practice–research relationship: a case of ambivalent attachment?' *Journal of Social Work 2,* 1, 105–122.

Raynor, P. (2002) 'What Works: Have We Moved On?' In D. Ward, J. Scott and N. Lacey (eds) *Probation: Working for Justice.* Oxford: Oxford University Press.

Read, J. and Clements, L. (1999) 'Research, the law and good practice in relation to disabled children: an approach to staff development in a local authority.' *Local Governance 25,* 2, 87–95.

Readhead, E. and Mather, C. (2006) *Discussion Document: A Potential Framework for Health, Local Council and Criminal Justice Staff.* Leeds: Care Services Improvement Partnership (CSIP).

Reder, P., Duncan, S. and Gray, M. (1993) *Beyond Blame. Child Abuse Tragedies Revisited.* London: Routledge.

Redmond, B. (2004) *Reflection in Action: Developing Reflective Practice in Health and Social Services.* Aldershot: Ashgate.

Rich, A. (1983) 'Compulsory Heterosexuality and Lesbian Existence.' In A. Snitow, C. Stansell and S. Thompson (eds) *Powers of Desire: The Politics of Sexuality.* New York: Monthly Review Press, 177–205.

Richmond, M.E. (1922) *Social Diagnosis.* New York: Russell Sage Foundation.

Risley-Curtis, C. and Heffernan, K. (2003) 'Gender biases in child welfare.' *Affilia 18,* 4, 395–410.

Ritzer, G. (2004) *The McDonaldization of Society.* Thousand Oaks, CA: Sage.

Rix, S., Jenkins, J. and Mahoney, J. (2006) *Taking a Whole Life Approach.* NIMHE, Eastern Region.

Roche, D. and Rankin, J. (2004) *Who Cares? Building the Social Care Workforce.* London: Institute for Public Policy Research.

Rose, G. (1989) 'High risk and population strategies of prevention: ethical considerations.' *Annals of Medicine 21,* 409–413.

Rothman, J.C. (1998) *From the Front Lines: Student Cases in Social Work Ethics.* Boston: Allyn and Bacon.

Royal College of Physicians of London (2000) 'Intermediate Care: Statement from the Royal College of Physicians of London.' Available at http://rpclondon.ac.uk/college/statements/statements _interm_care.htm (accessed 11 July 2007).

Rubin, A., Franklin, C. and Selber, K. (1992) 'Integrating research and practice into an interviewing skills project: an evaluation.' *Journal of Social Work Education 28,* 2, 141–152.

Rustin, M. (2005) 'Conceptual analysis of critical moments in Victoria Climbié's life.' *Child and Family Social Work 10,* 11–19.

Schneidman, E.S. (1989) 'Approaches and Commonalities of Suicide.' In Diekstra, F.W. (ed.) *Suicide and its Prevention: The Roles of Attitudes and Imitation.* Hamburg: Brill.

Schon, D. (1983) *The Reflective Practitioner: How Professionals Think in Action.* New York: Basic Books.

Schon, D. (1987) *Educating the Reflective Practitioner.* San Francisco, CA: Jossey-Bass.

Schope, R.D. (2005) 'Who's afraid of growing old? Gay and lesbian perceptions of ageing.' *Journal of Gerontological Social Work 45,* 4, 23–38.

Scottish Executive (2006a) *21st Century Social Work: Changing Lives Implementation Plan.* Edinburgh: Scottish Executive.

Scottish Executive (2006b) *Changing Lives: Report of the 21st Century Social Work Review.* Edinburgh: Scottish Executive.

Secretary of State for Social Services (1974) *Report of the Committee of Inquiry into the Care and Supervision Provided in Relation to Maria Colwell.* London: HMSO.

SEU/ODPM (2006) *A Sure Start to Later Life: Ending Inequalities for Older People.* London: HMSO.

Shardlow, N. (2002) 'Social Work.' In R. Adams, L. Dominelli and M. Payne (eds) *Social Work: Themes, Issues and Critical Debates.* Basingstoke: Palgrave.

Sheppard, D. (1996) *Learning the Lessons* (2nd edn). London: Zito Trust.

Sheppard, M., Newstead, S., Di Caccavo, A. and Ryan, K. (2000) 'Reflexivity and the development of process knowledge in social work: a classification and empirical study.' *British Journal of Social Work 30,* 4, 465–488.

Sixsmith, A. (1986) 'Independence and Home in Later Life.' In C. Phillipson, M. Bernard and P. Strang (eds) *Dependency and Interdependency in Old Age.* London: Croom Helm.

Skills for Care (2001) *Learning Disabilities Awards Framework.* Leeds: SfC.

Skills for Care (2005a) *Common Induction Standards.* Leeds: SfC.

Skills for Care (2005b) *Leadership and Management Strategy: Product Three* (2nd edn). Leeds: SfC.

Skills for Care/Children's Workforce Development Council (2006) *Continuing Professional Development for the Social Care Workforce: Employers' Guide.* Leeds: SfC/CWDC.

Skills for Health (2006) *Developing a Flexible Workforce to Support Better Healthcare and Health Care Services.* Bristol: Skills for Health.

Smaile, G. and Tuson, G. (1993) *Empowerment, Assessment Care Management and the Skilled Worker.* London: HMSO.

Smith, M. (1993) *Pressure, Power and Policy: State Autonomy and Policy Networks in Britain and the United States.* Hemel Hempstead: Harvester Wheatsheaf.

Smith, M. and Nursten, J. (1998) 'Social workers' experience of distress – moving towards change?' *British Journal of Social Work 28,* 3, 351–368.

Social Exclusion Unit (2004) *Mental Health and Social Exclusion.* London: OPDM.

Solomon, P. and Campbell, L. (2002) *Mindful Learning.* Thousand Oaks, CA: Corwin Press.

Soydan, H. (1999) *The History of Ideas in Social Work.* Birmingham: Venture Press Ltd.

Speight, N. and Wynne, J. (2000) 'Is the Children Act failing severely abused and neglected children?' *Archives of Disease in Childhood 82,* 192–196.

SSI/DoH (1991) *Care Management and Assessment: Practitioners' Guide.* London: HMSO.

Stavenga de Jong, J.A. and Wierstra, R.F.A. (2006) 'An exploration of the relationship between academic and experiential learning approaches in vocational education.' *British Journal of Educational Psychology 76,* 155–169.

Stepney, P. and Ford, M. (2000) *Social Work, Models, Methods and Theories: A Framework for Practice.* Lyme Regis: Russell House Publishing.

Sutherland, Sir S. (1999) *With Respect to Age: A Report by the Royal Commission on Long Term Care.* London: The Stationery Office.

SWAPltsn (2005) *SWAP Homepage: Social Policy and Social Work Subject Centre of the Higher Education Academy.* Available at http://www.swap.ac.uk/ (accessed 29 December 2006).

Taylor, I., Thomas, J. and Sage, H. (1999) 'Portfolios for learning and assessment: laying the foundations for continuing professional development.' *Social Work Education 18,* 2, 147–160.

Thomas, D. and Woods, H. (2003) *Working with People with Learning Disabilities*. London: Jessica Kingsley Publishers.

Thompson, N. (1996) *Theory and Practice in Health and Social Welfare*. Buckingham: Open University Press.

Thompson, N. (2000) *Theory and Practice in Human Sciences*. Buckinghamshire: Oxford University Press.

Thompson, N. (2005) *Understanding Social Work. Preparing for Practice*. Basingstoke: Palgrave Macmillan.

Thompson, N. (2006) *Anti-Discriminatory Practice* (4th edn). Basingstoke: Palgrave Macmillan.

Tolman, D.L., Spencer, R., Rosen-Reynoso, R. and Porche, M.V. (2003) 'Sowing the seeds of violence in heterosexual relationships: early adolescents narrate compulsory heterosexuality.' *Journal of Social Issues 59*, 1, 159–178.

Topss (2002) *The National Occupational Standards for Social Work*. Leeds: Training Organisation for the Personal Social Services.

Topss (2004) *What Leaders and Managers in Social Care Do – A Statement for a Leadership and Management Development Strategy for Social Care* (revised 2006). Product 1 of Leadership and Management: A Strategy for the Social Care Workforce. Leeds: Training Organisation for the Personal Social Services.

Topss/GSCC (2002) *Guidance on the Assessment of Practice in the Workplace*. London: GSCC.

Trotter, J. (2000) 'Speaking Out, Coming Out and Being Outed.' In P. Cox, S. Kershaw and J. Trotter (eds) *Child Sexual Assault: Feminist Perspectives*. Basingstoke: Palgrave.

Trotter, J. (2006) 'Violent crimes? Young people's experiences of homophobia and misogyny in secondary schools.' *Practice 18*, 4, 291–302.

Trotter, J. and Gilchrist, J. (1996) 'Assessing DipSW students: anti-discriminatory practice in relation to lesbian and gay issues.' *Social Work Education 15*, 1, 75–82.

Trotter, J., Brogatzki, L., Duggan, L., Foster, E. and Levie, J. (2006) 'Revealing disagreement and discomfort through auto-ethnography and personal narrative: sexuality in social work education and practice.' *Qualitative Social Work 5*, 369–388.

Turnell, A. and Edwards, S. (1999) *Signs of Safety: A Solution and Safety Oriented Approach to Child Protection Casework*. New York: W.W. Norton and Co.

Tyson, K.B. (1992) 'A new approach to relevant scientific research for practitioners: a heuristic paradigm.' *Social Work 37*, 6, 541–557.

UNISON (2005) *Factsheet: Bargaining for Lesbian, Gay and Bisexual Workers' Rights*. Available at http://www.unison.org.uk/acrobat/B1776.pdf (accessed 18 May 2006).

University of Helsinki (2006) *Welcome to the Department of Social Policy*. Available at http://www.valt.helsinki.fi/yhpo/english/index.htm (accessed 29 December 2006).

Utting, D. and Vennard, J. (2000) *What Works With Young Offenders in the Community*. Essex: Barnardo's.

Valuing People Support Team (2004) *Workbook on Person-Centred Care Management*. London: Valuing People Support Team.

Vaughan, G. (2000) 'Violence, Sexuality and Gay Male Domestic Violence.' In K. Buckley and P. Head (eds) *Myths, Risks and Sexuality: The Role of Sexuality in Working with People*. Lyme Regis: Russell House Publishing.

Vetter, N. (2003) 'Inappropriately delayed discharge from hospital: what do we know?' *British Medical Journal 326*, 927–928.

Vickery, A. (1976) 'A Unitary Approach to Social Work with the Mentally Disordered.' In R. Olsen (ed.) *Differential Approaches in Social Work with the Mentally Disordered*. Birmingham: BASW.

Waddell, M. (2006) *Living in Two Worlds: Psychodynamic Theory and Social Work Practice*. Available at http://human-nature.com/free-associations/waddell%20-%20living_in_two_worlds.htm (accessed 7 December 2006).

Wainstock, S.L. (1994) 'Swimming against the current: teaching research methodology to reluctant social work students.' *Journal of Teaching in Social Work 9*, 1, 3–16.

Walter, I., Nutley, S., Percy-Smith, J., McNeish, D. and Frost S. (2004) *Improving the Use of Research in Social Care Practice.* London: Social Care Institute for Excellence.

Ward, C. (2004) 'News feature.' *Learning Disability Practice 7*, 6, July, 8–9.

Warren, K. (2003) *Exploring the Concept of Recovery from the Perspective of People with Mental Health Problems.* Norwich: UEA Social Work Monograph 198.

Watson, F., Burrow, H. and Player, C. (2002) *Integrating Theory and Practice in Social Work Education.* London: Jessica Kingsley Publishers.

Watson, H. (2001) 'Partnership in Action: The New Challenge of the Youth Justice Reforms and Youth Offending Teams.' In L.-A. Cull and J. Rocke *(eds) The Law and Social Work*. Basingstoke: Palgrave, 244.

Webb, D. (1996) 'Regulation for Radicals: The State, CCETSW and the Academy.' In N. Parton (ed.) *Social Theory, Social Change and Social Work.* London: Routledge.

Weinstein, J. (1992) *Multi-Disciplinary Teams.* London: CCETSW.

Weinstein, J., Whittington, C. and Leiba, T. (2004) *Collaboration in Social Work Practice.* London: Jessica Kingsley Publishers.

Whitaker, D.S. and Archer, J.L. (1989) *Research by Social Workers: Capitalizing on Experience.* CCETSW Study 9. London: Central Council for Education and Training in Social Work (CCETSW).

White, C.P. (2004) 'Student portfolios: an alternative way of encouraging and evaluating student learning.' *New Directions for Teaching and Learning 100*, 37–43.

Williams, P. (2006) *Social Work with People with Learning Difficulties.* Exeter: Learning Matters.

Wilton, T. (2000) *Sexualities in Health and Social Care: A Textbook.* Buckingham: Open University Press.

Winter, R. and Maisch, M. (1996) *Professional Competence and Higher Education: The ASSET Programme.* London: Falmer Press.

Woodward, J. and Burnage, J. (2006) *'The Whole Life Recovery Project': An Opportunity to Use Your Mental Health Social Work Skills and Values in Practice.* Hertford: HPT.

Worden, J.W. (1991) *Grief Counselling and Grief Therapy.* New York: Springer Publishers.

Yellowly, M. and Henkel, M. (eds) (1995) *Learning and Teaching in Social Work – Towards Reflective Practice.* London: Jessica Kingsley Publishers.

Yoon, K.P. and Hwang, C.L. (1995) *Multiple Attribute Decision-Making: An Introduction.* Thousand Oaks, CA: Sage.

Young, J. (1999) *The Exclusive Society.* London: Sage.

Young, R. (1992) 'Psychotic Anxieties in Groups and Institutions.' Paper presented at the Psychoanalytic Week, the New Bulgarian University, Sofia.

Young, R. (1994) *Mental Space.* London: Process Press.

Youth Justice Board (YJB) (2005) *Managing Risk in the Community.* London: YJB.

Youth Justice Board (YJB) (2006) *Professional Certificate in Effective Practice in Youth Justice.* London: YJB.

Contributors

Robert Adams is Professor of Social Work in the School of Health and Social Care, University of Teesside. He has published widely on social work and social care, including three major edited texts on social work and books such as *Social Policy for Social Work and Services* and *Social Work and Empowerment*, now in its fourth edition. He is currently involved in research in service user and carer participation.

Linda de Chenu is a senior lecturer in social work and social policy at the University of Hertfordshire, and is currently involved in developing the PQ programme and the mental health pathway. Her research interests have included the response of social care staff to client self-harm, the development of national suicide prevention programmes, social exclusion, women and community work, and social work in schools.

Mary Crawley is a practising social worker within a children's charity. She gained her diploma in Social Work in 2002 from the University of Teesside and has completed the Post Qualification Award. Her specialised field is working with children and young people who are at risk of or who are abused through sexual exploitation.

Lesley Duggan has worked as a Graphic Designer, a Support Worker in Mental Health, a Learning Disability Nurse and as a Social Worker for Children & Families in a Protection and Support Unit. She gained a BA (Hons) in Social Work/Learning Disability Nursing in 2002 and is currently a Community Development Officer.

Ian Duncan completed 25 years' service as a Probation Officer and Senior Probation Officer, and was seconded to the University of Durham. He works part-time as a senior lecturer with the University of Teesside, and as a programme tutor and consultant with the Faculty of Health and Social Welfare, Open University. He has experience as a counsellor, trainer and practice teacher, and contributes to PQ awards as a mentor and assessor.

Emma Foster qualified as a social worker in 2000 and since then has continued to study and teach as a practice teacher and practitioner. She has worked in a variety of residential and fieldwork settings, specialising in work with young people and disability.

Jackie Gilchrist trained in social work at the London School of Economics and chose to work with offenders. She has taught and assessed over 50 students in practice as an on-site and off-site practice teacher. For the past 16 years she has assessed practice teachers and latterly runs the Practice Teaching Award programme at the University of Teesside.

Denis Hart is a visiting lecturer at the University of Teesside. He has worked for 16 years in residential child care, culminating in being Head of the Regional Assessment Centre, County Durham. He has taught at the Universities of Bristol and Trent. He has substantial experience in youth justice work and is a YJB-approved APIS trainer. He is co-author of *Mental Health Nursing*, with Stephen Kirby.

Amanda Hatton is Head of the Continuing Professional Development Programme, Skills for Care.

Maggie Jackson is a senior lecturer at the University of Teesside. She previously worked as a senior practitioner for the Psychological Service in Redcar and Cleveland. She has published a number of papers in her particular interest: death education.

Vicki Lawson-Brown is a director of Lawson-Brown and Nugent Partners, which specialises in workplace investigation and mediation in cases of bullying, harassment, dignity at work grievances, disciplinary issues and conflict management. She is also senior lecturer in Health Studies at Sunderland University, an associate lecturer with the Open University and a regional inspector with the GSCC. She is a disciplinary panel member for the Council for Registration of Forensic Practitioners, a trustee for the charity Witness, and ombudsman for the European Patents Office. Her research interests include the use of language in complaints responses and the involvement of people who use services within the regulatory framework.

Nigel Leech is senior lecturer in social work and human relations at the University of Teesside. His interests include the dynamics of trauma, psychotherapy and applying aspects of psychoanalytical theory towards an understanding of aspects of society and institutions. His publications include articles in the *Journal of Social Work Practice, Social Work Education, History and Philosophy of Psychology* and *Journal of Historical Motivations and the Social Fabric*.

Martin Leveridge was a social worker in and around Liverpool before coming to Teesside. He is a University Teaching Fellow and has been an active member of the North East PQ Consortium since its inception. He has published papers, nationally and internationally, on learning and teaching in social work. His current teaching interests centre on community care and older people. He is currently researching the growing division between statutory social work, based around form-filling, and more relationship-based work in the independent sector.

Jo Levie is a practising social worker in a children and families fieldwork team. She gained her BA (Hons) in Social Work Studies from Teesside University in 2000. She has a particular interest in working with looked after children and young people.

Brian Littlechild is Professor of Social Work at the University of Hertfordshire. He teaches on undergraduate and postgraduate social work programmes, and has published and carried out research in relation to assessment, most recently into the use of risk assessment tools in mental health work. He has taught and published on risk assessment issues both in the UK and internationally.

Maire Maisch works at Anglia Ruskin University where she is head of the Department of Social Work and Social Care. She has been involved in social work post-qualifying education and development since its inception in the early 1990s. One of her main areas of interest has been in work-based learning, which eventually led to the publication of a book entitled *Professional Competence and Higher Education: The ASSET Programme* (Winter and Maisch 1996). More recently she has become involved in learning and teaching online, and this is the subject of her doctorate.

Dr Terry Murphy is a senior lecturer in social work at the University of Teesside. Since entering social work in 1983 he has worked as a practitioner, researcher and manager in child protection in England and Northern Ireland. He has acted as a child protection consultant to UNICEF and social work services in the UK and Canada. He has a particular interest in human service practice with and by men.

David Nulty is an independent PQ mentor-assessor and public-sector consultant working in north-west England and North Wales. He worked in both the statutory and voluntary sectors as a social worker, trainer and training manager prior to moving into independent practice.

Geoff Owens is the manager of the North East Post-Qualifying Consortium.

Malcolm Payne is Director, Psycho-social and Spiritual Care, St Christopher's Hospice, London, Emeritus Professor at Manchester Metropolitan University and Honorary Professor, Kingston University, having previously worked in probation, social services, and the national and local voluntary sector, including mental health care. He is also docent in social work at the University of Helsinki, Finland. He is author of many articles and books, including *Modern Social Work Theory* (Palgrave Macmillan, 3rd edn, 2005) and *What is Professional Social Work?* (Policy Press, 2nd edn, 2006).

Michael Preston-Shoot is Professor of Social Work and Dean of the Faculty of Health and Social Sciences at the University of Bedfordshire. He is chair of the Joint University Council Social Work Education, which represents the perspectives of social work education in higher education institutions. He was editor of *Social Work Education: The International Journal* between 1993 and 2006, and is managing editor of the *European Journal of Social Work*. He was awarded a National Teaching Fellowship by the Higher Education Academy in 2005. His research and writing has concentrated on the interface between law and social work practice, on which in 2005 he co-authored a systematic review of teaching, learning and assessment of law in social work education for the Social Care Institute for Excellence. He has also undertaken research and published in the areas of social work education, group work, and on the needs and service outcomes for young people in public care and older people requiring care in the community.

Mary Rayner is a senior lecturer in Social Science at the University of Teesside. Her major interests are the restructuring of the welfare state, the key role of social work in the postmodern welfare state, and practical ethics. She has a conviction that ethics and moral philosophy must firmly underpin all welfare interventions and the actions of professionals responsible for delivering them.

James Reid is a senior lecturer in social work at the University of Teesside. He teaches on undergraduate and post-qualification social work programmes, most recently developing teaching on contemporary assessment issues for a Specialist post-qualification programme. His wider interests also include ethical approaches to practice, reflection and social work with fathers.

Paula Sobiechowska is a Senior Lecturer in Social Work in the Faculty of Health and Social Care at Anglia Ruskin University. She has been involved with the PQ framework since its inception in the early 1990s – much of this work is described in the publication 'Work-Based Learning: In Search of an Effective Model' (with M. Maisch) in *Educational Action Research – An International Journal* (Special Edition July 2007). Her interest is in supporting the development of professional practitioners as learners and shapers of policy and practice.

Wade Tovey is Head of social work in the School of Health and Social Care at the University of Teesside. He has leadership and consultancy interests in participation for people who use services and carers, youth inclusion, adult protection, partnership working and flexible learning. He is chair of the Learning Resource Network (NE), a member of the Executive of Skills for Care (NE) and a board member of the Open Learning Foundation.

Joy Trotter is Reader in Social Work at the University of Teesside. Her interests are in sexuality and gender, child sexual abuse and domestic violence. Her publications include *'No-one's Listening': Mothers, Fathers and Child Sexual Abuse* (Whiting and Birch), *Child Sexual Assault: Feminist Perspectives* (Palgrave), and *Confronting Prejudice: Lesbian and Gay Issues in Social Work Education* (Ashgate). Her social work experience has been in generic, psychiatric and child protection work.

Mike Wren is a senior lecturer in social work at the University of Teesside, after being in social work practice for 19 years. He has worked across a range of service user groups, including children with special needs, education social work, adults with learning disabilities and latterly older people. He is course coordinator for joint programmes in social work learning disabilities/mental health nursing. His interests include transitions to adulthood, intermediate care, and inter-professional working in social work and nursing.

Subject Index

Author Index